IMAGES
of America

IRONDEQUOIT

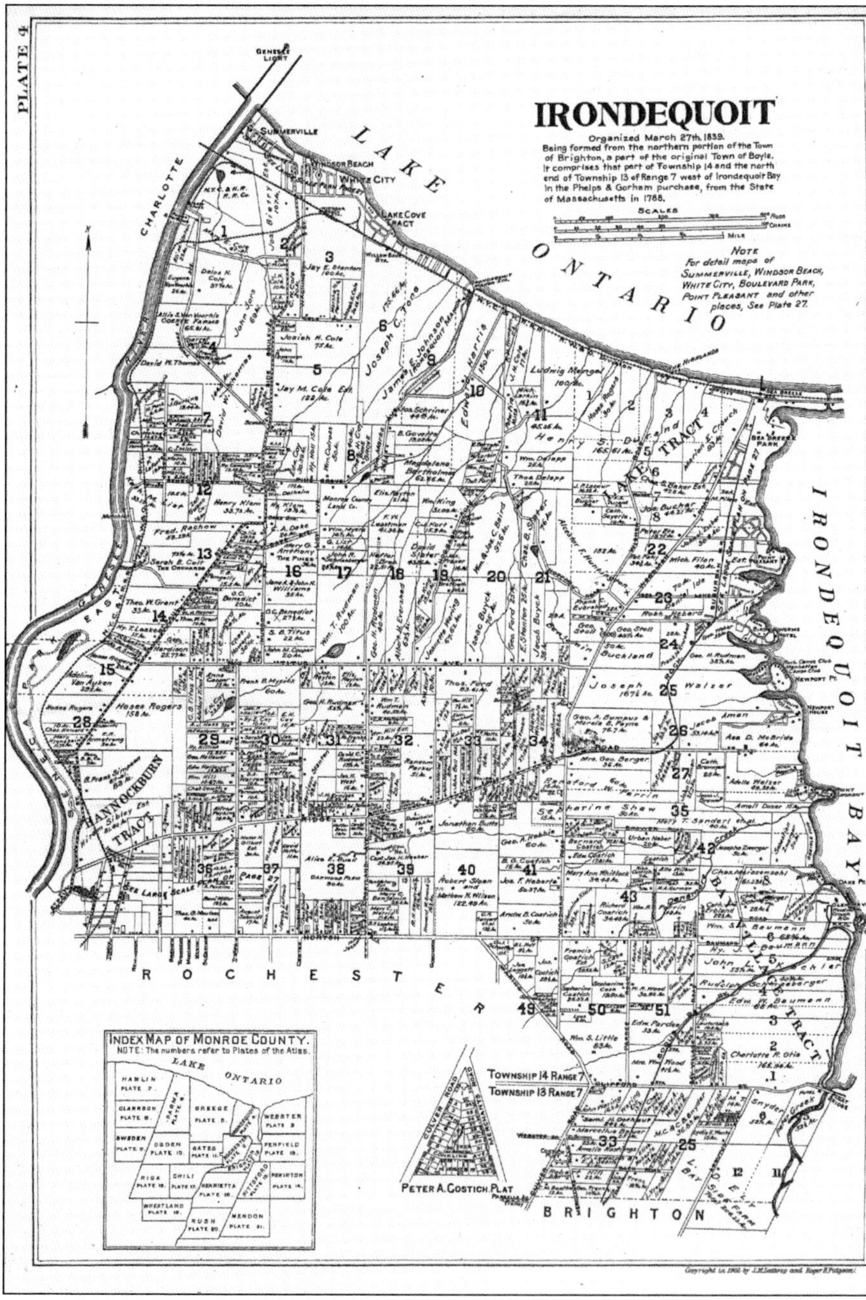

This 1902 map illustrates the economic and social development of Irondequoit as an agricultural community specializing in market gardening. Irondequoit eventually gained the reputation as "the garden spot of western New York" due in large part to the perseverance of early settlers.

On the cover: Summer rest was the objective at White City, which began in 1870. The 300-tent colony was named for the temporary white tents that residents called home for the summer months. The tent that appears on the cover is the summer retreat of Professor Stephen Wilkinson, a local music teacher. White City played a pivotal role in Irondequoit's transformation to a resort area in the late 19th and early 20th centuries. (Courtesy of the archives of the Irondequoit town historian.)

IMAGES
of America

IRONDEQUOIT

Thomas Cole Richens
and Patricia S. Wayne

ARCADIA
PUBLISHING

ISBN 978-0-7385-4918-7

Published by Arcadia Publishing
Charleston, South Carolina

Printed in the United States of America

Library of Congress Control Number: 2006930544

For all general information, please contact Arcadia Publishing:
Telephone 843-853-2070
Fax 843-853-0044
E-mail sales@arcadiapublishing.com
For customer service and orders:
Toll-Free 1-888-313-2665

Visit us on the Internet at www.arcadiapublishing.com

"To the citizens of Irondequoit, in honor of the pioneers who left their peaceful homes and relocated before 1809 to this fever breeding, desolate, and forbidding land and with their successors cleared the forests and excited the earth to production, thereby making it a garden spot and one of the best places in the world to live; to the people who call Irondequoit home today; and to those who strive to preserve local, regional, and national history and recognize the importance of preserving the past for the future." – Linda Van Voorhis

CONTENTS

ACKNOWLEDGMENTS

So many friends, family members, and colleagues deserve thanks for their inspiration, encouragement, and support, not only in relation to this book but in general. First and foremost, my deepest thanks goes to Randy, Barbara, and Sarah Richens. Without their unconditional love and support, this book would not exist. Thank you to Alice Cassidy for her love, humor, and for sharing her childhood stories, and the extended Cassidy family for being more like brothers and sisters than aunts, uncles, and cousins. Much gratitude goes to Dr. Russell A. Judkins for his knowledge, faith, integrity, and guidance. Thank you to Professors David Day, Tom Proietti, James Hancock, and Ed Buscemi of Monroe Community College for encouraging critical and creative thinking within their students. Also thank you to Dr. Ellen Kintz, Beverly Rex Burley, and the State University of New York, Geneseo Anthropology Department; Leatrice Kemp and the Rochester Museum and Science Center; Diane Lucas, Linda Seavy, and the Lavery Library at St. John Fisher College; the Milne Library at State University of New York, Geneseo; the musicians, artists, and close friends in the Rochester area who devote themselves to creating something tangible and unique; and Linda Cain, John Cole, and Kathleen Cole Broman for their assistance. Finally, thank you to Pam O'Neil, Tiffany Howe, and the staff at Arcadia Publishing for allowing this project to come to life.

—Thomas Cole Richens

I am very grateful to many individuals who have supported my efforts through the years, but I would feel very remiss naming them for fear of unintentionally omitting someone. My thanks to the members of the Irondequoit Historical Society, the Landmark Society, the administration of the Town of Irondequoit, my patient family, and the citizens of Irondequoit who believe as I do that preserving the past for the future is a goal for which we should all work.

—Patricia S. Wayne

INTRODUCTION

Irondequoit's history and development is best understood by dividing it into several major phases. Each has had profound effects on the growth of the community and present economic, cultural, and physical aspects. The Pre-Columbian phase is where we begin. Before the arrival of Europeans, the land was the territory of the Senecas, one of the six tribes of the Iroquois Confederacy. The Senecas hunted but never established permanent settlements in the area. Marshes, ponds, and swamps originally covered the landscape and provided a variety of game and waterfowl. The surrounding bodies of water teemed with fish. The name Irondequoit is derived from the Seneca word *Gerundegut* that translates as "where the land and waters meet."

With the arrival of the first Europeans, this area, and the North American continent would forever be changed. Accompanied by missionaries, the young French explorer René Robert Cavelier Sieur de La Salle first sailed into Irondequoit Bay in 1669 with hopes of recruiting Seneca guides and securing the fur trade. In 1687, Louis XIV nominated the Marquis Denonville, governor-general of Canada, to lead a punitive expedition to the mouth of Irondequoit Bay, and a battle ensued south in Victor. The accounts of the conflict vary among historians; however relations between the French and Iroquois never recovered and England gained a crucial position towards the domination of North America.

After the American Revolution, the Phelps-Gorham Purchase in 1788 would play a key role both in the development of Irondequoit and most of western New York. Two enterprising veterans, Oliver Phelps and Nathaniel Gorham, purchased roughly two and a half million acres stretching from Sodus Bay on the east to 12 miles beyond the Genesee River on the west, from Lake Ontario to the north, to Tioga Point, Pennsylvania, in the south. To secure their purchase, Phelps and Gorham negotiated first with the state of Massachusetts, which controlled the land, then reached an agreement with the Council of Six Nations. A deed was executed on July 8, 1788, which stated that the tribes would receive $5,000 in cash and an annual amount of $500. After a survey of the tract, the holding was divided into townships six miles square, numbered one to 14, and were sold off. It is unlikely that the Six Nations ever received any of the annual payments.

Tory Walker was the area's first European settler and fought during the Revolution with the British forces led by Col. Walter Butler and his ally Chief Joseph Brandt of the Iroquois Confederacy. Walker built a cabin near the mouth of the Genesee River in 1791 near the Pilot Tree (a landmark to locate the Genesee River) but soon left the area and headed north to Canada. Other settlers had more vision and in the early to mid-1800s, approximately 100 cabins were scattered throughout the area. Many early settlers endured great hardships and loss, but their perseverance lead to the rise of market gardening, the era's most vital to the development of Irondequoit. Early settlers drained marshlands, filled ravines, and the rich soil eventually lent itself to produce crops with large yields on small acreage. A cobblestone blacksmith shop was built in the early 1830s to service the small farming community and still stands in the same location today, protected by local preservation laws. By 1839, enough settlers had cleared the land and built homes to justify the establishment of Irondequoit as a separate entity from Brighton. The first town meeting was held at the corner of Culver and Ridge Roads, in a tavern owned by Samuel Tompkins, on April 2, 1839, and Irondequoit was established by an act of New York State legislature.

Prosperity reigned and early farms produced potatoes, asparagus, peas, beans, corn, tomatoes, cucumbers, celery, and squash, and provided hams, flour, cornmeal, and cider. Names like Hooker, Bietry, Pardee, Rudman, Cole, Rogers, Cooper, and Titus are some examples of the families that prospered during this golden age. Wheat fields and open farmland stretched over the land and the success of the Irondequoit farmers was reflected in the large gracious houses they built. Farmers with larger acreage concentrated on fruits. The Irondequoit melon, first produced on the farm of William Sutton, was unrivaled for its sweetness and even shipped to the Savoy Hotel in London. It is said that the first telephone in Irondequoit was installed by a Rochester hotel owner to speed delivery of the luscious fruit. These agricultural explosions are what stabilized and aided the social growth of Irondequoit.

In 1865, George Allen built an impressive three-story hotel with three balconies on land overlooking Lake Ontario and Irondequoit Bay. Allen's Hotel became known as the Sea Breeze House, because customers remarked they came to the hotel to enjoy "the sea breeze." This marks the beginning of the resort era. In time, the western shore of Irondequoit Bay boasted resorts such as Glen Haven Park and the Newport House. The development of mass transit would bring even more changes and more people to Irondequoit, and breathe life into the era that forever changed the landscape and attitudes towards Irondequoit. In 1893, the Rochester and Irondequoit Railroad opened an electric trolley line from the city line north on St. Paul Boulevard to Lake Ontario. The Windsor Improvement Company purchased land from the Bietry's at Windsor Beach and Summerville, and in a masterful plan to increase passengers, the company offered large wooden platforms for rent. Vacationers rented the platforms and erected tents for summer retreats. The company laid out streets, planted trees, beautified the grounds, brought in electricity, and furnished faucets for water at the end of each street. The area became known as White City, a 300-tent colony named for its characteristic white tents.

The period that seems most familiar started in the 1920s and accelerated after the end of World War II. The rich farmland was sold off to real estate developers to supply housing for returning veterans and their families. Irondequoit's market gardeners, who faced increased taxes, an exploding population, and a changing economy, could hardly resist the high prices they were offered for their land. The large sprawling farmhouses gave way to accommodate potential suburbanites. Over the years, the landscape has been transformed and the farms have gradually disappeared. Today only three farm markets remain, selling produce trucked in from outside of the town.

These numerous and drastic changes have all left their mark on the area, but Irondequoit has endured and the ambience of the town still remains, which attracts families and defines this unique and thriving community. Hopefully, *Irondequoit* provides an appreciation for the days that have passed, encourages an interest in local history, and provides some warm reflection and fond memories to those who flip through its pages.

One

Where the Land and Waters Meet

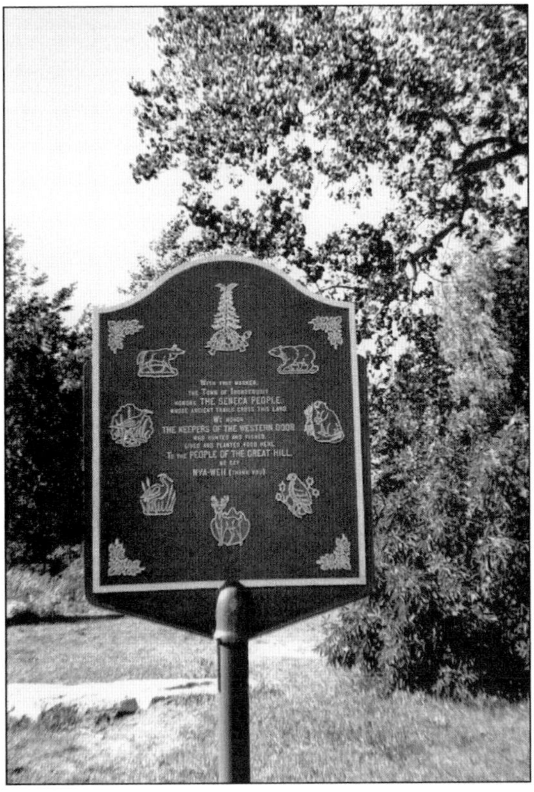

This commemorative marker was placed by Kathy Taddeo's fourth-grade class from Iroquois School in 2002 at Irondequoit Bay. It reads, "With this marker, the town of Irondequoit honors the Seneca people, whose ancient trails cross this land. We honor the keepers of the western door who hunted and fished, lived and planted food here. To the people of the great hill, we say *nya-weh* (thank you)."

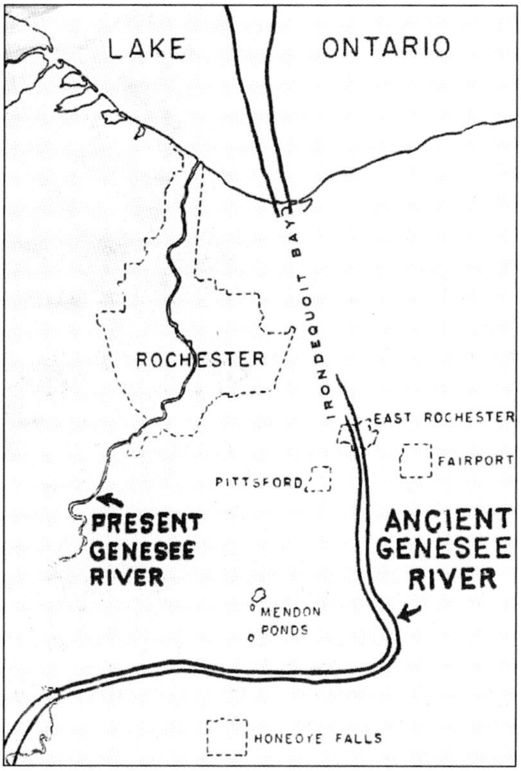

This University of Rochester map was originally published in Maude West's book *The Irondequoit Story*. It shows that the Genesee River once flowed north, turning eastward through what is now Rush and then northward again through East Rochester and Ellison Park. An ice sheet covered the area, and as it advanced and retreated, it deposited so much debris that the river cut a new path to Lake Ontario, leaving Irondequoit Bay in its present form.

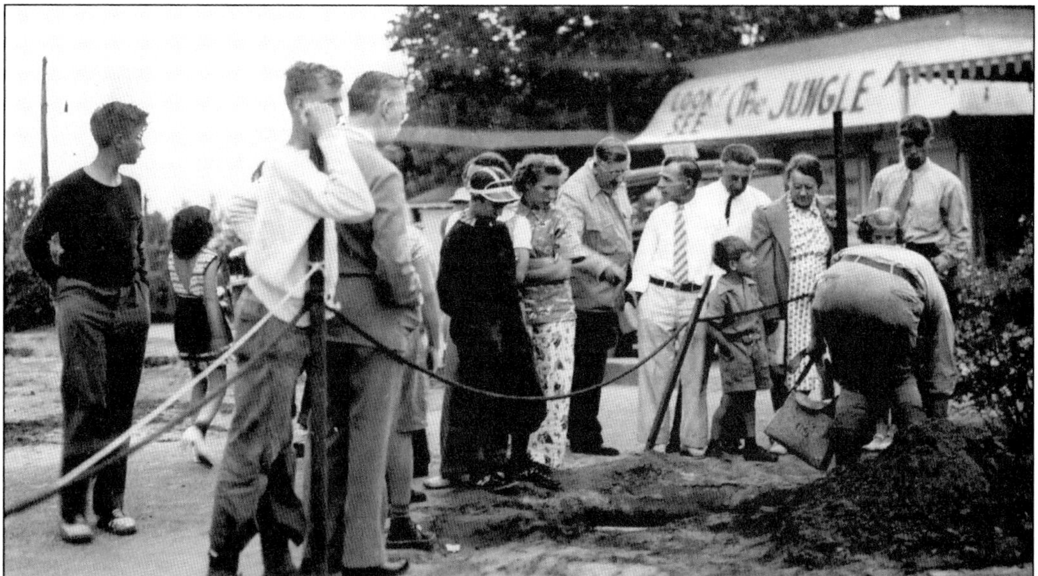

In the spring of 1939, an accidental discovery in Sea Breeze Park led to the excavation of a cemetery containing nine skeletons from the early woodland Point Peninsula culture of 1000 BC. The excavation also uncovered Hopewellian goods making the site an important link between the Hopewell area and the Northeast. Later residents of the area arrived about 150 years before the first Europeans and several Native American tribes eventually formed the Iroquois Confederacy.

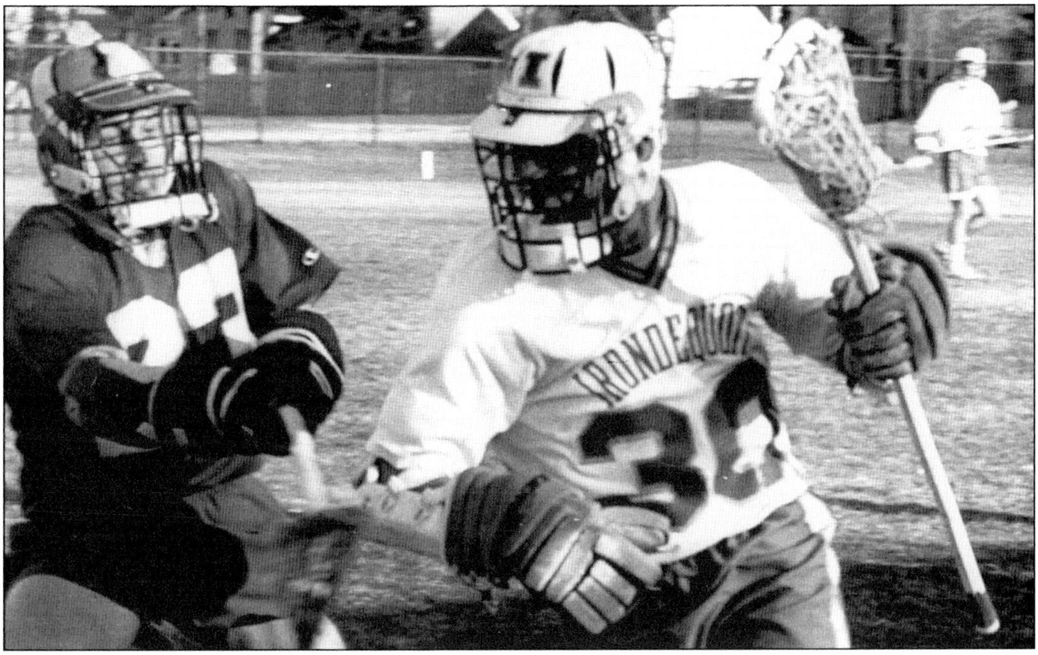

The Iroquois developed a complex society with competitive games, the most famous was lacrosse, but a much rougher version than is played today. It perhaps is no coincidence that Irondequoit High School was one of the first in the county to introduce lacrosse as a high school sport. Greg Hill (pictured above) of Irondequoit gave his all against Canandaigua in 1987.

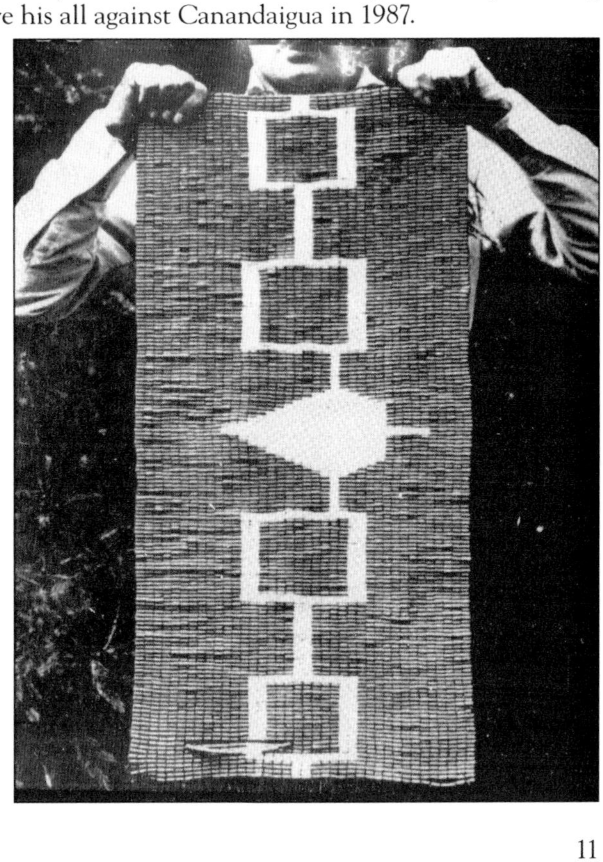

Wampum belts with white, purple, and black beads traditionally made from shells were used as a form of currency among the Iroquois. The belts also symbolized the ideals of the Iroquois Confederacy. White stood for peace, health, and riches, and the purple and black represented sorrow or sympathy for another's sorrow. The belts were not used after 1661 as currency but are highly valued today. This one represents the five nations of the Iroquois Confederacy: the Mohawks, Oneidas, Onondagas, Cayugas, and Senecas. Later the Tuscaroras migrated from North Carolina and became the sixth nation.

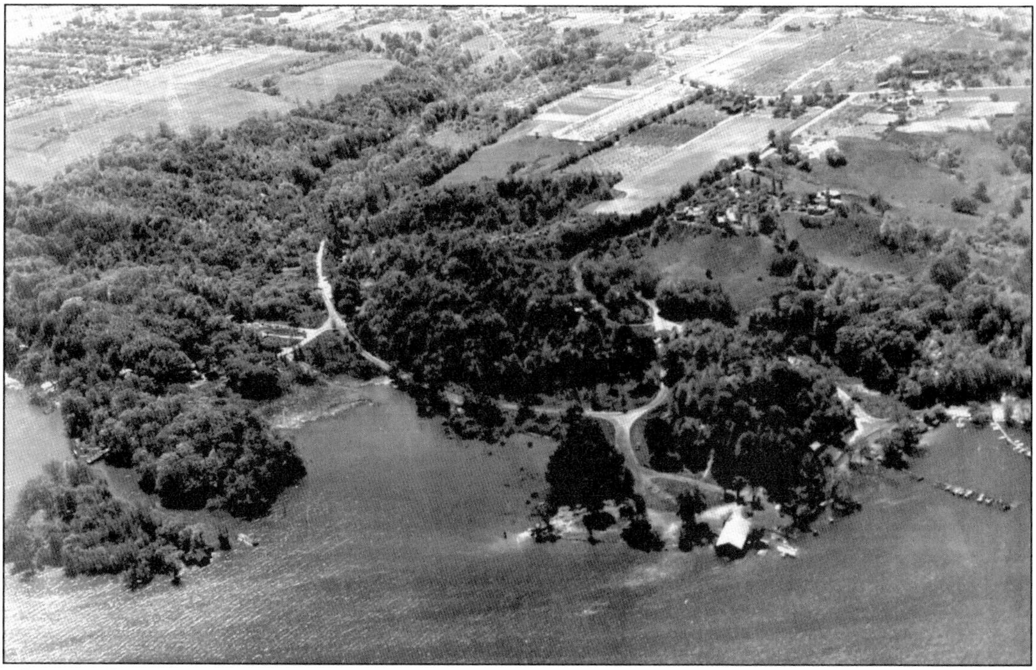

The Irondequoit Bay area was a vibrant hunting ground for the Senecas. The bay, lake, and marshes were plentiful with wildfowl, game, and fish. Despite the abundance of fish and game, the heart of the Seneca settlement was not here, but south in Victor.

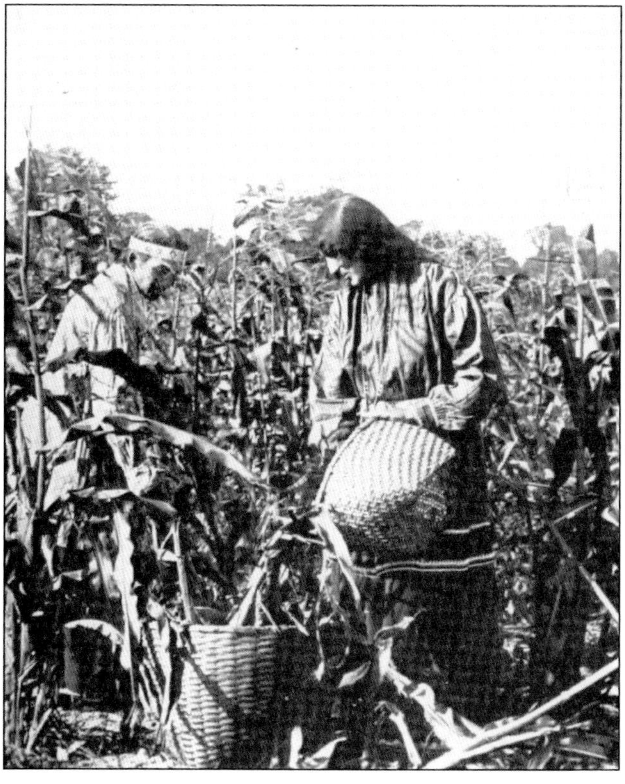

The position of women in the tribes of the Iroquois Confederacy was unique and gender roles were clearly defined. Women bore and nurtured the children, tilled fields, planted the crops, and made clothing, baskets, and sleeping mats. Each longhouse contained one clan that took its name from an animal and when a man married, he moved into the longhouse of his wife's clan. Women were given great influence in the governing of the clan and the chief was chosen by clan mothers. The oldest and most respected of the clan mothers could also depose a chief.

On August 10, 1669, a remarkable expedition entered Irondequoit Bay. Seven canoes carried the first white men seen in this area. Its leader was a 36-year-old Frenchman, René Robert Cavalier Sieur de La Salle (pictured here), who had immigrated to Montreal to join his brother, a member of the Sulpician order of priests that virtually controlled Montreal. La Salle persuaded the Sulpicians to allow for an expedition to the Ohio Valley. Seizing the opportunity to broaden the strength of the Catholic Church, they agreed. However, they attached to the expedition a newly arrived member, René Brehant de Galinée. Galinée was a mathematician, chronicler, and a mapmaker. To modern historians, the most important of Galinée's talents was that of journalist. His diary still makes informative and entertaining reading.

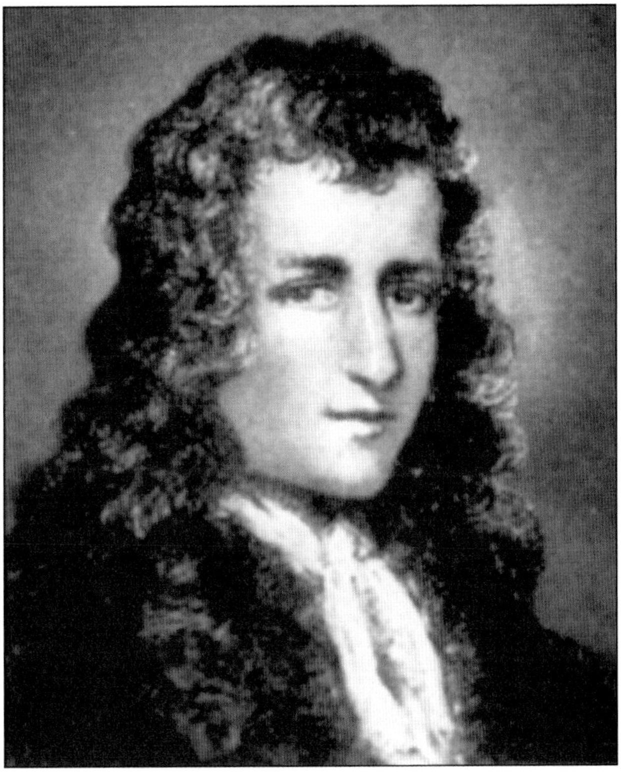

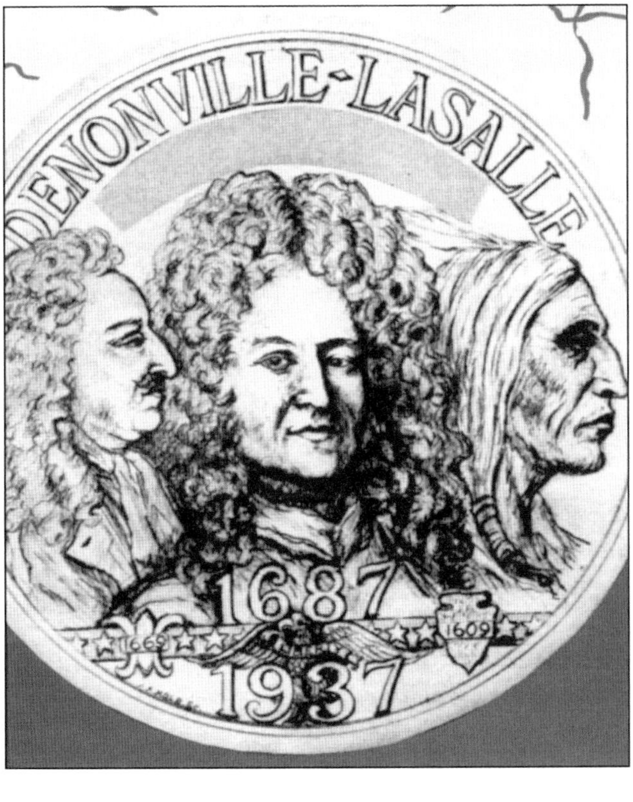

Marquis de Denonville was the next Frenchman to influence the fate of the Senecas who, under direct orders from Louis XIV, landed at Irondequoit Bay with a large force of 3,000. Denonville built a fort at the mouth of the bay, left a force of 400 to guard it, and then proceeded south. Accounts of the battle with the Senecas vary. Some records say that the Senecas withdrew leaving their villages undefended and that Denonville's forces burned all the crops. Other accounts claim a great battle raged with heavy loss of life on both sides. One thing is certain: the Senecas never trusted the French again and allied with the British in the struggle to control North America. This image was designed in 1937 to commemorate the 250th anniversary of the expeditions by the New York State Archaeological Association.

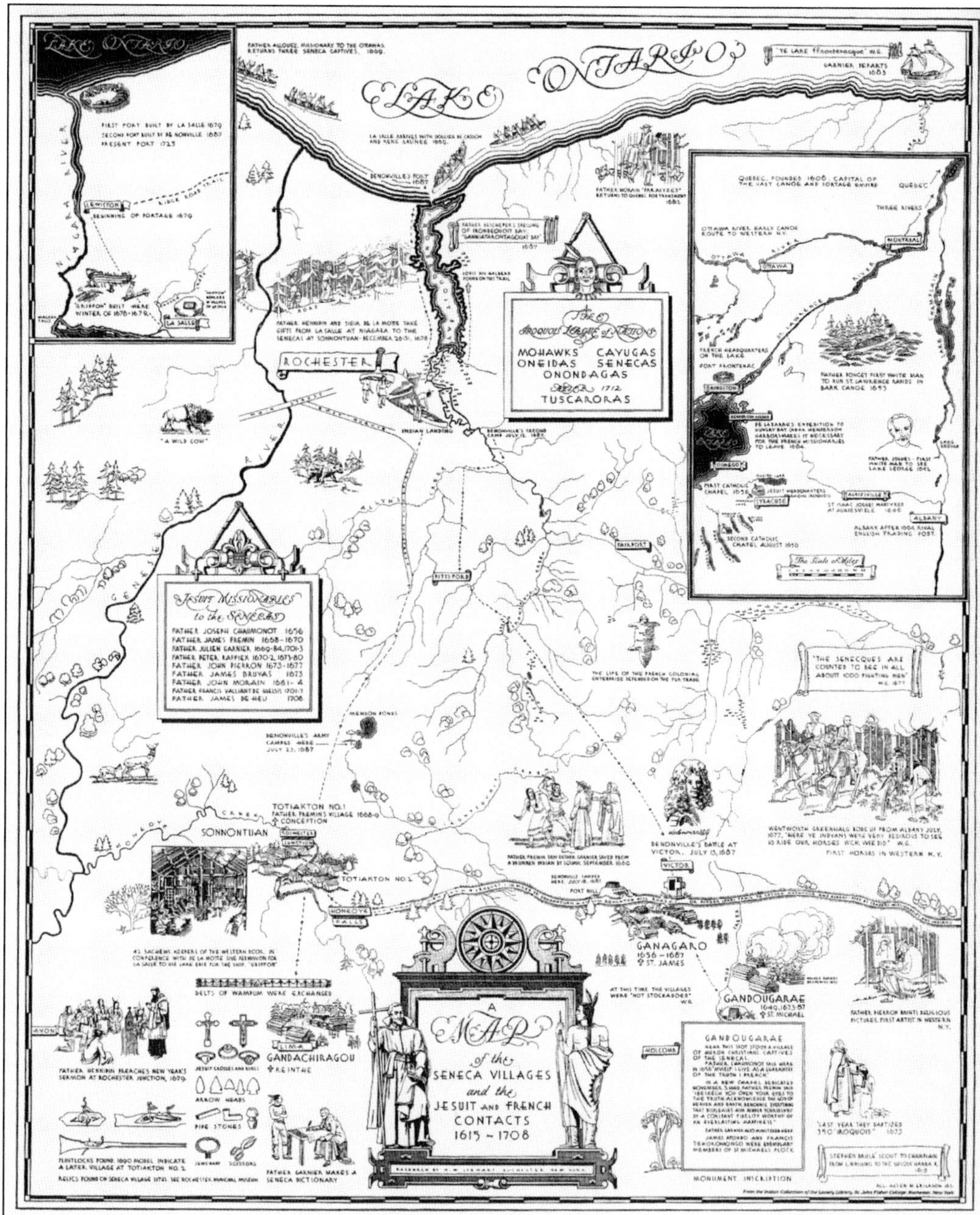

This map illustrates the routes of René Robert Cavalier Sieur de La Salle, Marquis de Denonville, the Iroquois League of Nations, and other early European contact with Native Americans. (Courtesy of the Laverly Library at St. John Fisher College.)

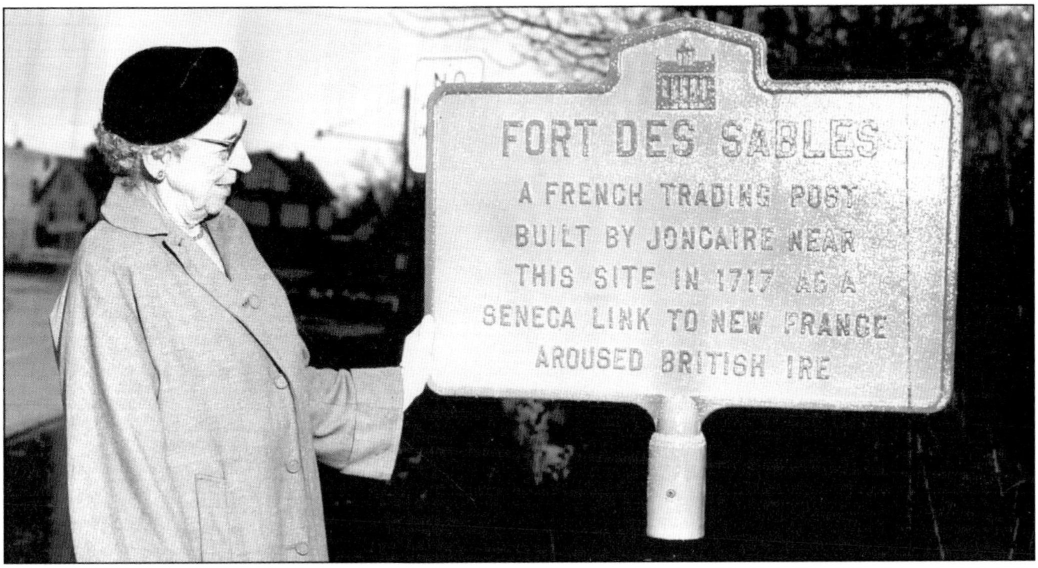

In 1717, the French, under the leadership of Louis Thomas Joincaire, did return to build a trading post at Sea Breeze called Fort des Sables. Joincaire had been a captive of the Senecas but escaped death because they admired his courage and strength. He became a great interpreter and official agent between the Senecas and the French. In this photograph, former Irondequoit town historian Maude West points out the historic marker installed in 1957.

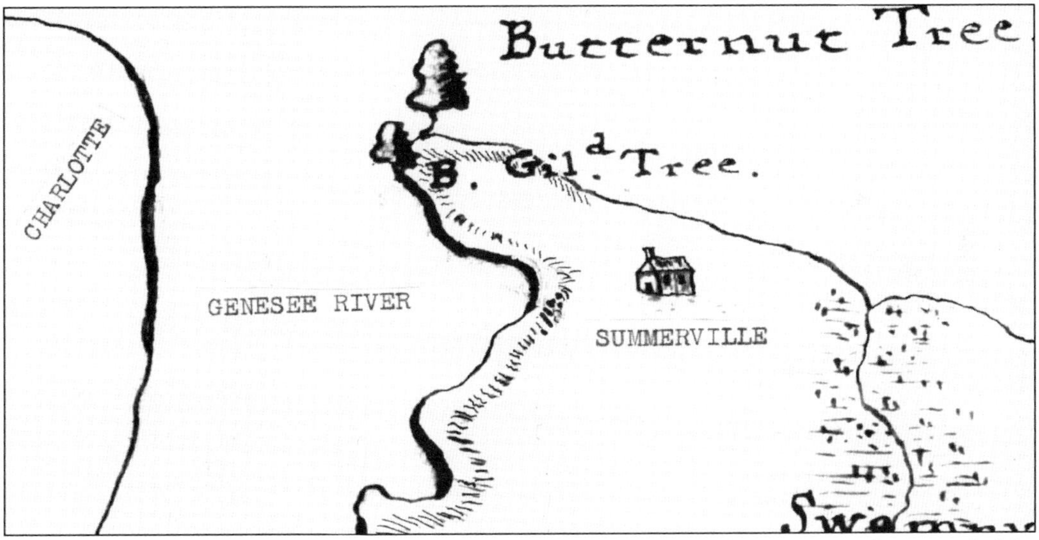

The American Revolution hardly touched the wilderness of Irondequoit. British troops led by John and Walter Butler and the Iroquois allies led by Chief Joseph Brandt spread terror along the frontier in the southern tier and western Pennsylvania. George Washington sent Gen. John Sullivan and a force of 5,000 to rid the area of this force. Sullivan destroyed the Seneca villages and defeated the British. The first white man to live in this area was a veteran of Butler's Rangers, and was known as Tory Walker. He settled at the mouth of the Genesee River and survived by hunting, fishing, trapping, and growing a bit of corn. Walker insisted on boasting about his time with the Rangers. At a trading post in Canandaigua he said the wrong thing to Horatio Jones who suffered as a captive of the Iroquois. Jones threw an axe at Walker barely missing his head. Walker decided that the area was becoming too settled for comfort and moved to Canada.

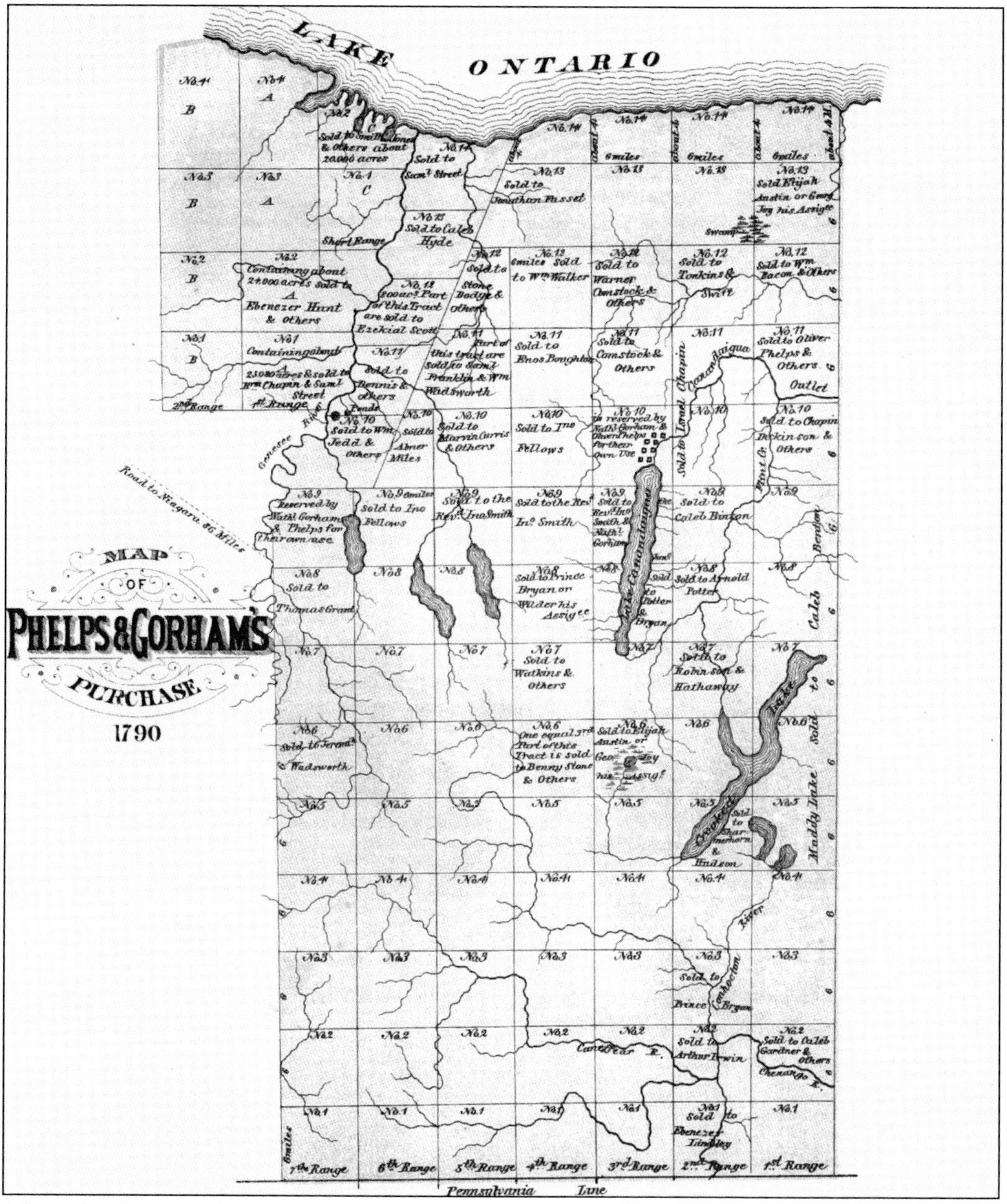

Oliver Phelps served as deputy commissioner of the colonial army during the American Revolution and Nathaniel Gorham had been a delegate to the Continental Congress from Massachusetts. These connections helped them secure the purchase of approximately two and a half million acres in western New York in 1788. Their holdings extended from Sodus Bay on the east to 12 miles beyond the Genesee River on the west, from Lake Ontario on the north all the way to Tioga Point, Pennsylvania, on the south. After a survey of the tract, the area was divided into townships six miles square, and numbered from one to 14, starting from the Pennsylvania line north to Lake Ontario. In 1792, the land that later became Monroe County had seven towns labeled Northfield.

Two

Pioneer Spirit

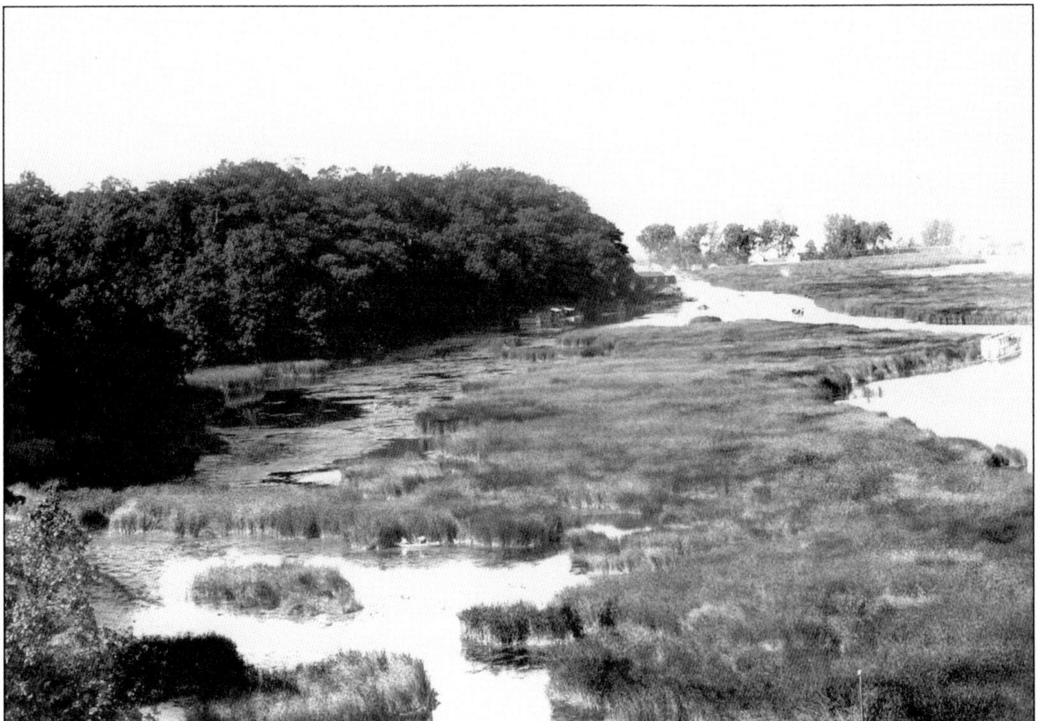

"I would not take it as a gift for it is worth nothing. It is full of wolves, panthers and other inhospitable inhabitants." This is a quote from James Wadsworth who, in 1795, explored the woods of Irondequoit with the view of purchasing a large amount of land for speculation.

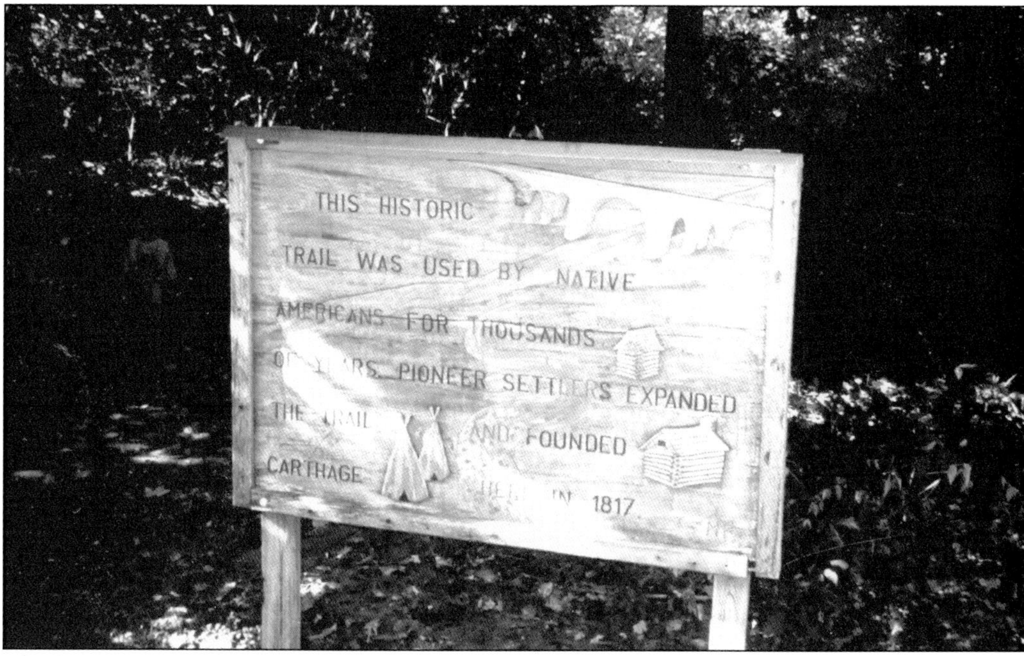

The first regional settlement was developed on the east side of the Genesee River near the lower falls. Following an old Native American trail pioneers established the town of Carthage in 1817. By 1821, the town had grown from 331 persons to 2,000. In 1834, the village was incorporated into the city of Rochester.

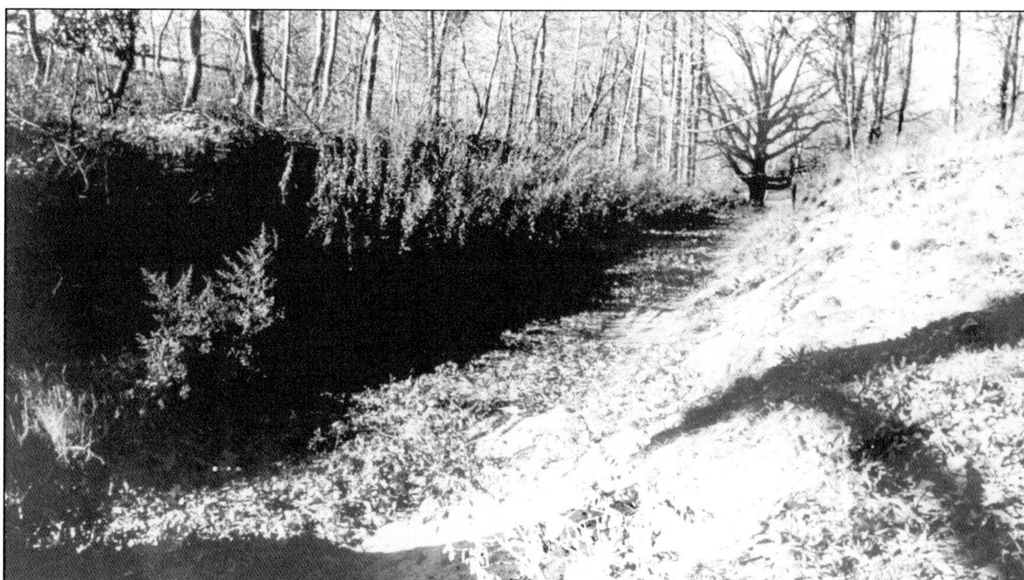

Canandaigua was the jumping off point for pioneers moving to the lower Genesee area. The merchants of this bustling frontier town made a decent living supplying goods to settlers to sustain them while they cleared the land for their new homes. In 1804, the merchants cut a road to the mouth of the Genesee River to facilitate shipping goods to Canada and to aid settlers. Those going to Carthage followed the Native American trail from Merchants Road up the river to Carthage.

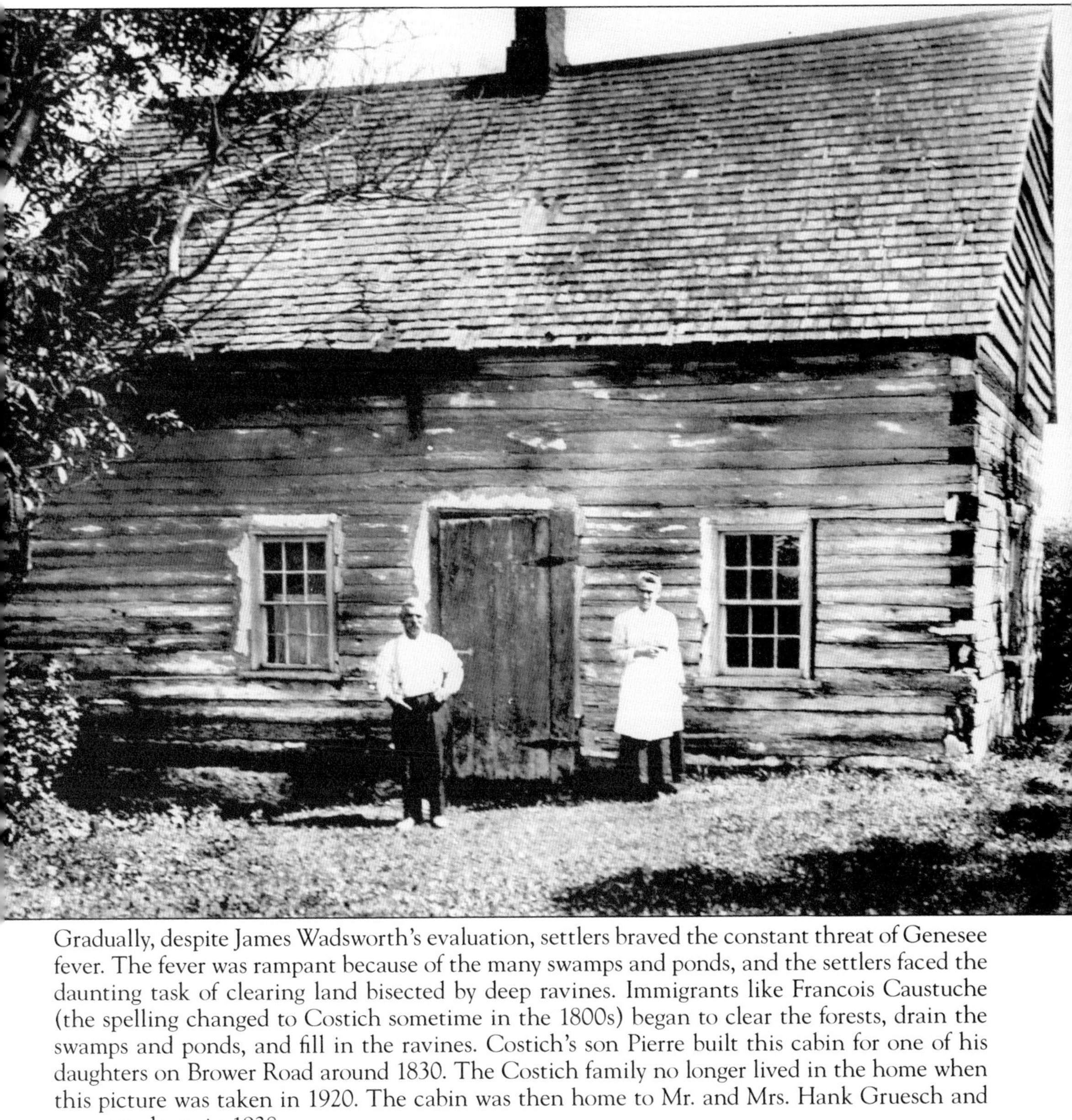

Gradually, despite James Wadsworth's evaluation, settlers braved the constant threat of Genesee fever. The fever was rampant because of the many swamps and ponds, and the settlers faced the daunting task of clearing land bisected by deep ravines. Immigrants like Francois Caustuche (the spelling changed to Costich sometime in the 1800s) began to clear the forests, drain the swamps and ponds, and fill in the ravines. Costich's son Pierre built this cabin for one of his daughters on Brower Road around 1830. The Costich family no longer lived in the home when this picture was taken in 1920. The cabin was then home to Mr. and Mrs. Hank Gruesch and was torn down in 1938.

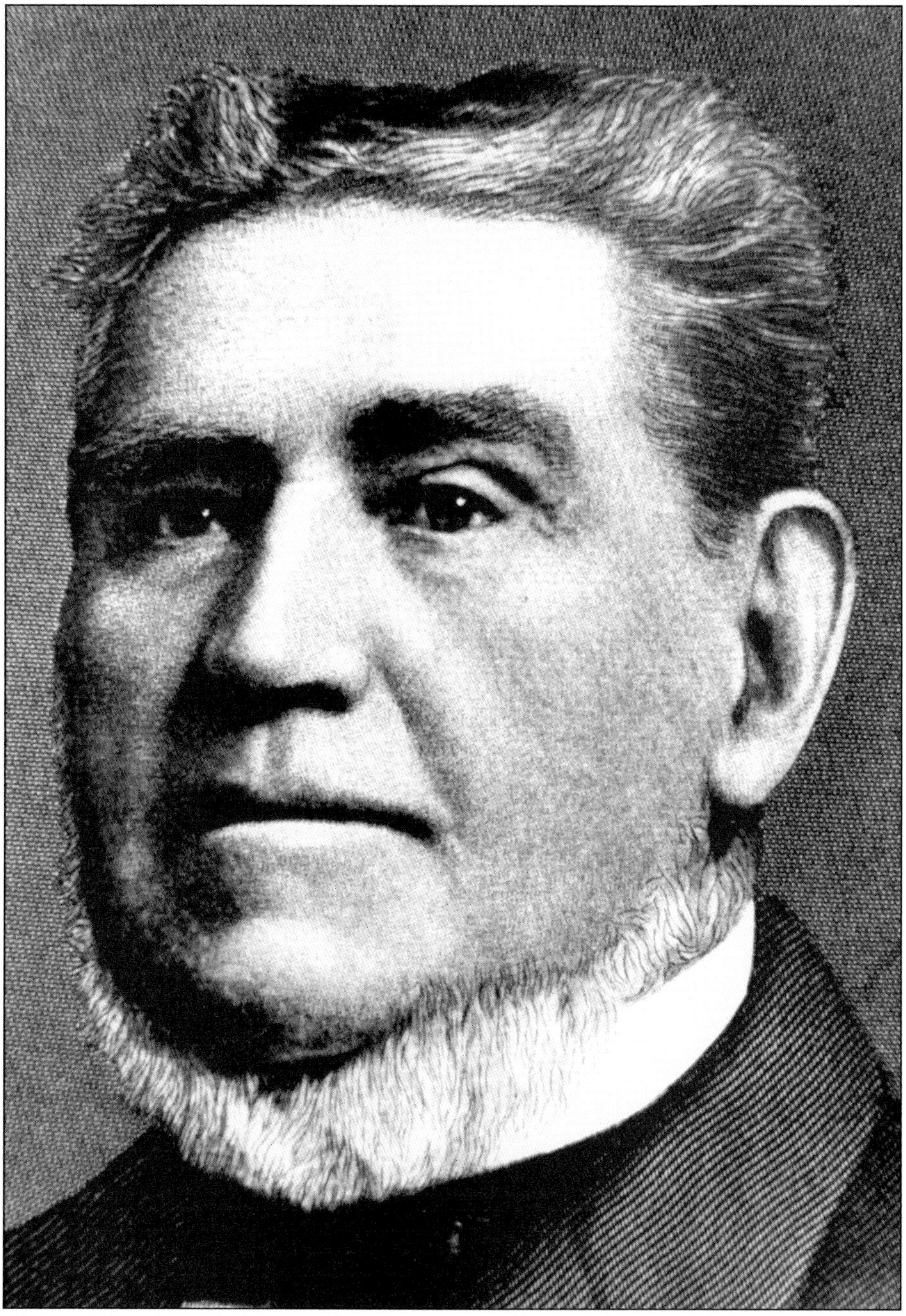

Hosea Rogers's family settled in Carthage in 1809 and he was born in a log house in 1812. After Hosea's father, Ezra Rogers, died, his brothers started a shipbuilding business on the Genesee River, and Hosea, while still a boy, sailed on his first voyage aboard the *Caroline*, the first ship the Rogers brothers built. By 1836, Hosea was able to purchase 85 acres in Irondequoit. He was one of the early settlers who petitioned the New York State legislature to allow Irondequoit to separate from the town of Brighton, which happened in 1839. He eventually owned land on Lake Ontario, the Union racetrack, one of the largest peach orchards in town, and a sawmill on the east side of Stanton Pond.

In 1812, Joseph Vinton left Connecticut by horseback and bought three acres of land in Webster. He abandoned Webster when he decided that floating timber across Irondequoit Bay to sell to early settlers was inefficient, and he shifted his business to the Irondequoit side of the bay and built a sawmill to process lumber. In 1841, he converted the sawmill into a resort hotel. The Newport House was the first hotel on Irondequoit Bay and is the only one of the early resorts remaining today. Vinton also expanded his business interests by planting vineyards on the shores of the bay and by distilling port and sherry from the grapes.

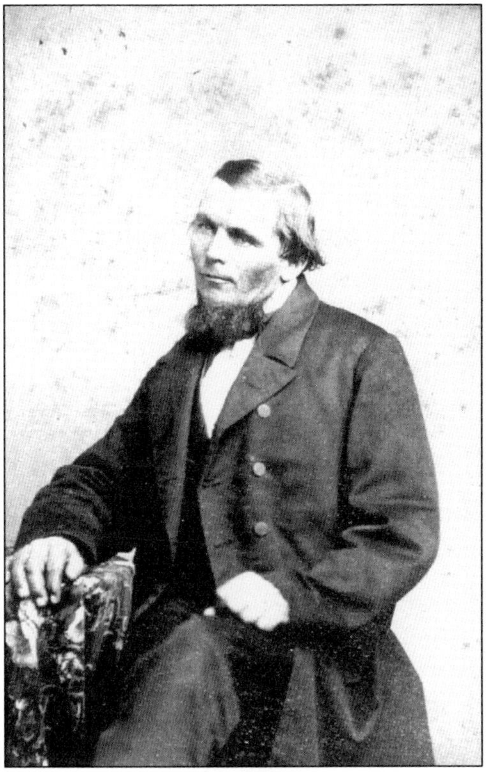

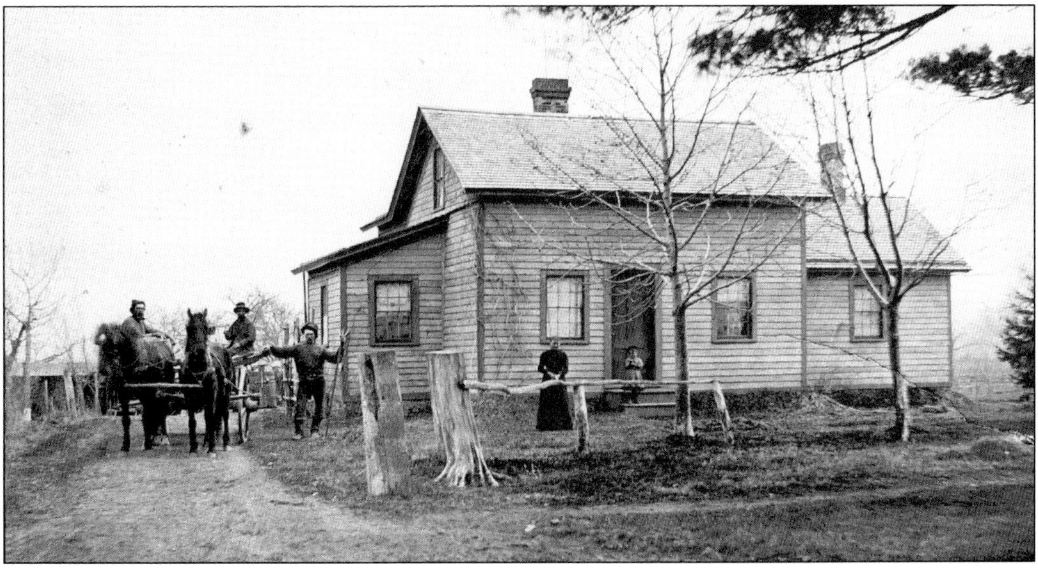

This early home was built by the Holland family in 1830 on Ridge Road East. It was later purchased in 1870 by Louis J. Dubelbeiss and his wife Caroline. Like many of the early houses, the frame consisted mostly of hewn logs between the split boards to hold the plaster and clapboards. The house was lined with brick and had a deep cellar under the whole house. The little boy in the doorway is Louis J. Dubelbeiss at the age of three. His mother Caroline is standing at the left, and Louis Dubelbeiss Sr. is standing next to the wagon. The two men behind the wagon were hired to work in the vineyards on the farm.

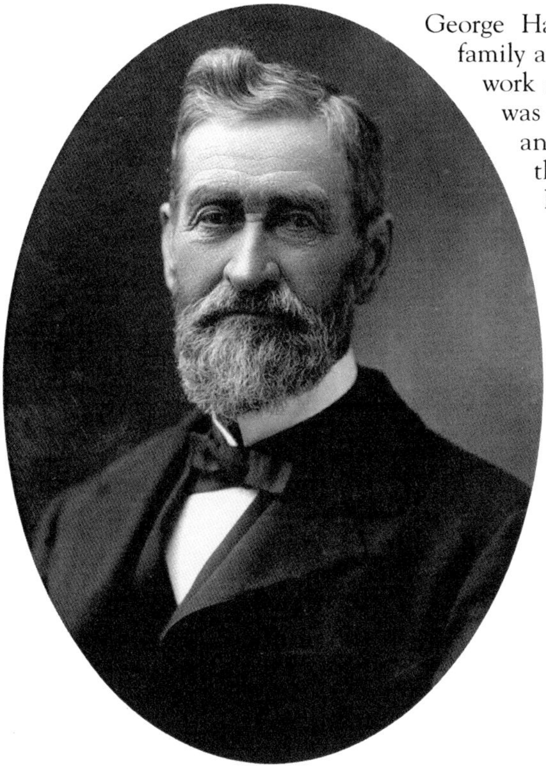

George Hardison emigrated from England with his family and eventually settled in Irondequoit, finding work as a ship builder with Hosea Rogers. Travel was necessary in his line of work, which took him and his family to several ports and residences on the Great Lakes. Their permanent residence, however, was a "big white farmhouse" at the corner of St. Paul Boulevard and Titus Avenue in Irondequoit. In the Cole family history recorded by June Cole Stanton, she writes that George Hardison "was a very impressive figure, and at one time, was mayor of Charlotte." Hardison Road in Irondequoit is named for his family.

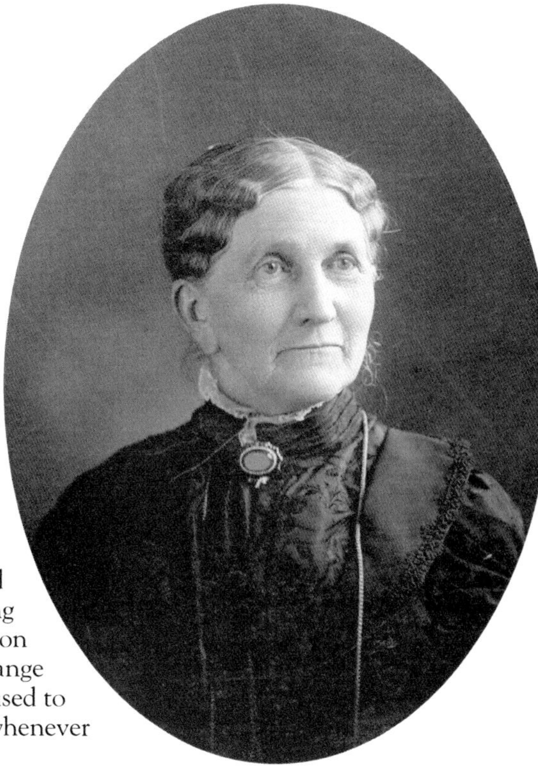

Pictured here is George Hardison's wife, Eliza. The couple lived on Titus Avenue and this is where their niece Lily Hardison, who they raised, married Mason Cole. June Cole Stanton fondly recalls stories she was told of her mother's wedding in the Cole family history. "My mother was married at the house on Titus Avenue and I have heard her tell of a home wedding. She was wearing a silk dress and there were orange blossoms on the cake. She kept the remains of those orange blossoms in a box in her dresser drawer. We used to sneak into her bedroom and look at them whenever we could get the opportunity."

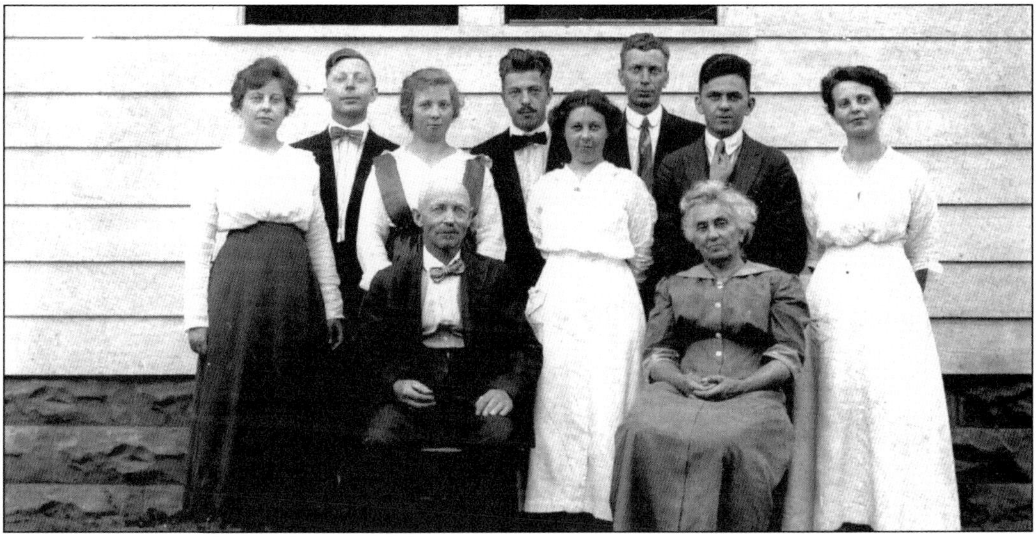

The Coles, one of several pioneer families in Irondequoit, once owned between 500 and 1,500 acres in the area. Above is the family of Mason (1858–1921) and Lily Hardison Cole (1856–1932), who are both seated. Eight of their nine children appear in this photograph. They are, from left to right, Harriet Cole Pettengill (1881–1958), John H. Cole (1888–1933), Ruby Cole Finlay (1893–1984), Mason Cole Jr. (1896–1964), Sara Cole Flack (1895–1975), Edward M. "Ted" Cole (1885–1970), Clyde N. Cole (1898–1949), and June Cole Stanton (1890–1974). Clarice Cole Deppisch (1883–1964) is not shown, but appears on page 31. Colebrook Road (formerly Cole Road) in Irondequoit is named for the family.

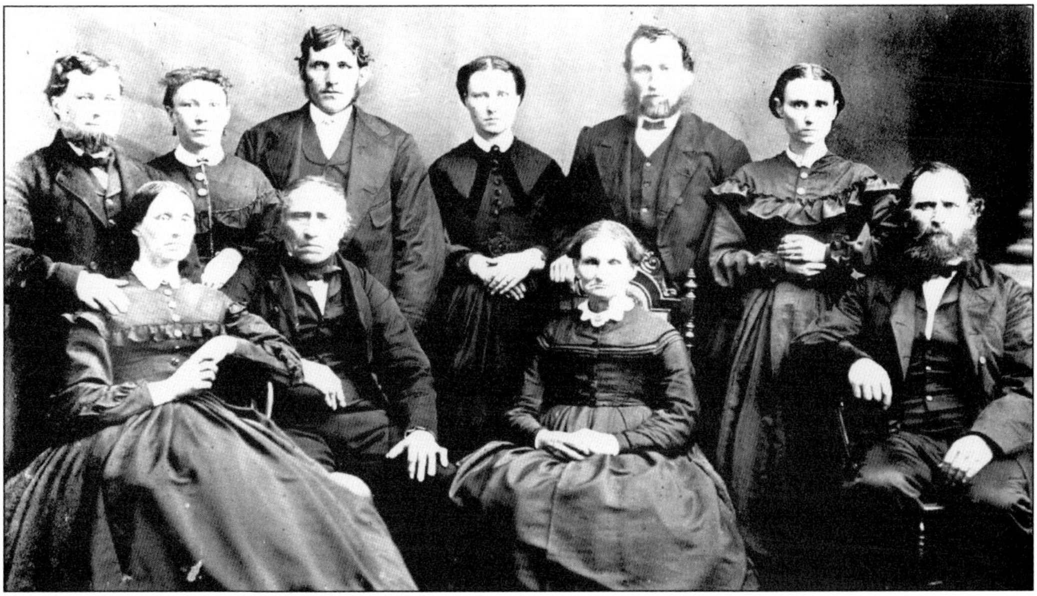

Henry and Ester Stanton came from Norwich, Connecticut, on their honeymoon riding double on horseback in 1814, and reportedly had the first frame house in Irondequoit. They are pictured here around the time of the Civil War with their eight children. From left to right are (first row) Eunice, Henry, Ester, and Charles; (second row) Ezra, Mary, George, Prescilla, Harrison, and Eliza. Their grim expressions may have been because of bad teeth, tight corsets, hoop skirts, or having to pose for an hour before the photographer was ready.

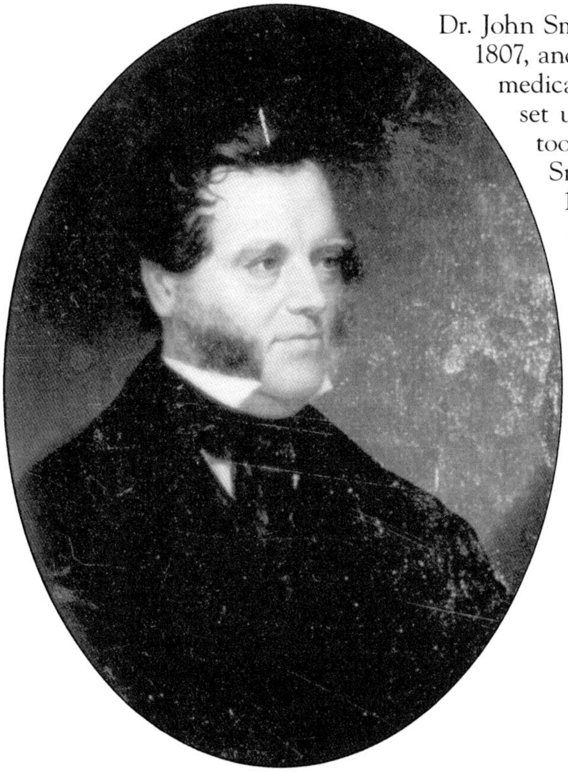

Dr. John Smyles was born in Edinburgh, Scotland, in 1807, and was a graduate of Edinburgh University's medical school. He came to Irondequoit in 1835, set up his practice on Empire Boulevard, and took up a partnership in a local drugstore. Smyles served as town supervisor in 1853, 1858, and 1859, and was one of the leading abolitionists in the area. His home still stands on Empire Boulevard.

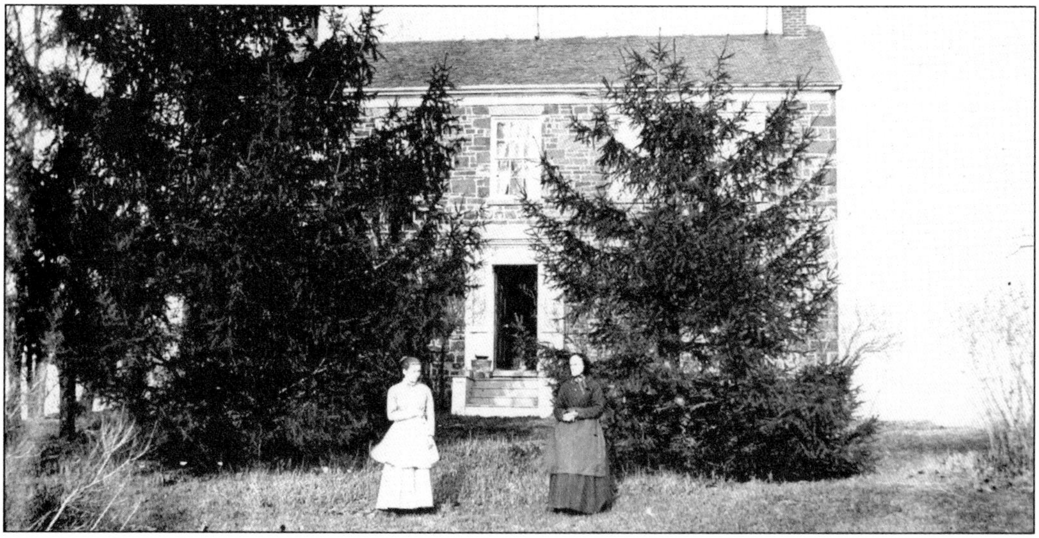

In 1823, Alexander Hooker purchased a farm on what is now Portland Avenue from Jesse Tainter. Tainter was more than willing to sell after the great loss he suffered due to Genesee Fever. As Tainter put it, "most of my family is buried on the sand ridge in back of the house." Hooker was not discouraged and used the profits from the lumber he cleared to pay for draining the swamp on his farm. He became a town leader, served as town clerk, and donated land for the first town cemetery and one of the town's first schoolhouses. Hooker built a beautiful fieldstone house for his wife Lucy and family to replace the run-down cabin that had been their home when they purchased the farm.

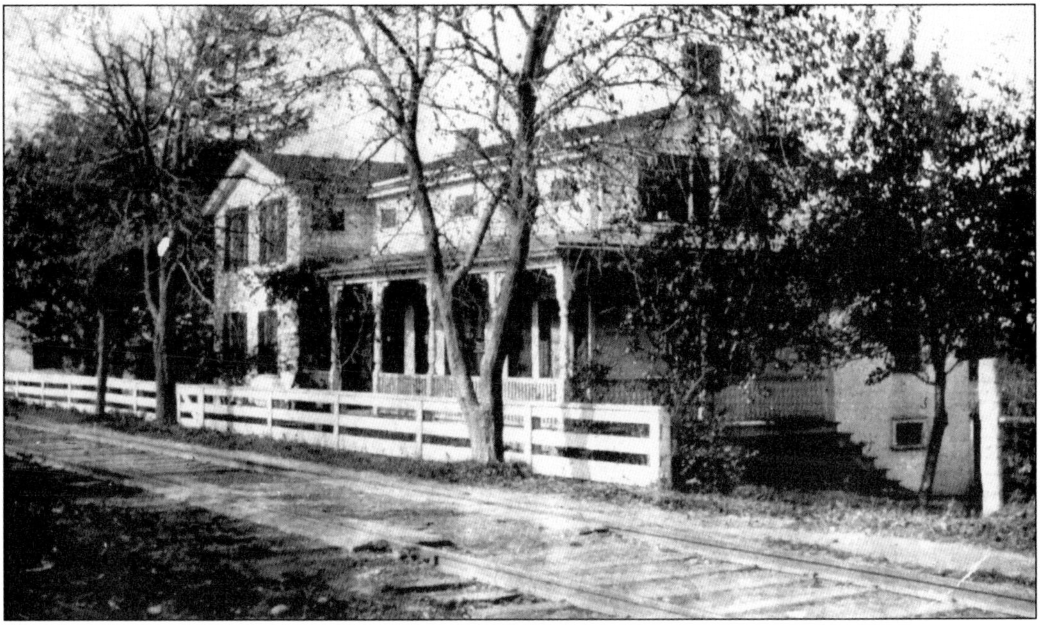

This home once stood at 1480 Ridge Road East and was built in 1856 by Lucy Bundy. She sold the home to Cleveland Bradstreet in 1874. The interesting feature of the picture is the trolley line going right past the front of the house. Trolleys changed Irondequoit from just a farming community to a vacation destination, bringing vacationers to resort hotels on the shores of Lake Ontario and Irondequoit Bay and to the growing amusement park at Sea Breeze.

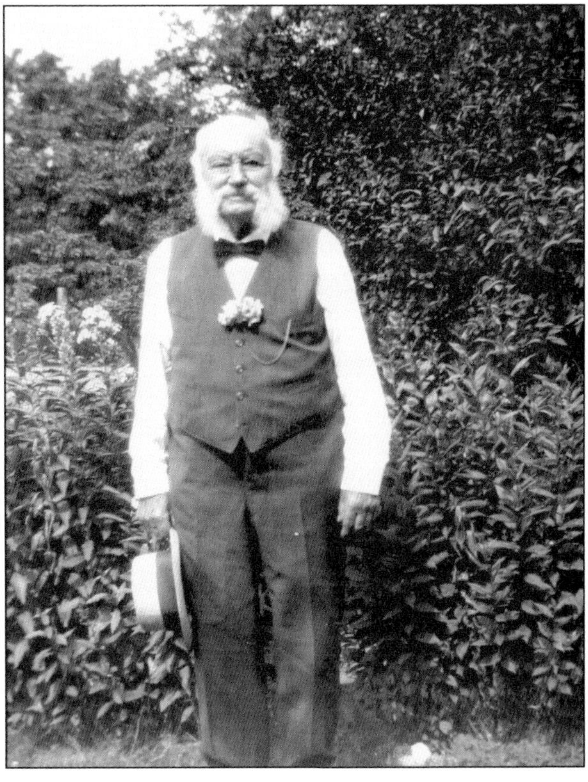

One of the most prominent of the market gardeners was George Cooper. In 1911, at the age of 85, he wrote recollections of his 81 years spent in Irondequoit. He was born in England in 1827 and came to America when he was three years old. The family moved to Irondequoit in 1837. Cooper married Phoebe Janet Titus and began raising trees and growing vegetables. He sold his produce and trees on Main and Front Streets in Rochester. His produce included grapes, currents, raspberries, rhubarb, asparagus, boxwood, cabbage, and tomato plants, plus sage and thyme. His memoirs are a great source of information about the early farming days. George Cooper died in 1922 at the age of 95 and is shown here at his home on Cooper Road.

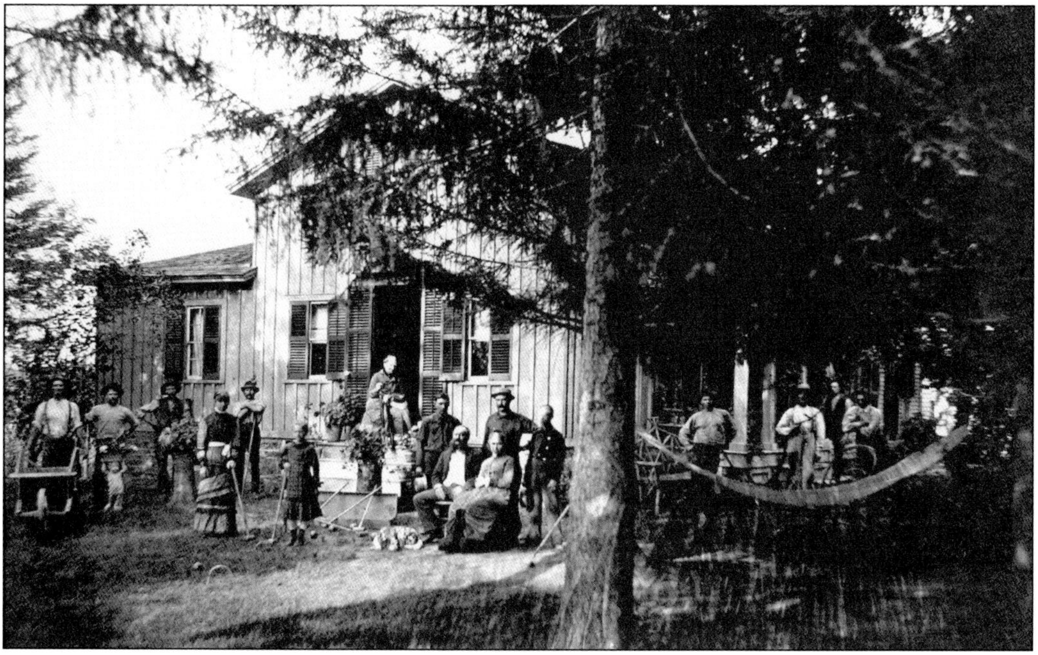

There is an old adage that "all work and no play, makes Jack a dull boy." Certainly the Cooper and Titus families believed this was true when they gave a picnic for their hired hands on their farms. Emmaline Sherry, the mother of George Titus, is seated in the doorway and George Titus and his wife, Phoebe, are seated on the lawn.

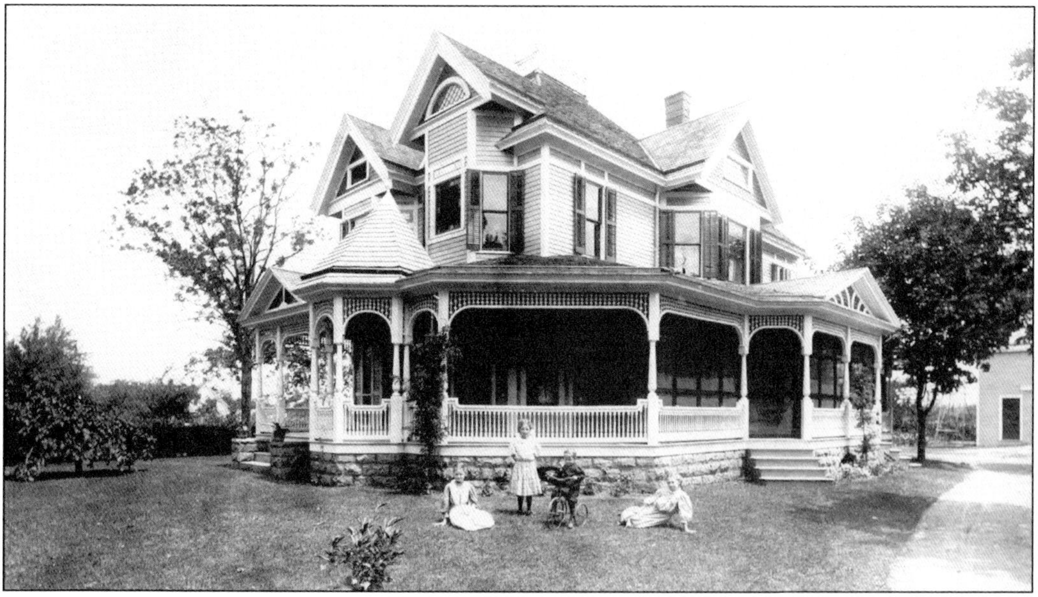

This gracious family home located at 1754 Hudson Avenue was the residence of the William Hallauer family in 1907. The wide porch or veranda was characteristic of the less-frantic lifestyle of the early 20th century. People had time, despite the lack of so-called labor-saving devices, to sit on the front porch on a cool summer evening with neighbors and family. The wooden beadwork trim at the top of the porch and the delicate spindle railing illustrate craftsmanship that is difficult to duplicate today.

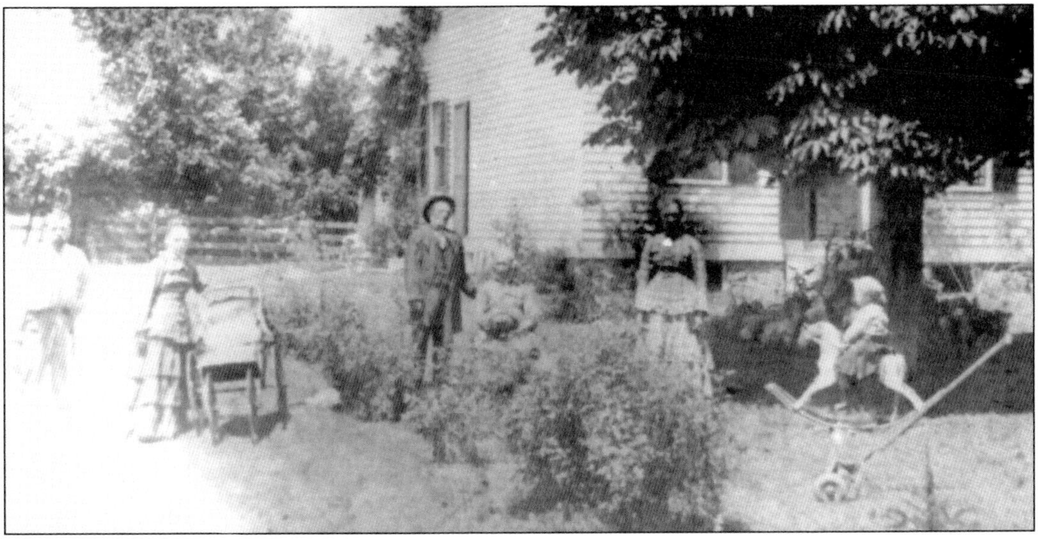

In 1827, Sidney Grant gave up his role as a teacher and moved to Irondequoit, purchasing a farm at what is now 3219 St. Paul Boulevard. He and his wife, Adelade Hayward Grant, who were both interested in education, turned their kitchen into a makeshift classroom where they taught adults who could not read or write. Adelade was the president of the Women's Christian Temperance Union and founder of the local Sunday school movement. This photograph, taken in 1876, shows the Grant family. From left to right are oldest son Frank with his wife Eva Drake Grant, Sidney, Adeline, and Mate Wilson, a tailoress in one of the early clothing factories. The child on the rocking horse is Frank and Eva's son, Pierce.

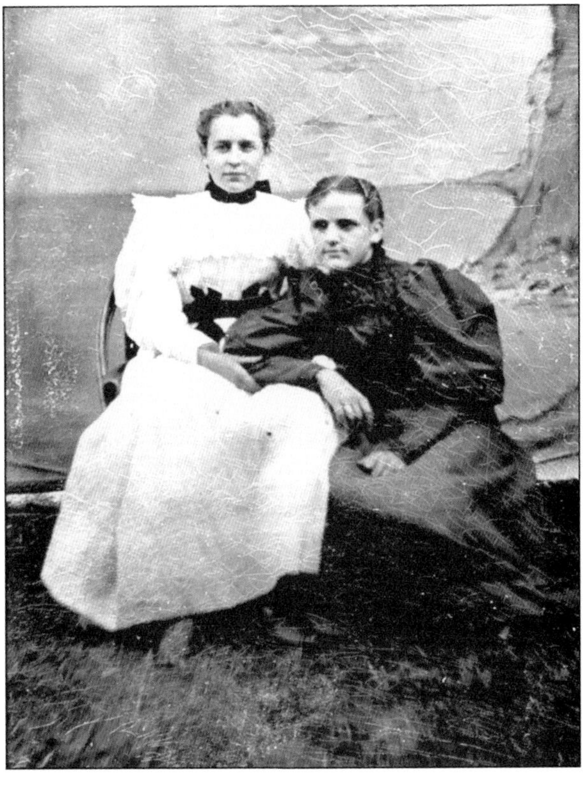

This engaging tin type shows two young ladies from pioneer families, Lucy Lamming and Eva Rudman. Lucy Lamming's mother Lillian Rudman married David Lamming, and Lucy married Otto Bitters. Eva Rudman's father, William Rudman was Lucy Lamming's mother's brother, making the girls cousins. As Irondequoit grew, many of the early settlers inter-married and newcomers were cautioned to be careful of gossip because one never knew who was related to whom.

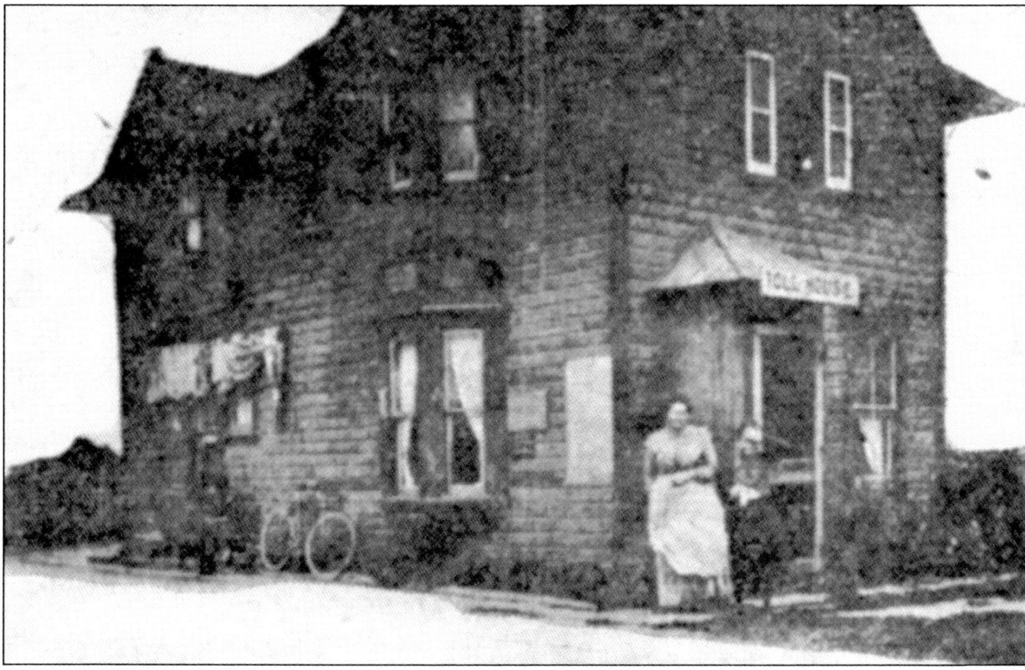

An old newspaper article revealed the difficulties of traveling St. Paul Boulevard in the past. When the town assumed control of the boulevard the toll house was moved to 48 Wimbledon Drive.

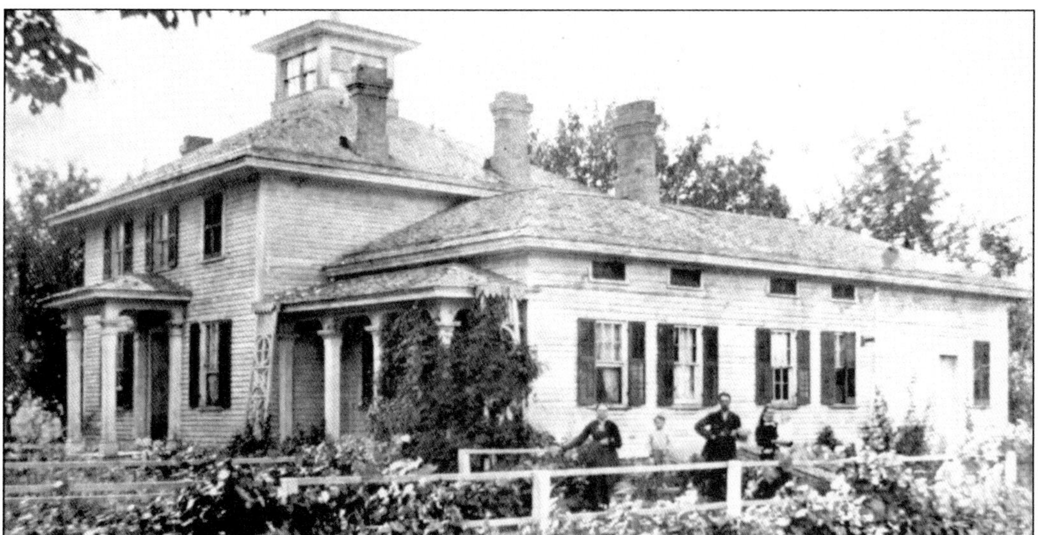

One of the many early families of Irondequoit that prospered through hard work on the land were the Coys. This lovely home was built by James and Maria Coy in 1847. The large addition was added in 1850. A stand of white pine trees, not visible in this 1870 picture, led to the naming of the street as Pinegrove Avenue. From 1905 to 1907, the extensive peach orchards in Irondequoit bore no fruit because of killing frost at budding time. The only orchard that produced fruit was the Coy orchard, protected by the modifying effect of Lake Ontario. In 1943, this family home was torn down and the Coy farm, like many others, became only a memory.

One of the indications of a growing prosperous middle class in Irondequoit was the ability to pay for studio photographs. The dapper man on the left was Canadian-born Archibald Bellamy who, after graduating from Queen's Medical College in Kingston, Ontario, came to Irondequoit to practice medicine. Bellamy lived with John Ernisse, a prosperous market gardener and lifelong resident of Irondequoit. Bellamy's office was at 1255 Ridge Road East. He died in April 1913, at age 42.

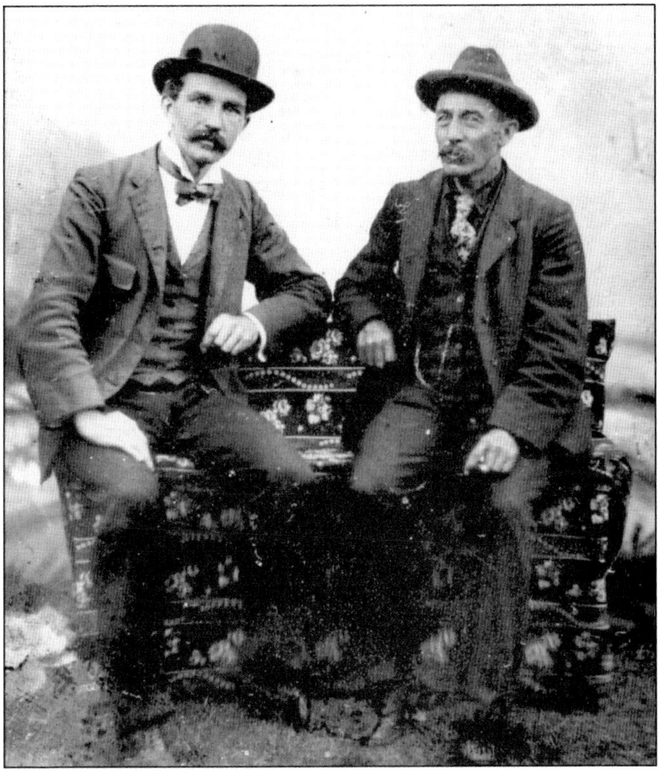

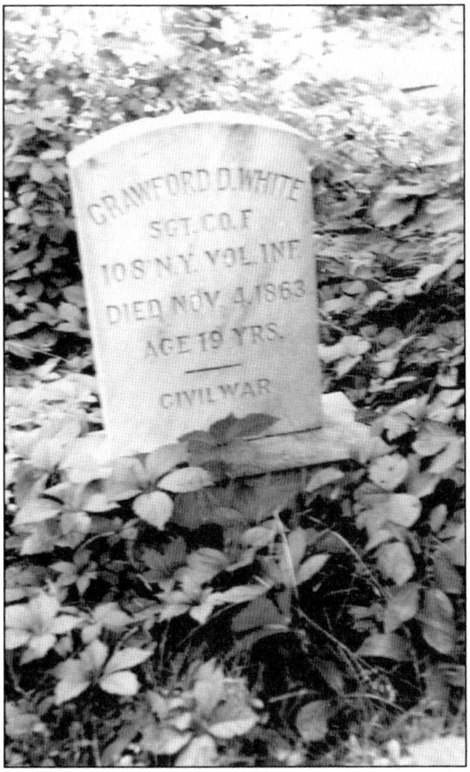

In 1861, the nation was torn apart over the issues of states' rights and slavery. Irondequoit was called upon to make sacrifices to preserve the union. While there is no proof that stations on the Underground Railroad existed in the town, many prominent citizens were abolitionists, including Dr. John Smyles. Army recruiters set up a tent at the corner of Culver and Ridge Roads and 108 young men served the cause. This was a severe strain on an agricultural community of just over 5,000. Crawford White was 18 when he enlisted. He was captured and imprisoned in Richmond where he became ill and was exchanged. He died in 1863, shortly after he returned to Irondequoit, and is buried in the Pioneer Cemetery.

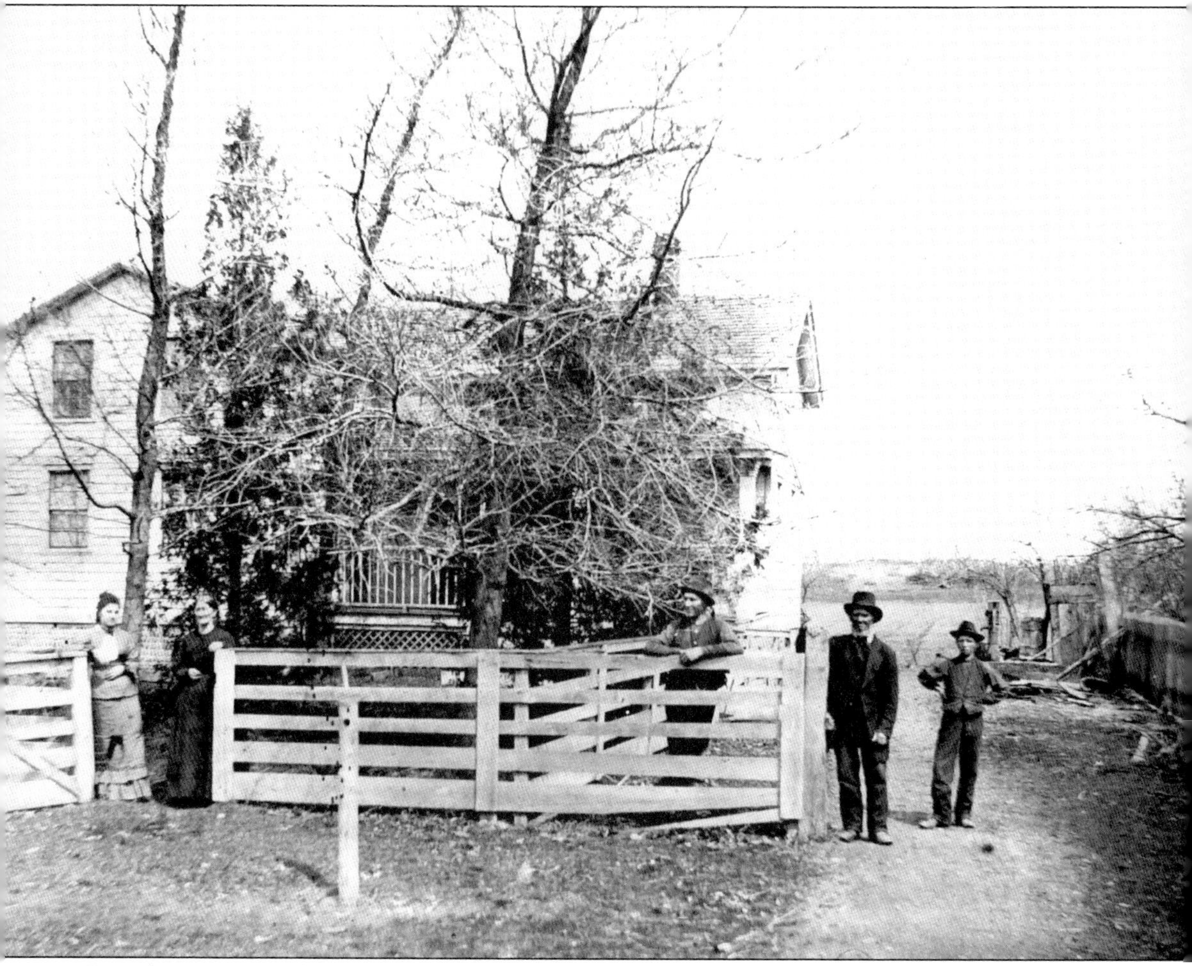

Benedict Aman and his family left France and moved to Irondequoit in 1825. Four generations of the Aman family lived in this home at 2626 Ridge Road East. Pictured here are Benedict, Jacob, and Rupert Aman. The home was torn down when the Keeler Street expressway was built in 1971. Benedict and his wife, Barbara Mosher (seen second from left), had 11 children. One of his sons, Joseph, served as justice of the peace in 1884 and as town supervisor from 1901 to 1905. The Aman family still lives in Irondequoit and operates a farm market on Ridge Road East.

Three

Market Gardening and Community Growth

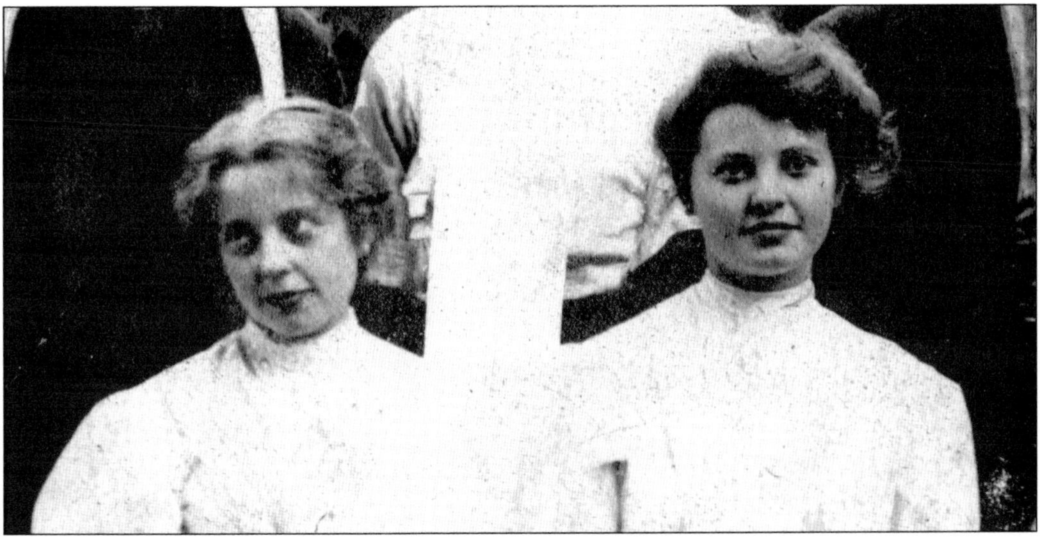

"We always had lots of vegetables and fruit since my father was a truck farmer. My father, in the summertime would take his produce to the Market in the city. On a Sunday afternoon we used to sit out on the porch. I think that is one of the good things this generation is missing—sitting on the porch with the family and taking walks to the woods. Now people are always seeking ways to amuse themselves. In those days, we really had time to know ourselves and each other. We had a wonderful family picnic in August every year. The whole family on both sides would come. We had a great big table on Grandpas front lawn. Everyone brought their home-made specialties. Aunt Hattie brought a four layer cake. Ma specialized in a mustard pickle, always in 2 quart jars. Aunt Eliza always made brown bread." This excerpt was taken from *Cole Family Memories*, written in 1970, by June Lily Cole Stanton (right). Pictured with her in the early 1900s is her sister Clarice Cole Deppisch.

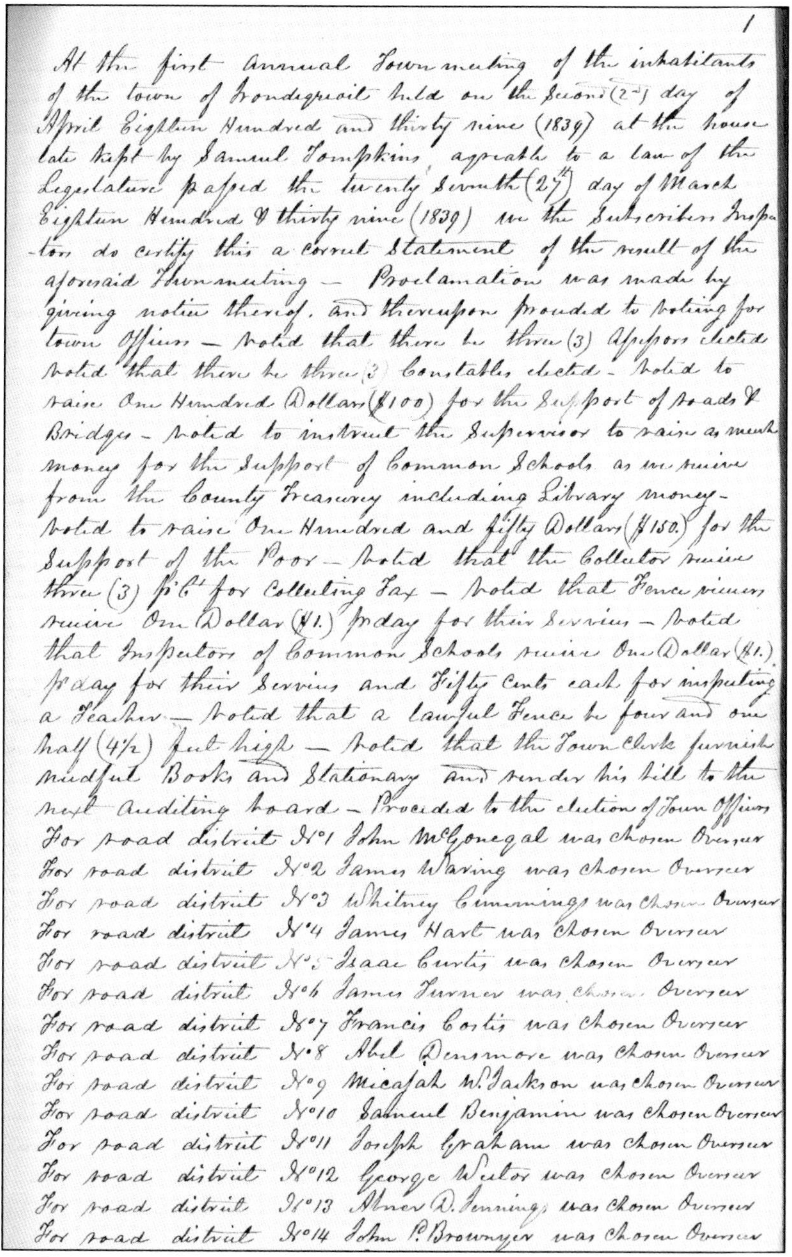

1

At the first Annual Town meeting of the inhabitants of the town of Irondequoit held on the Second (2nd) day of April Eighteen Hundred and thirty nine (1839) at the house late kept by Samuel Tompkins agreeable to a law of the Legislature passed the twenty Seventh (27th) day of March Eighteen Hundred & thirty nine (1839) we the Subscribers Inspectors do certify this a correct Statement of the result of the aforesaid Town meeting — Proclamation was made by giving notice thereof, and thereupon proceeded to voting for town Officers — Voted that there be three (3) Assessors elected Voted that there be three (3) Constables elected — Voted to raise One Hundred Dollars ($100) for the Support of roads & Bridges — voted to instruct the Supervisor to raise as much money for the Support of Common Schools as we receive from the County Treasurey including Library money — Voted to raise One Hundred and fifty Dollars ($150.) for the Support of the Poor — Voted that the Collector receive three (3) pr Ct for Collecting Tax — Voted that Fence viewers receive One Dollar ($1.) pr day for their Services — Voted that Inspectors of Common Schools receive One Dollar ($1.) pr day for their Services and Fifty Cents each for inspecting a Teacher — Voted that a lawful Fence be four and one half (4½) feet high — Voted that the Town Clerk furnish needful Books and Stationary and render his bill to the next auditing board — Proceeded to the election of Town Officers

For road district No 1 John McGonegal was Chosen Overseer
For road district No 2 James Waring was Chosen Overseer
For road district No 3 Whitney Cummings was Chosen Overseer
For road district No 4 James Hart was Chosen Overseer
For road district No 5 Isaac Curtis was Chosen Overseer
For road district No 6 James Turner was Chosen Overseer
For road district No 7 Francis Curtis was Chosen Overseer
For road district No 8 Abel Densmore was Chosen Overseer
For road district No 9 Micajah W. Jackson was Chosen Overseer
For road district No 10 Samuel Benjamin was Chosen Overseer
For road district No 11 Joseph Graham was Chosen Overseer
For road district No 12 George Weitor was Chosen Overseer
For road district No 13 Abner D. Jennings was Chosen Overseer
For road district No 14 John P. Brownyer was Chosen Overseer

On April 2, 1839, as many male citizens as possible crowded into an Irondequoit tavern owned by Samuel Tompkins at the corner of Ridge and Culver Roads. Alexander Hooker, town clerk, kept meticulous notes as indicated by this beginning paragraph. The phrase "a house kept by" indicated that Tompkins was a tavern keeper and his tavern was probably the only building in town that could accommodate the citizens who had come to participate in the organization of their new town government. They dealt with the problems of road maintenance, education, care of the poor, and the election of a town supervisor. That election ended in a tie between William Shepherd and Joseph Graham. In a subsequent run-off election, William Shepherd became the first supervisor. The intersection of Ridge and Culver Roads was the center of the small community for years to come.

Gertude Rudman proudly displayed part of a bumper Irondequoit peach crop in 1913. She is all decked out in pantaloons, petticoats, high button shoes, black stockings, and a giant hair bow, typical little girl fashion for that era.

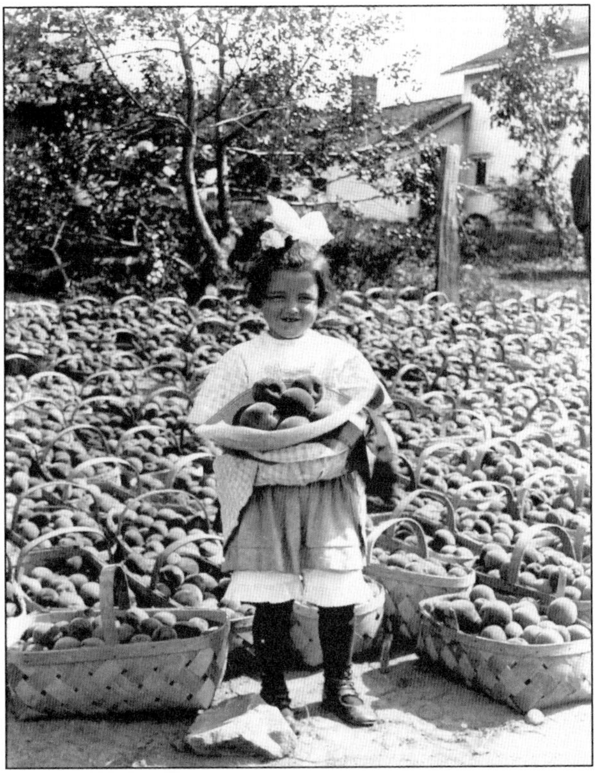

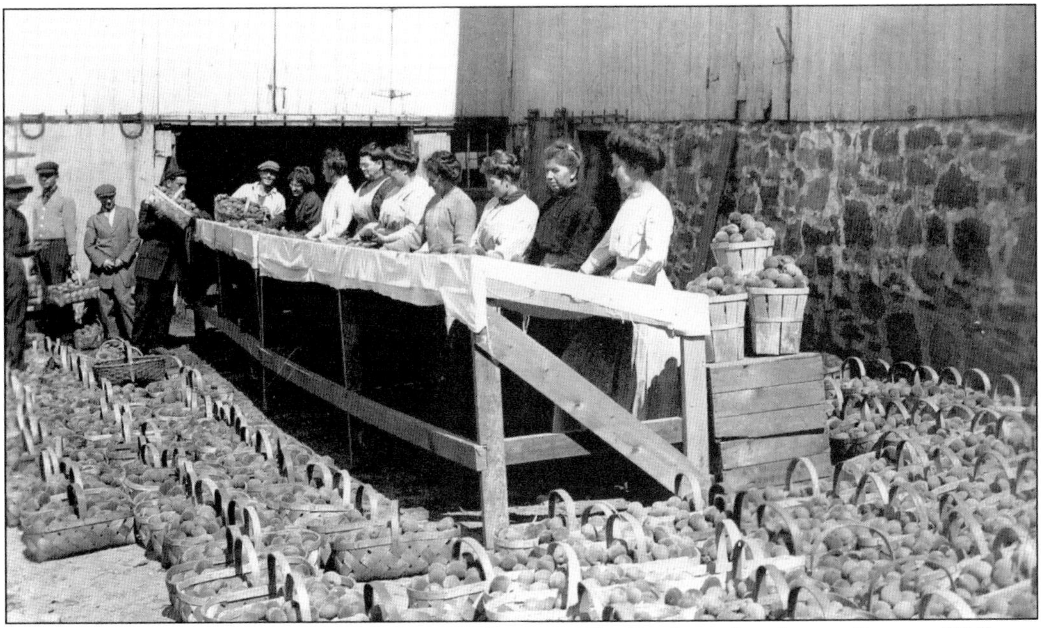

Peaches were a major crop for Irondequoit farmers. The Rudman brothers—George, William, and Roy—were known as "the peach kings of western New York." Their orchards covered 150 acres, occupying all the land to the west of Oakview Drive from Titus Avenue to List Avenue. These women sorted the luscious fruit before packaging them into baskets for market. All the women wore long sleeves because peach fuzz on bare arms was an itchy proposition.

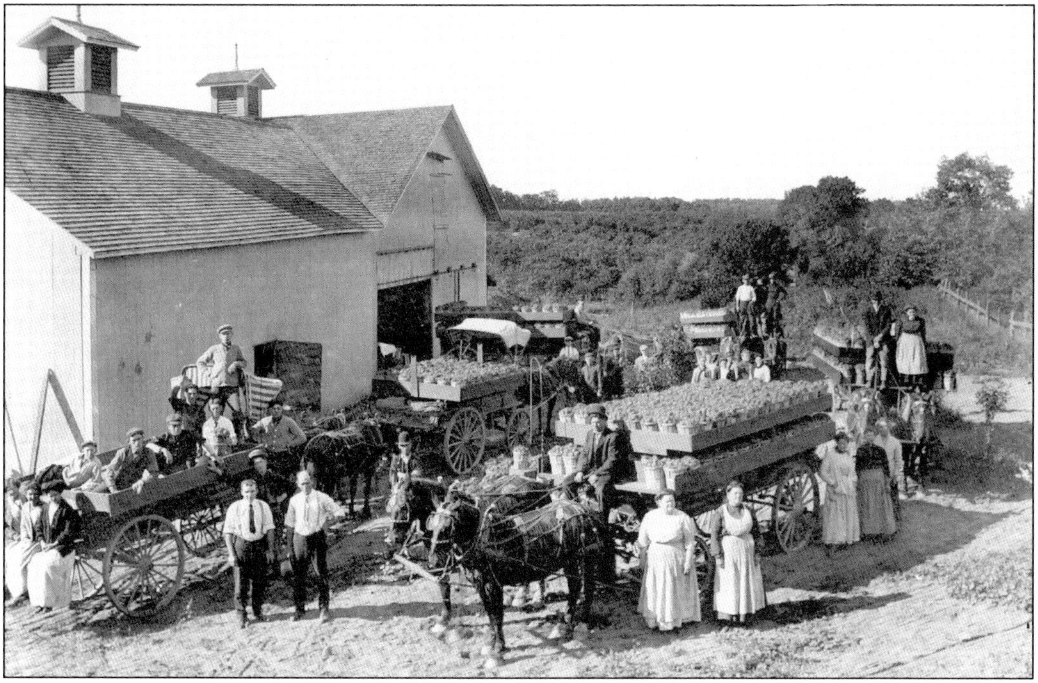

Tree-ripened peaches needed to be moved quickly to market before the soft fruit rotted. Picking and packing them so they would not bruise was a challenging task. A large work force was needed at harvest time to fill and load the baskets for delivery to the public market, which was then located at the site of the present Liberty Pole on Main Street.

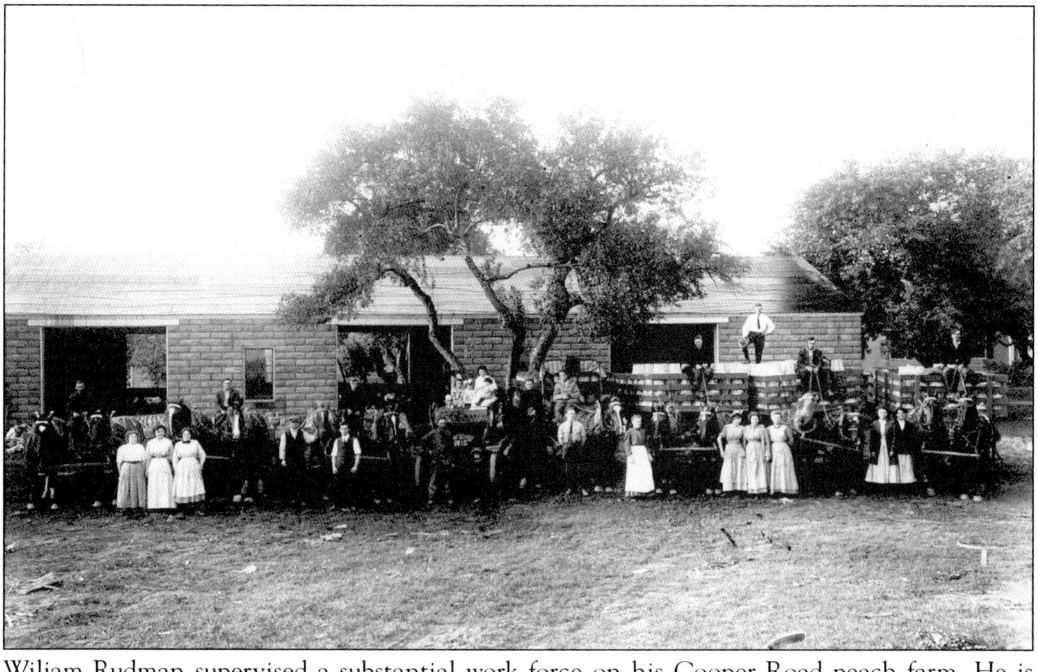

Wiliam Rudman supervised a substantial work force on his Cooper Road peach farm. He is pictured in the front seat of his car (center) with his wife, Hattie Stanton Rudman, and children Gertude, Sarah, and Avis in the back seat.

The Irondequoit melon had the reputation of being the sweetest, juiciest melon grown in the United States. In 1924, Charles Ernisse posed with this delicious fruit. A hard lesson was learned when the melons were decimated by a virus which spread because many of the farmers planted the melons in the same fields year after year. The very softness of the melon that made it so juicy also made shipping difficult. These two factors dealt a fatal blow to the production of the Irondequoit melons, and by 1940 they had disappeared from the market.

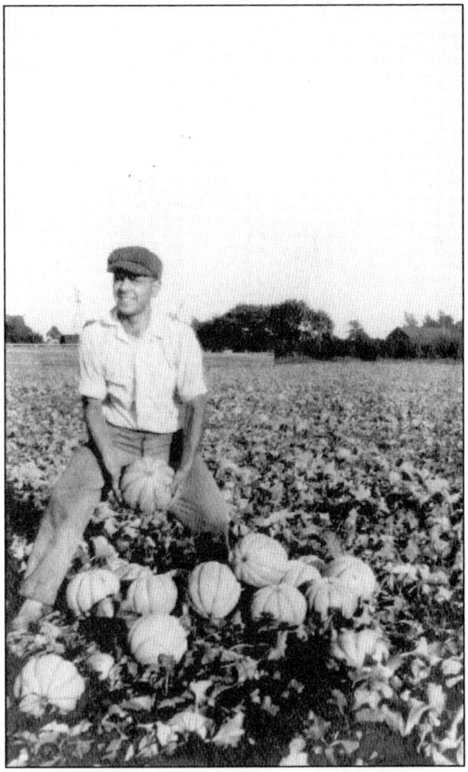

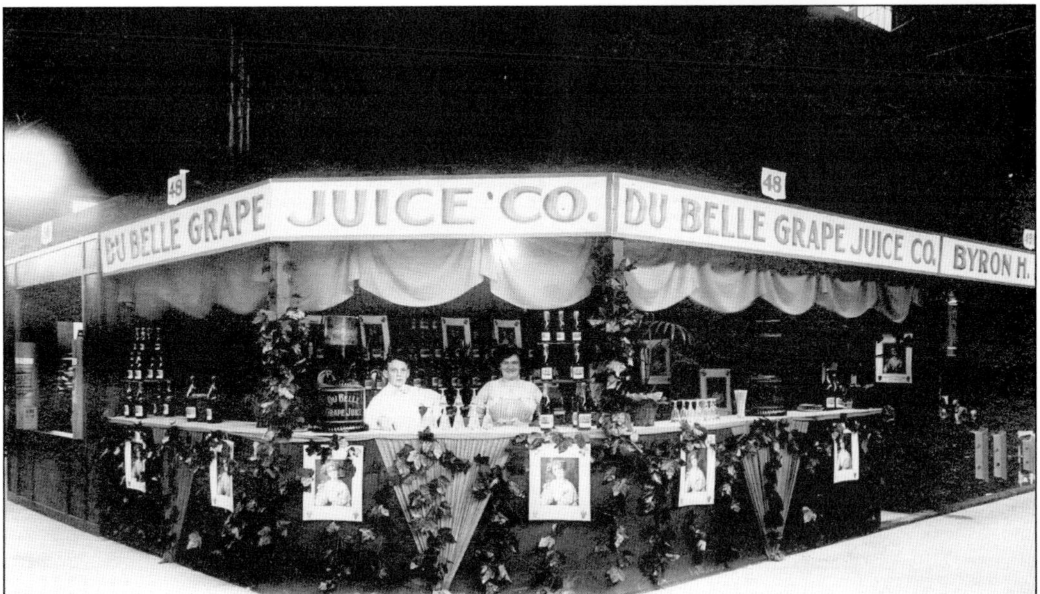

In 1912, the Du Belle Grape Juice Company set up this display at the Rochester Exhibition. The company was owned by the Dubelbeiss family who had been vintners of port and sherry wine with vineyards on the banks of Irondequoit Bay. In 1910, Louis Dubelbeiss discontinued the wine business and later moved to Fredonia, New York, and produced unfermented grape juice.

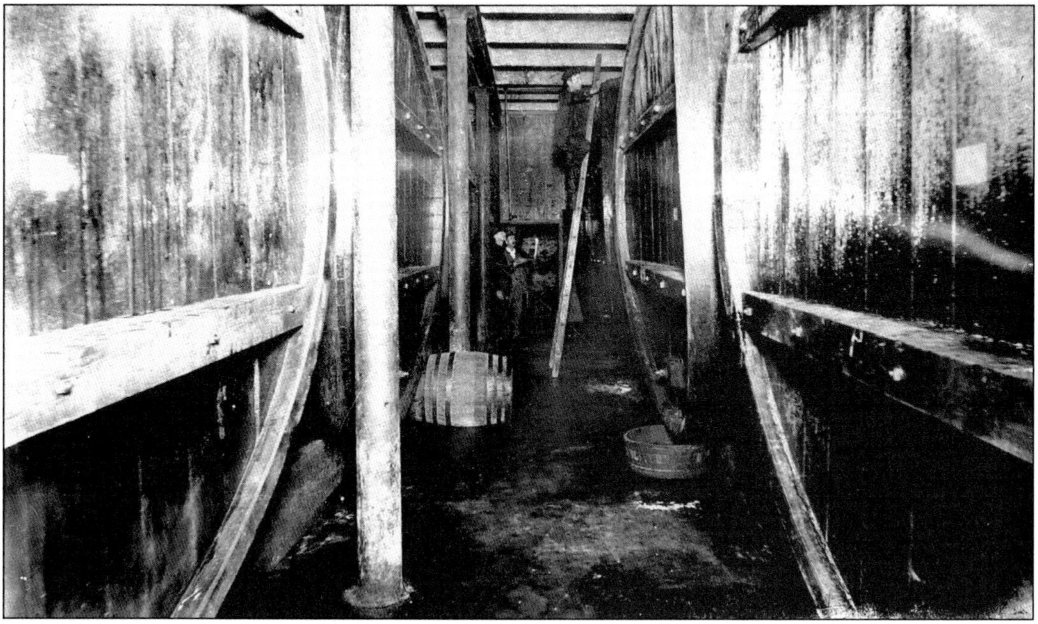

Asa Macbride was born in Steuben County in 1832. As a young man he worked in a store near Keuka Lake and became interested in the growing of grapes and processing them into wine. He moved to Rochester and was so impressed by the Vinton vineyards that he purchased 45 acres from Joseph Vinton and went into the wine business. By 1899, he formed the Irondequoit Wine Company, whose huge vats are pictured here. The claim that the business was established in 1832 came from the date of the Vinton vineyards that he purchased.

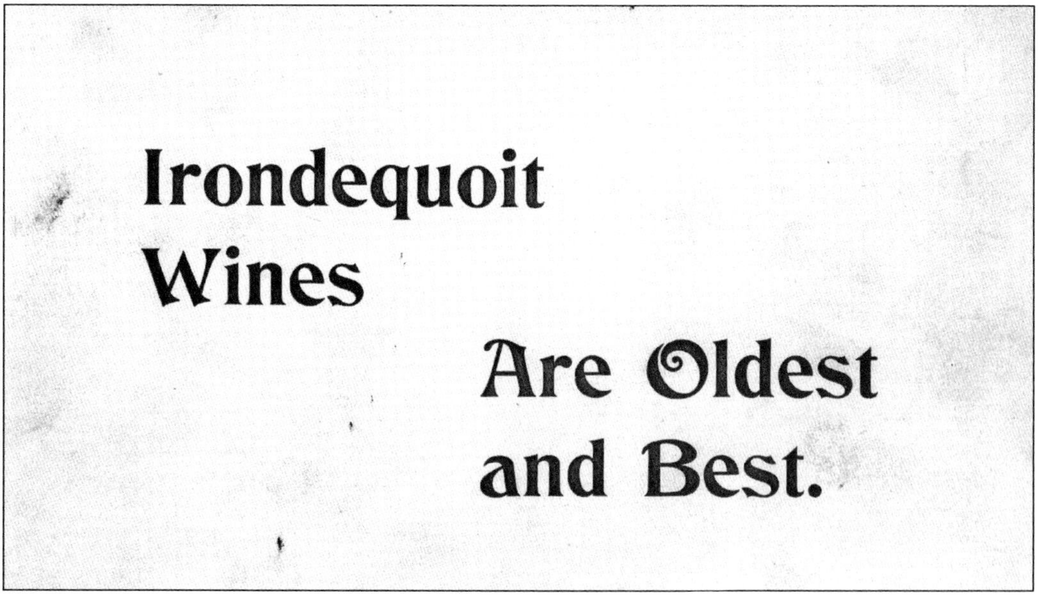

Irondequoit
Wines
Are Oldest
and Best.

On the back of the picture is the slogan "Irondequoit Wines are the Oldest and the Best." Like his neighbor Louis Dueblebeiss, MacBride also sold his wines only for home consumption and to druggists for medicinal purposes. The demand was enough to warrant the building of a new wine cellar on level ground above the bay. In 1909, the company began the manufacture of fruit juices, cordials, and ginger ale.

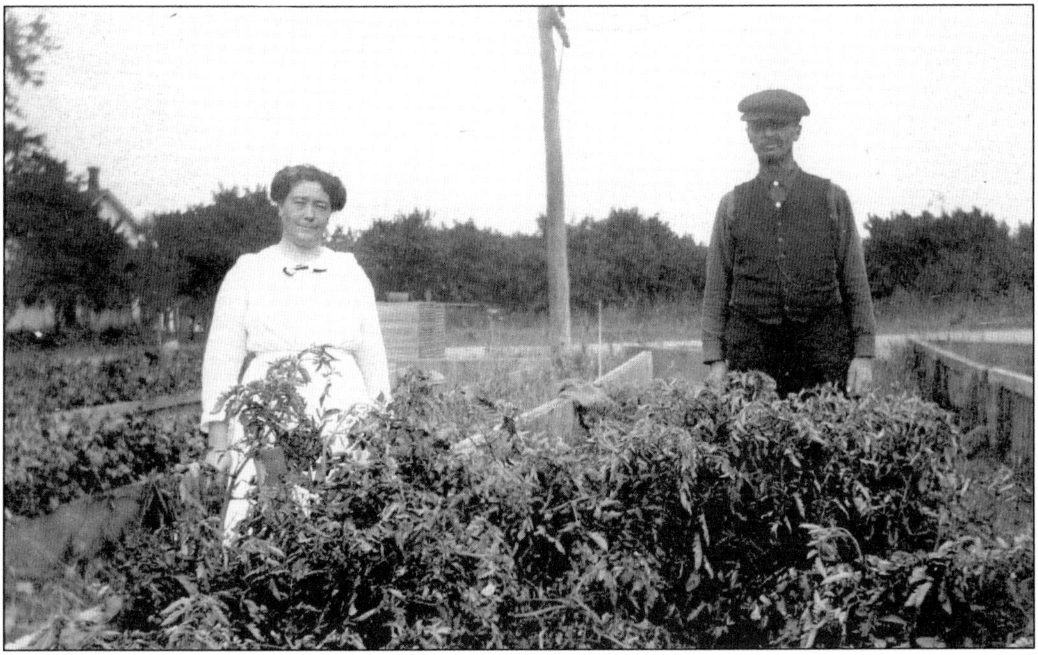

In 1914, Orlo and Emma Benedict posed with their tomato crop. The Benedicts were typical market gardeners whose farms were of small acreage but who specialized in crops that would produce a large yield from holdings that averaged about 50 acres. The Benedict farm was located at the present site of Irondequoit High School.

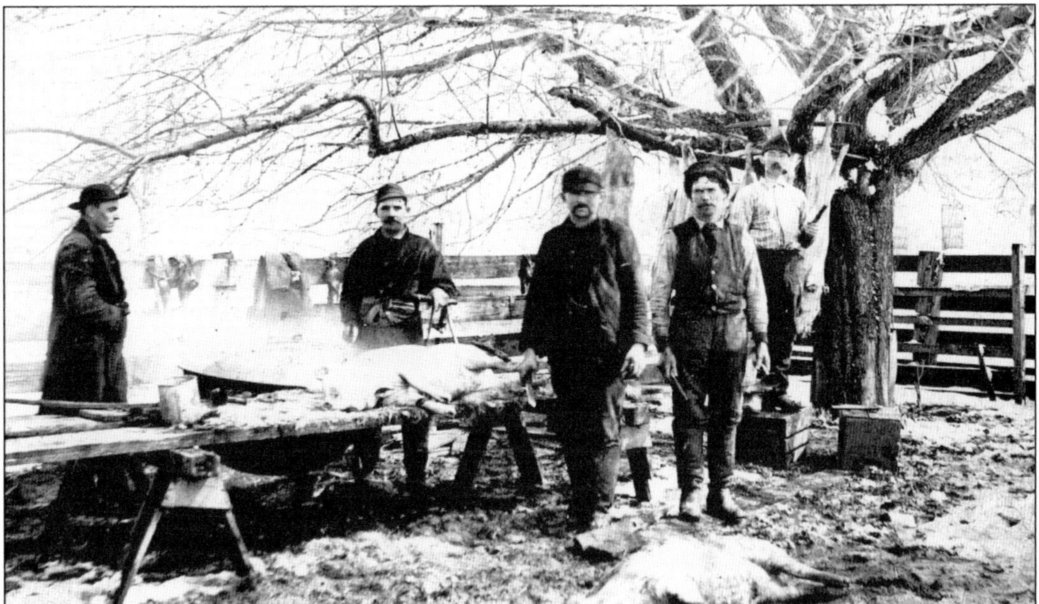

Today's grocery shoppers select their meat from packages wrapped in plastic from counters laden with all varieties. In this setting it is easy to forget that the killing of animals was involved in producing the product. But in farming communities, butchering of farm animals for food was not so sterile. On the List farm in 1942, the men gathered to ready a meat supply for the coming months by killing pigs and preparing them for market.

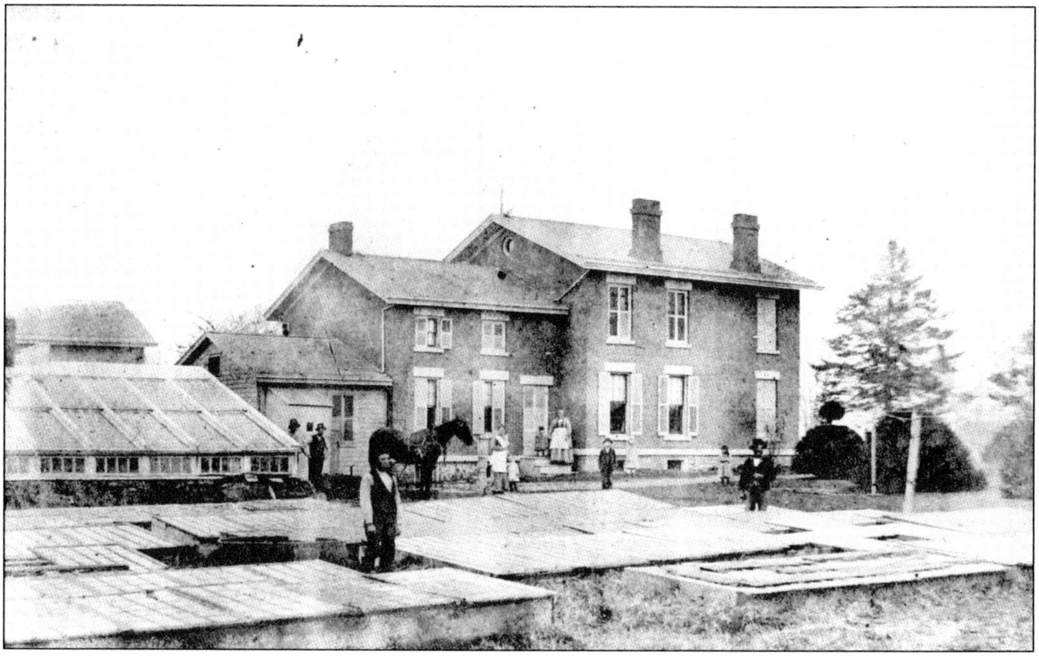

Many farmers grew their own seedlings for plantings and augmented their income by growing vegetables during the off-season in greenhouses. At David Rudman's home on Portland Avenue workers were transferring plants from the greenhouses to the cold frames to prepare for planting in the spring.

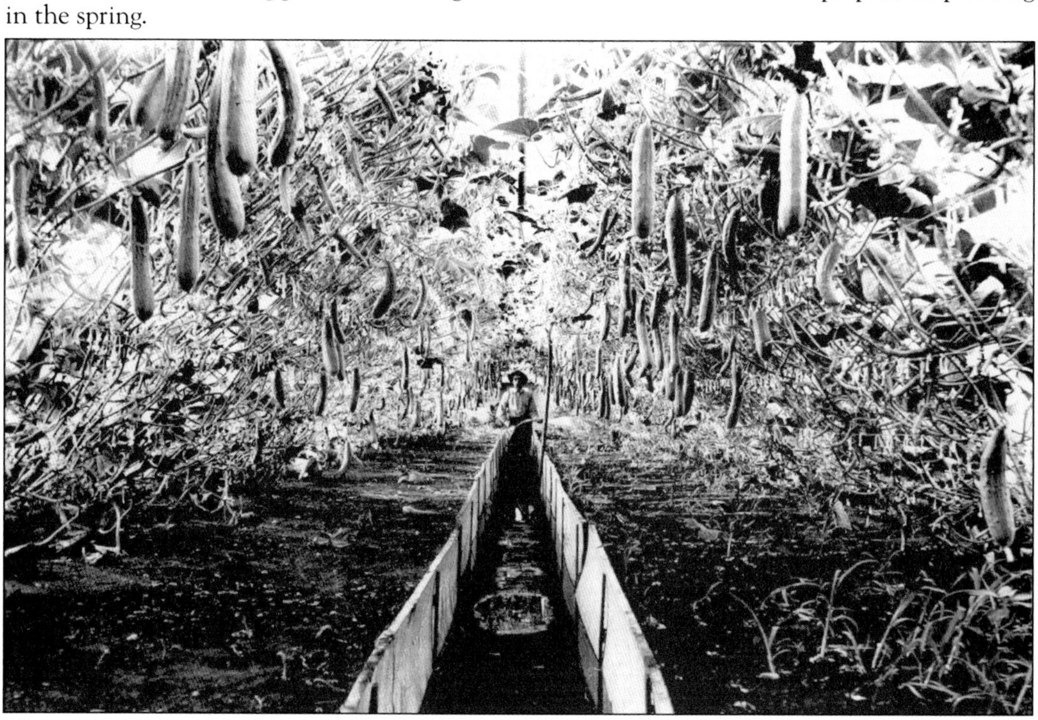

This picture of the Heffer greenhouse illustrates the trend toward producing crops for market in the off growing season. Heffer seems to have had a bumper crop of cucumbers for stores during the winter months.

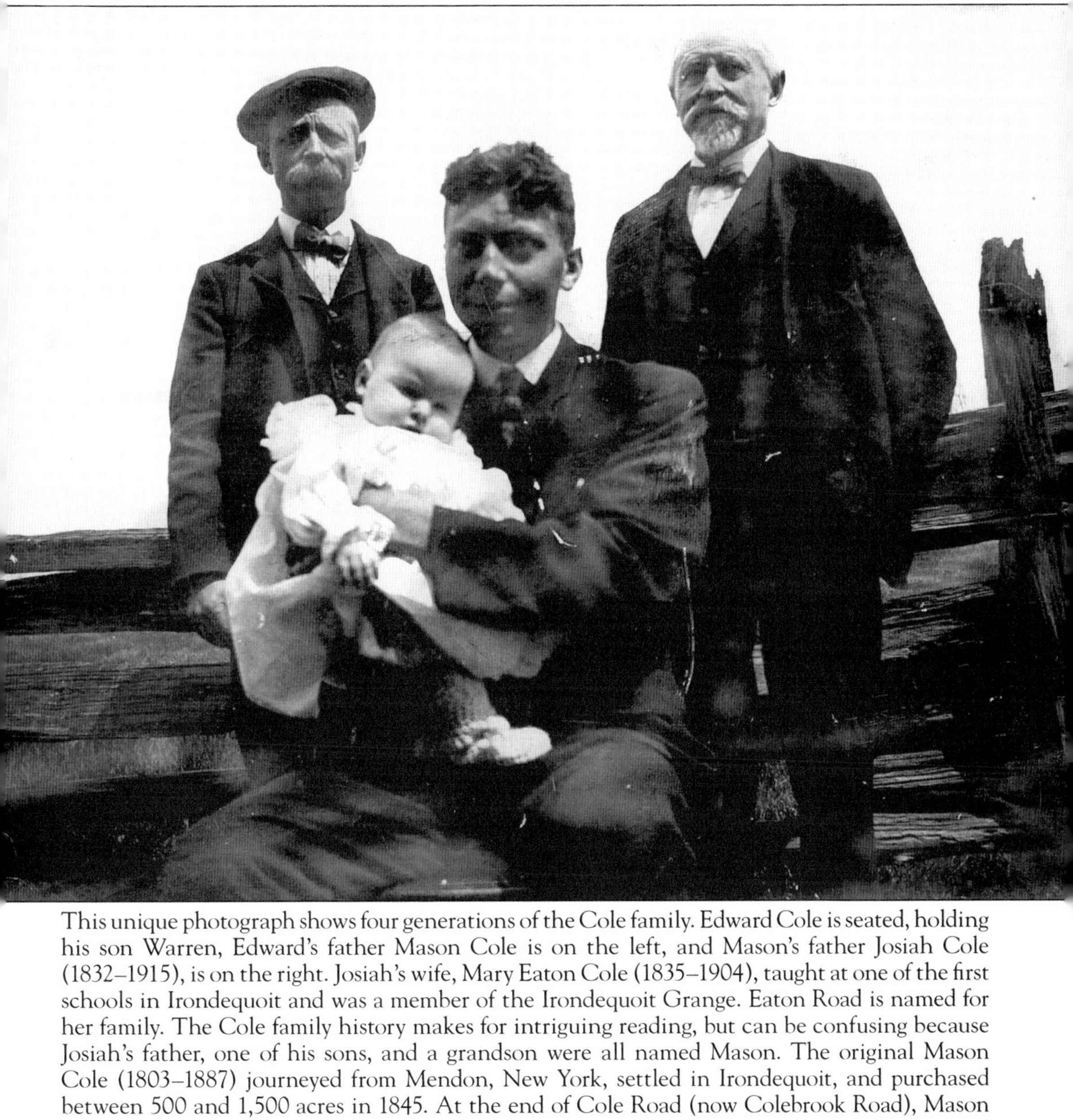

This unique photograph shows four generations of the Cole family. Edward Cole is seated, holding his son Warren, Edward's father Mason Cole is on the left, and Mason's father Josiah Cole (1832–1915), is on the right. Josiah's wife, Mary Eaton Cole (1835–1904), taught at one of the first schools in Irondequoit and was a member of the Irondequoit Grange. Eaton Road is named for her family. The Cole family history makes for intriguing reading, but can be confusing because Josiah's father, one of his sons, and a grandson were all named Mason. The original Mason Cole (1803–1887) journeyed from Mendon, New York, settled in Irondequoit, and purchased between 500 and 1,500 acres in 1845. At the end of Cole Road (now Colebrook Road), Mason built a large house, a farm with large yellow barns (a Cole trademark), a blacksmith shop, and a sawmill. He grew fruit, vegetables, and tobacco. Mason also sold ice cut from his ponds to summer residents and kept a pair of peacocks on his front lawn. Over the years, the property was divided between members of the Cole family, who donated land for one of the first schools in the area, Summerville, and St. Paul Boulevard.

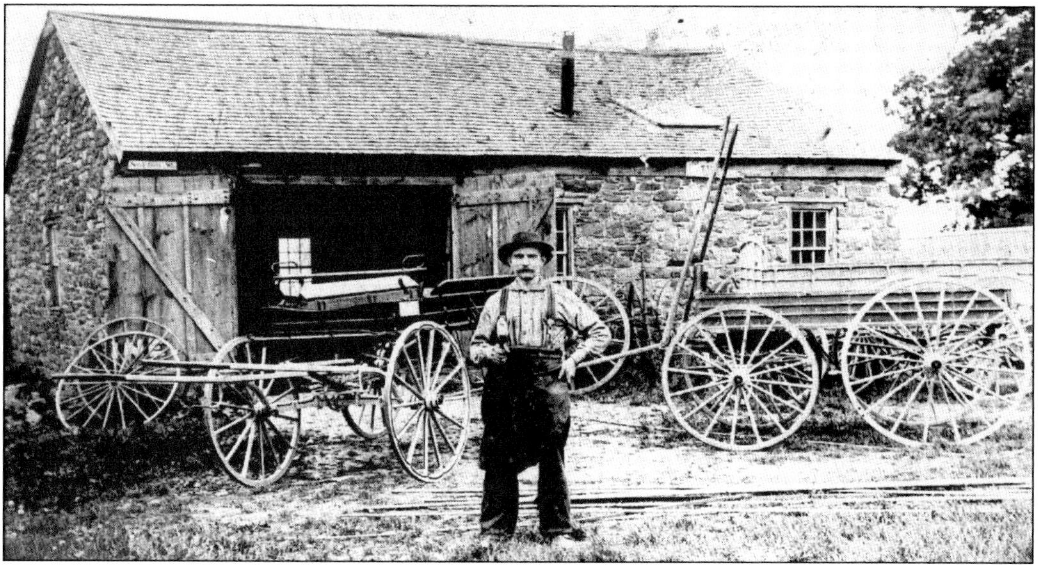

The oldest building in Irondequoit is a cobblestone blacksmith shop on Ridge Road East near Culver Road, but it was not the only blacksmith to serve the needs of the farmers of the town. An 1852 map reveals the location of the other shop located on the northeast corner of Portland Avenue and Norton Street. In 1895, it was purchased by Henry Rothman, who is shown here. He was not only a blacksmith but also a wagon maker supplying many wagons to the farmers in the area. The wagon on the right was the most popular model. He retired in 1920 and the building was torn down.

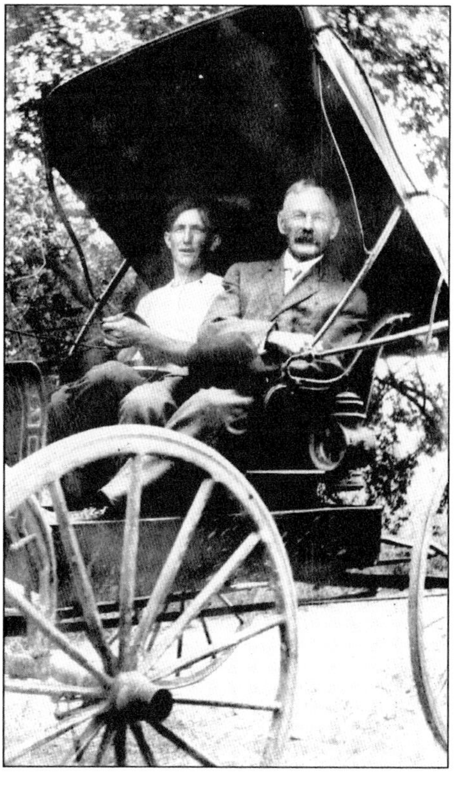

This photograph gives a good idea of what transportation might have been like in the early 1900s. It is different from the SUVs that dominate the roadways today, but it is an affordable option considering today's gasoline prices. The two passengers are unidentified.

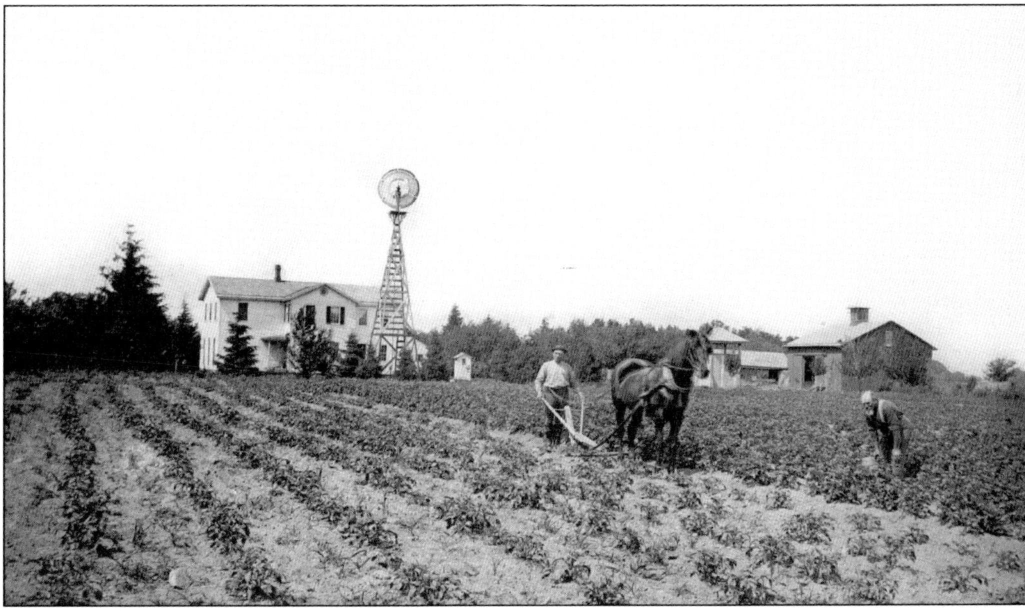

This is a typical farm scene of the late 1880s. The date is around 1885 on the List farm at 560 List Avenue. On the right, examining the new plants is John List. Operating the horse drawn cultivator is George List. Shortly after this picture was taken, the Lists sold the farm to the Myers family, who still own the property.

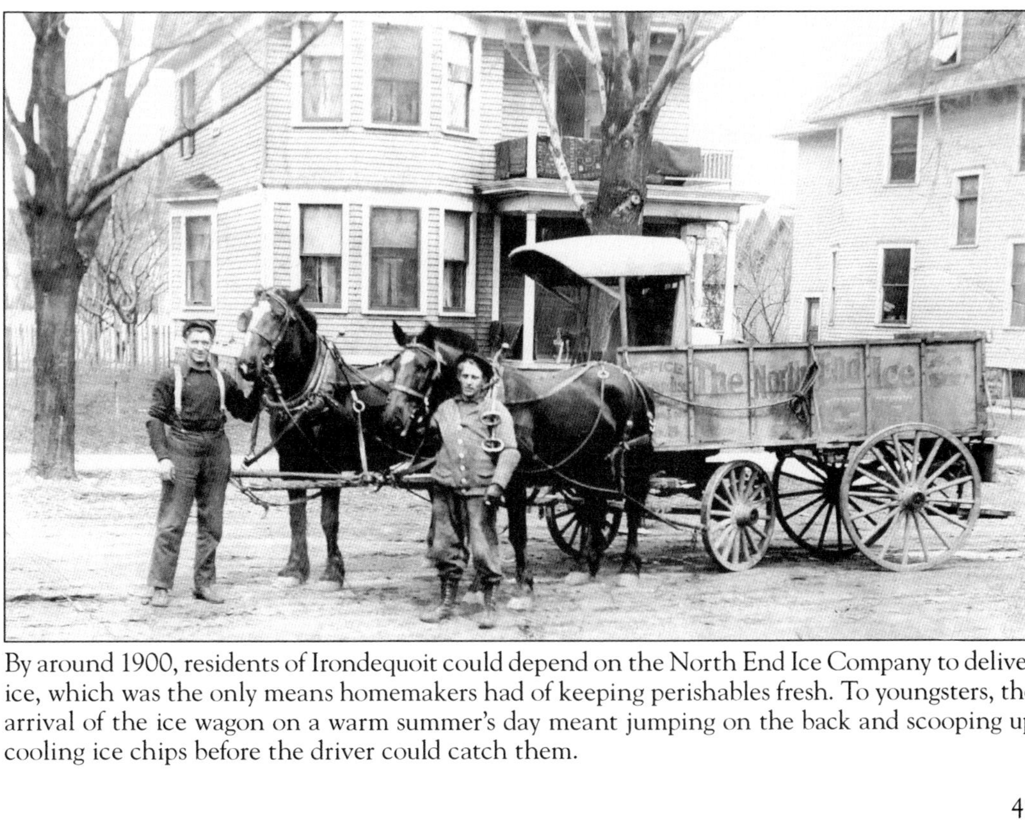

By around 1900, residents of Irondequoit could depend on the North End Ice Company to deliver ice, which was the only means homemakers had of keeping perishables fresh. To youngsters, the arrival of the ice wagon on a warm summer's day meant jumping on the back and scooping up cooling ice chips before the driver could catch them.

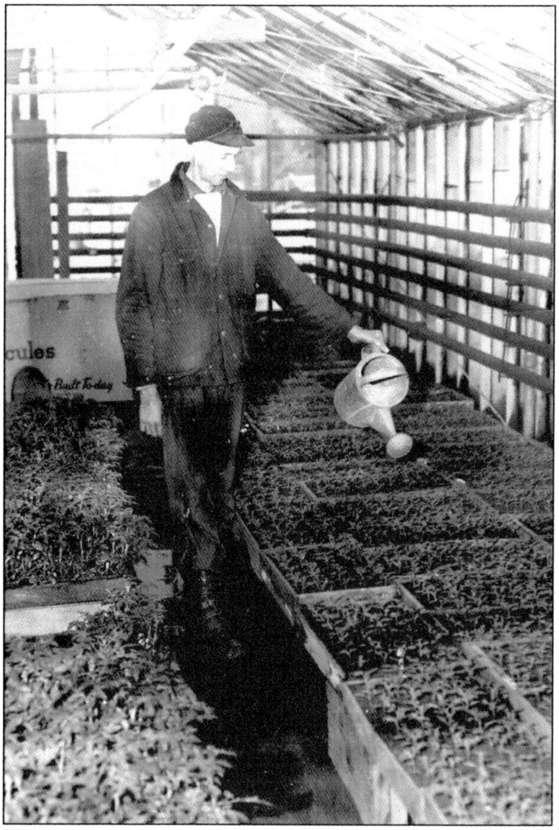

By the mid-1900s, farmers in Irondequoit had augmented their income by greenhouse farming, which allowed them to get ahead of other farmers by having young plants ready for transfer to the fields when it was time for spring planting. This photograph is of one of the Heffer family's greenhouses.

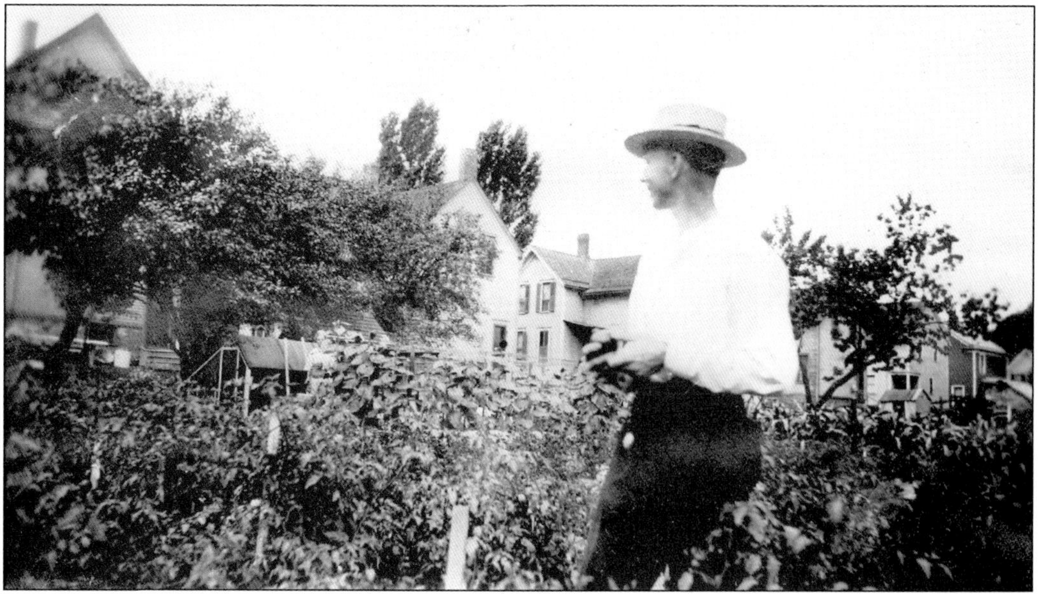

Edward "Ted" Cole (1885–1970) inherited his love for gardening and growing flowers from his father Mason Cole. Ted (a nickname for family and close friends) later owned land in nearby Greece at Dewey Avenue and Eastland Road, where he and his wife Luella Barrett Cole raised their three children, Warren Eugene (1905–1973), Audrey Alana (1908–1986), and Phyllis Mae, (1915–1996).

Many farm families not only raised pigs, chickens, turkeys, and cattle to provide a source of meat, but also added to the larder by hunting wild game. This young man, slightly overdressed for his picture, poses beside a young deer that will provide venison for the winter table. Deer still are found in Irondequoit but hunting, except for conservation purposes, is forbidden.

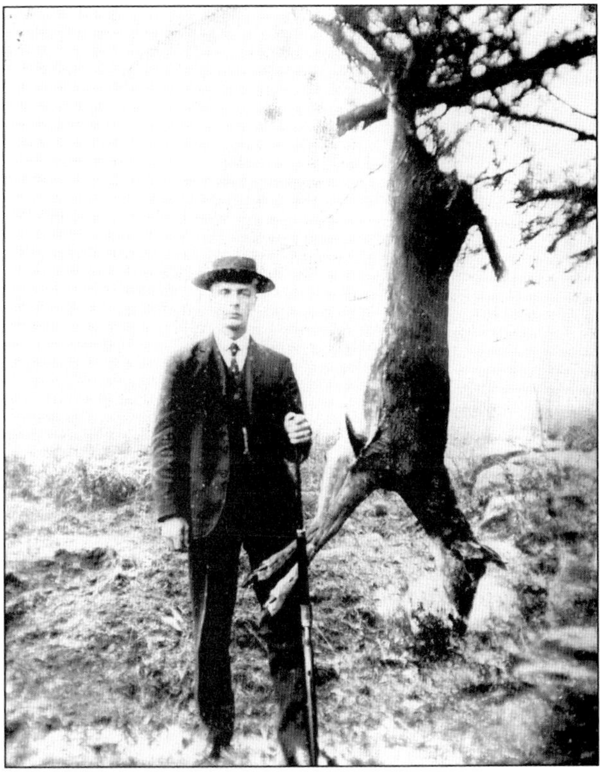

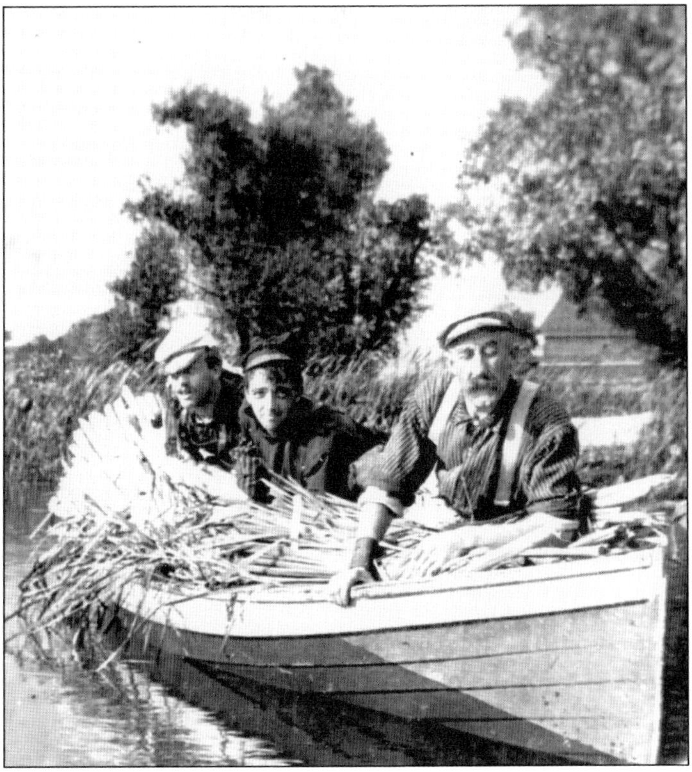

Bullrushes growing along the shores of Irondequoit Bay provided another source of income for residents. Most of them grew around the mouth of the bay at the outlet and the Float Bridge area. In late fall, and even when the snow began, "flag cutters" sold the rushes to barrel makers for caulking. The dried rush butt would swell when it came in contact with liquid, thus preventing leaks. Rushes were also used by furniture makers for woven chair seats. Though cutting the rushes was hard on the hands and the weather was often miserable, a cutter could make $1,000 to $2,000 a year, which, at the time, was good pay. High waters in the 1940s flooded the bullrush beds and the industry died out.

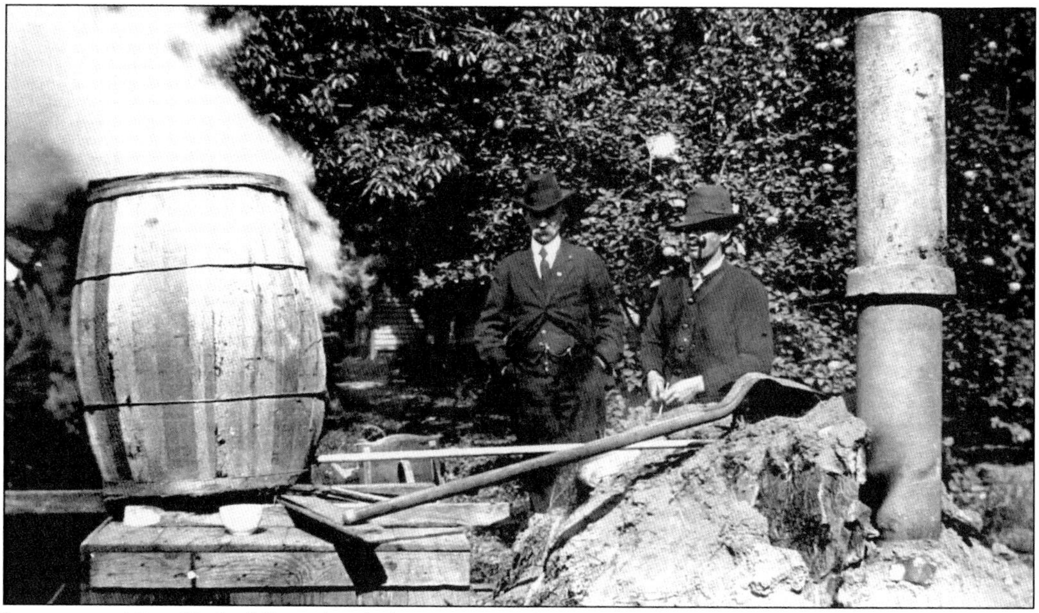

In western New York, fall is clambake season. Who can resist bags of steamed or raw clams on the half-shell supplemented by corn on the cob and barbecued chicken? If the price is right, lobster is also a nice addition. In 1913, mouths were watering on the Leake farm in anticipation of the feast that would come out of this homemade steamer.

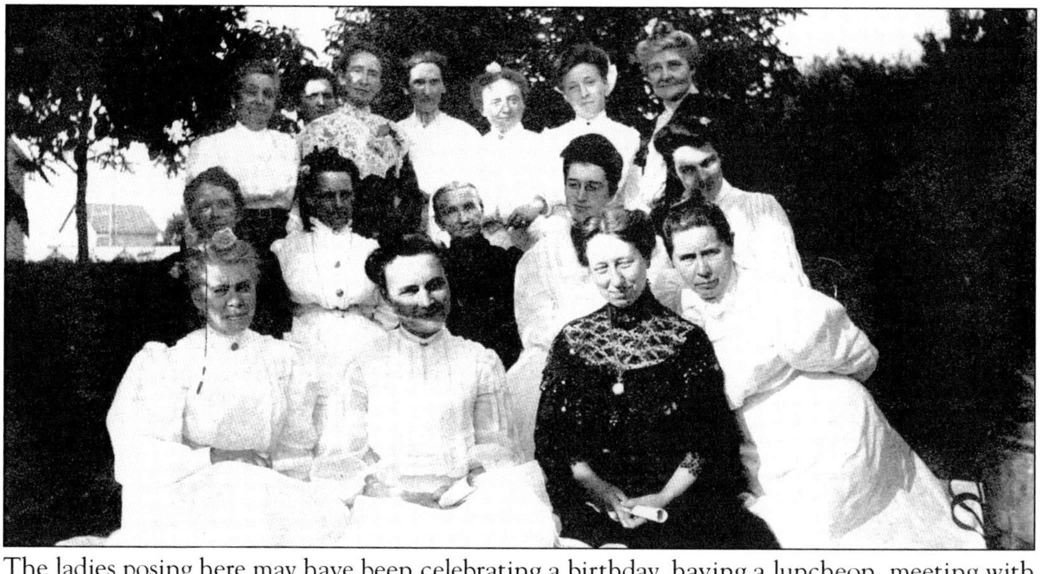

The ladies posing here may have been celebrating a birthday, having a luncheon, meeting with a church group, or welcoming a newcomer to the community. Whatever the occasion, they are dressed in their best finery, billowing white muslin or black net, with their long hair piled high or braided and twisted on the back of the head. It is obviously a warm summer day and despite the fact that they all were undoubtedly corseted and wearing at least two petticoats, they seem calm and collected. From left to right, they are (first row) Amelia Sherry, Sarah Hill Killick, Stella Metcalfe, and Emma Titus; (second row) unidentified, Mary Hill Hallauer, Dr. Bellamy's mother Victoria Bellamy, Maude West, and Edna Anthony; (third row) three unidentified women, Ella Rudman Anderson, unidentified, Ethel Metcalfe, and Mary Anthony, Edna's mother.

Ann Cooper Leake was George Cooper's sister and was first married to Gilbert J. Leake. Upon his death she married Henry Thomas Leake, Gilbert's brother. Such marriages were not uncommon since widows in those days did not have many options in the work force and often sought security in second marriages with in-laws they already knew and perhaps loved.

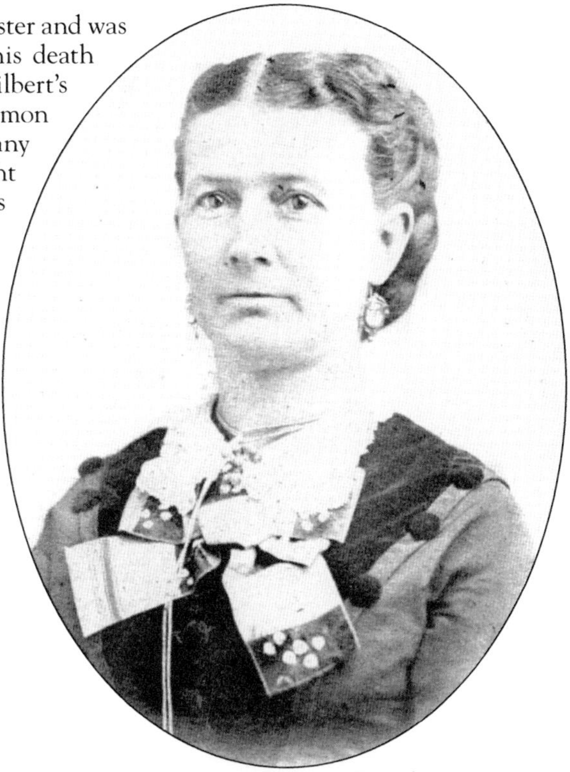

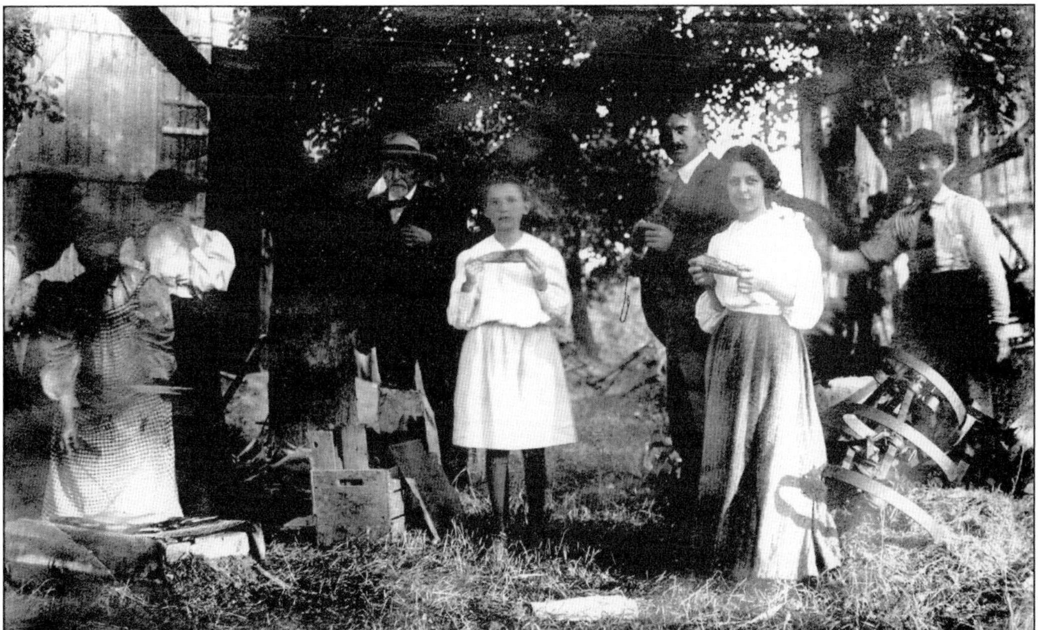

Enjoying the fruits of their labor at a family corn roast in the early 1900s, the Cole family posed for a quick photograph. A popular means of communication in those days was a post card, with phrases like, "corn roast on Sunday, the boys will be over to get you," written on the back.

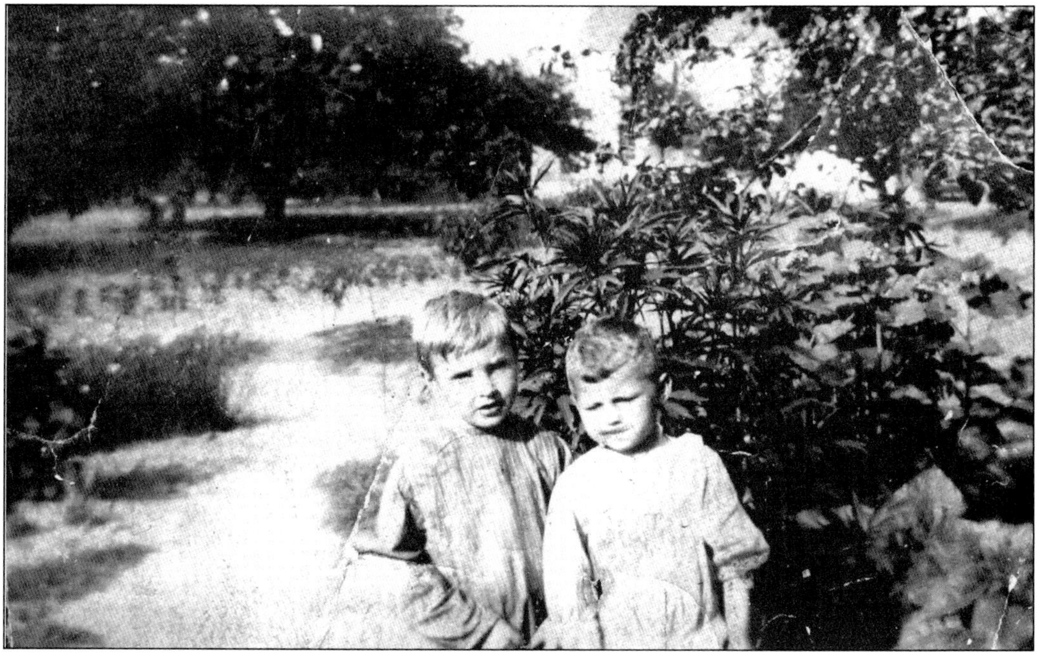

This photograph was recued from a fast deteriorating family album. It offers a good idea of what much of Irondequoit looked like in the early 1900s. Orchards and rich fields of fruit and vegetables covered the landscape, but gave way to the development of the 1940s and 1950s. Warren Cole is on the left, with an unidentified childhood friend.

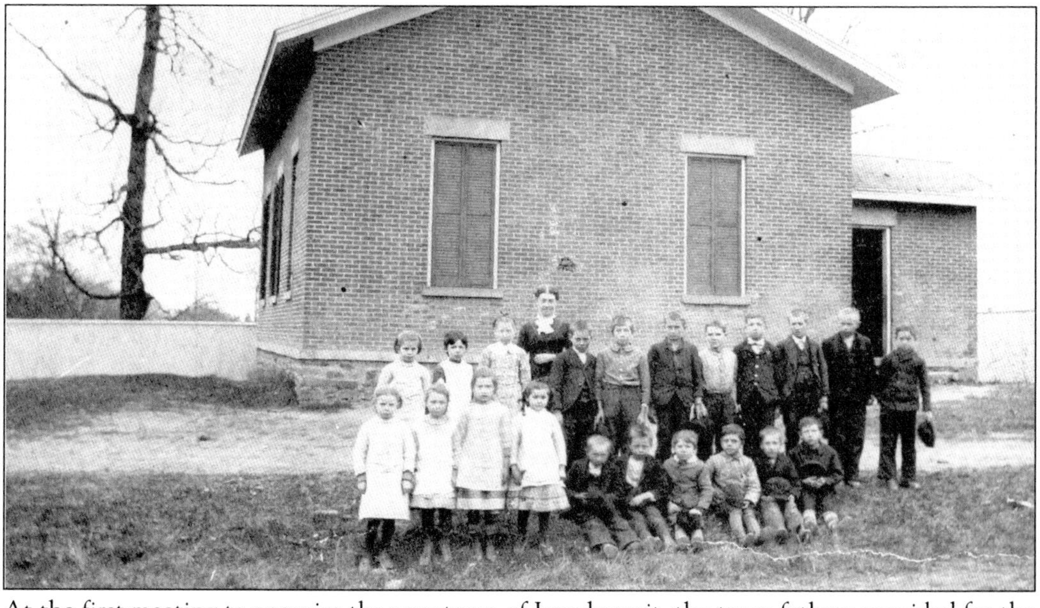

At the first meeting to organize the new town of Irondequoit, the town fathers provided for the education of tis children. School commissioners were elected and divided the town into four school districts. District No. 1 was located in the southwest part of the township. The first meeting to set up the district was held in the blacksmith shop on East Ridge Road on October 11, 1864. The Bell school was dedicated in April 1865, and was named for the efforts of the ladies of the district to raise money for a cupola and a bell.

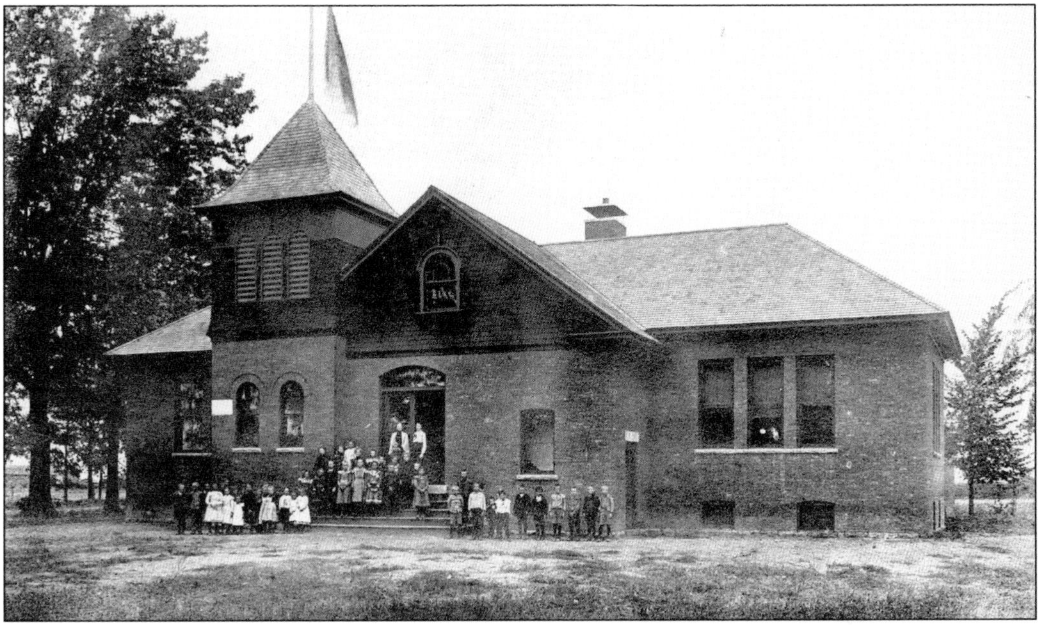

District No. 4 was formed at a meeting at Mason Cole's house on November 18, 1847. This school was built in January 1868, and in 1876 money was raised to add a cupola and a bell. Bells in these 19th-century schools were a necessity to alert students that school was starting and to call them in from recess and lunch. This picture was donated by Carl Martens, whose mother Dora Marks Martens attended the school

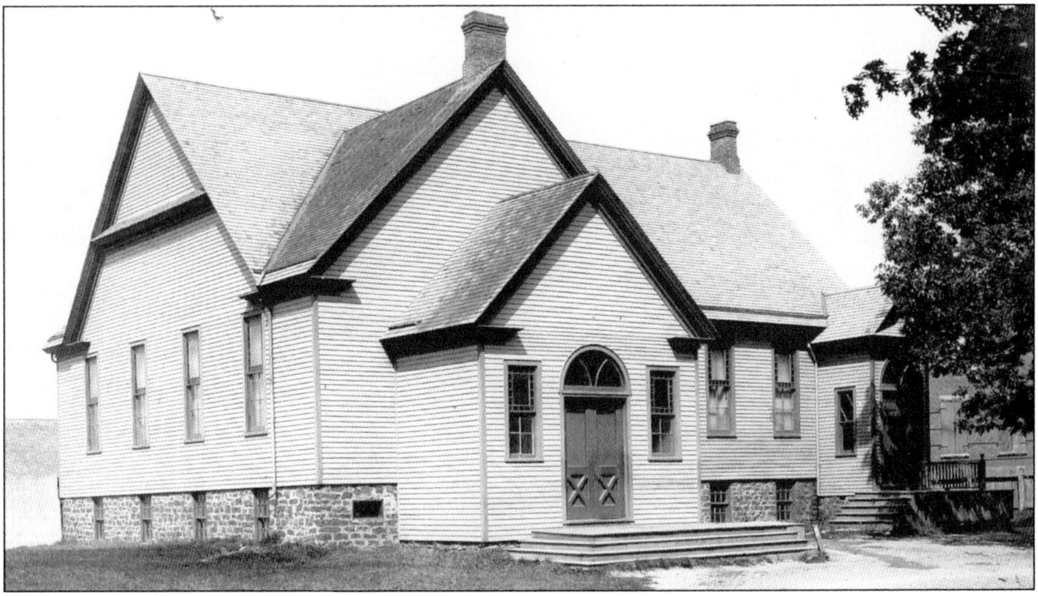

The Women's Christian Temperance Union was a national organization formed in 1874 to combat what was thought to be the rising threat of alcoholism. The chapter in Irondequoit began shortly after and built the first hall in 1884. It was not only the meeting place for the Women's Christian Temperance Union but also a social center used by all ages for the interdenominational west-side Sunday school. The organization not only campaigned to end the consumption of alcohol but extended aid to immigrants and later instructed women how to vote.

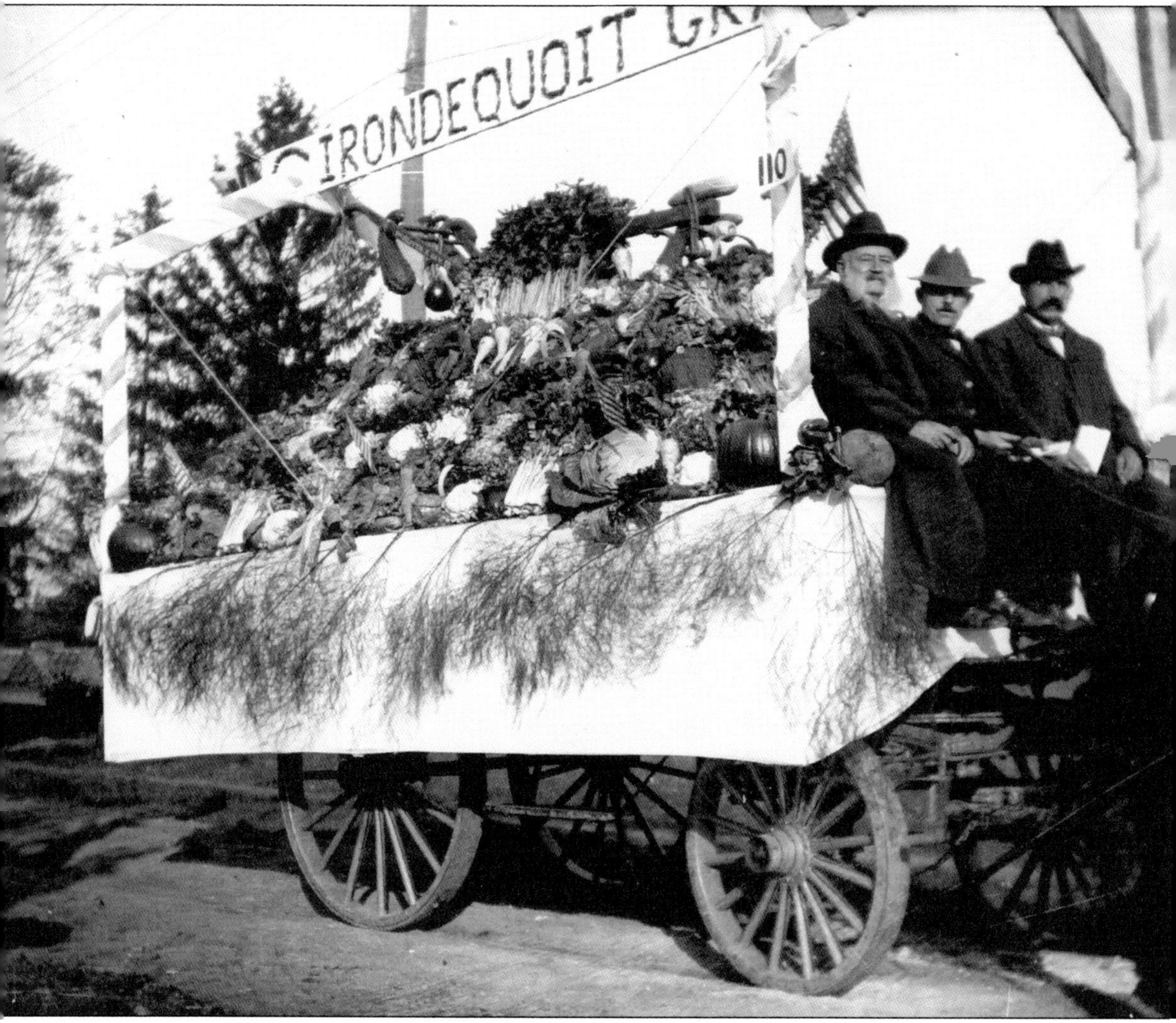

Across Titus Avenue from the Women's Christian Temperance Union building was the Grange Hall. This national organization was founded in 1867 to give voice to the needs of the American farmer. The formal title for the organziation was the Order of Patrons of Husbandry, and on the national scene it lobbied for agricultural interests.

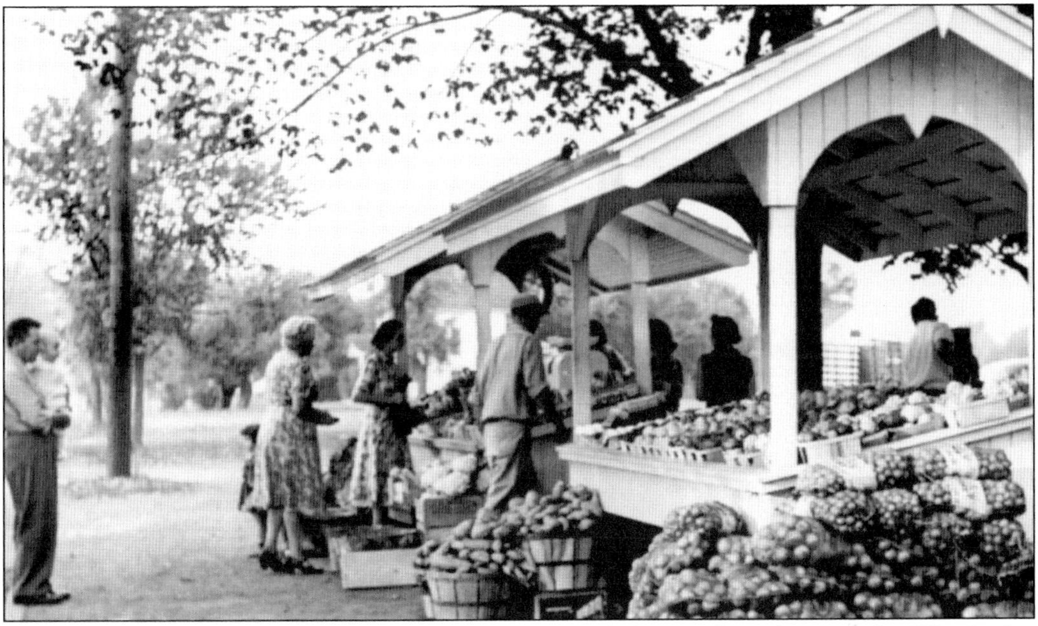

One of the most prominent farm families who entered the retail market was the Wambachs. Their ancestors included the Costich (or Caustuche) family who came to Irondequoit about 1828. The Wambachs have been farmers, nurserymen, and retailers for four generations, and the family still operates a market on Culver Road. This photograph was taken in the 1930s. Peter Wambach Sr. said the stand started when his father George dropped him off at the end of the farmland with a few boxes of berries to sell to people traveling on Culver Road.

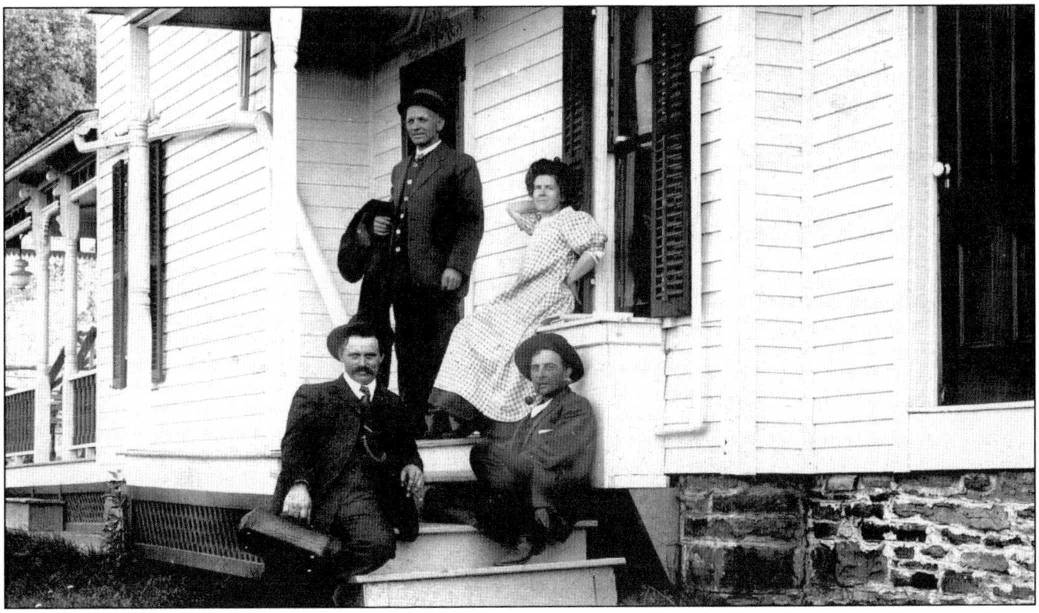

The Hallauers, like the Wambachs, were long-time farmers in Irondequoit, with the exception of William standing here ready to go town. He sold produce from Irondequoit to middlemen. He certainly looks like a prosperous salesman about to call on customers.

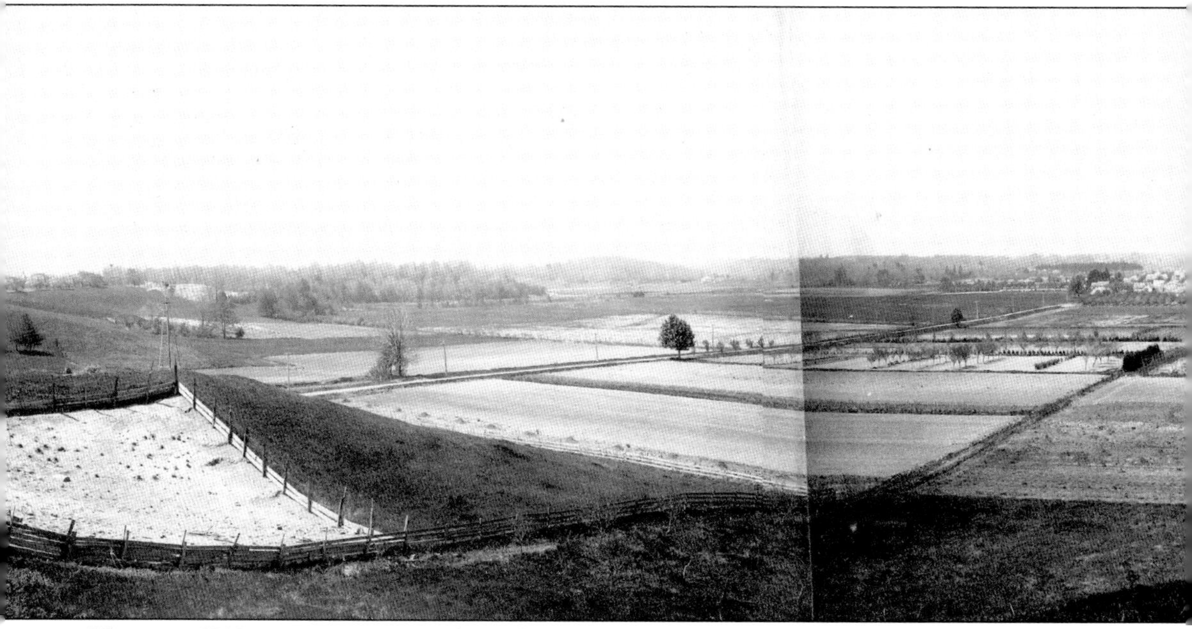

This rare 1898 panoramic view of Irondequoit farmland actually consists of three photographs that were carefully matched and mounted on poster board. The photographs, titled *Springtime in Irondequoit* were owned by George Marks until his wife donated them to the town historian on February 24, 1971. The attached note reveals just how extraordinary this piece is and reads as follows: "This picture was taken in spring 1898 overlooking (then known as) Moulson Flats—or Seneca Park Avenue—west of St. Paul Blvd- from a spot on Herb Leary's property just north of

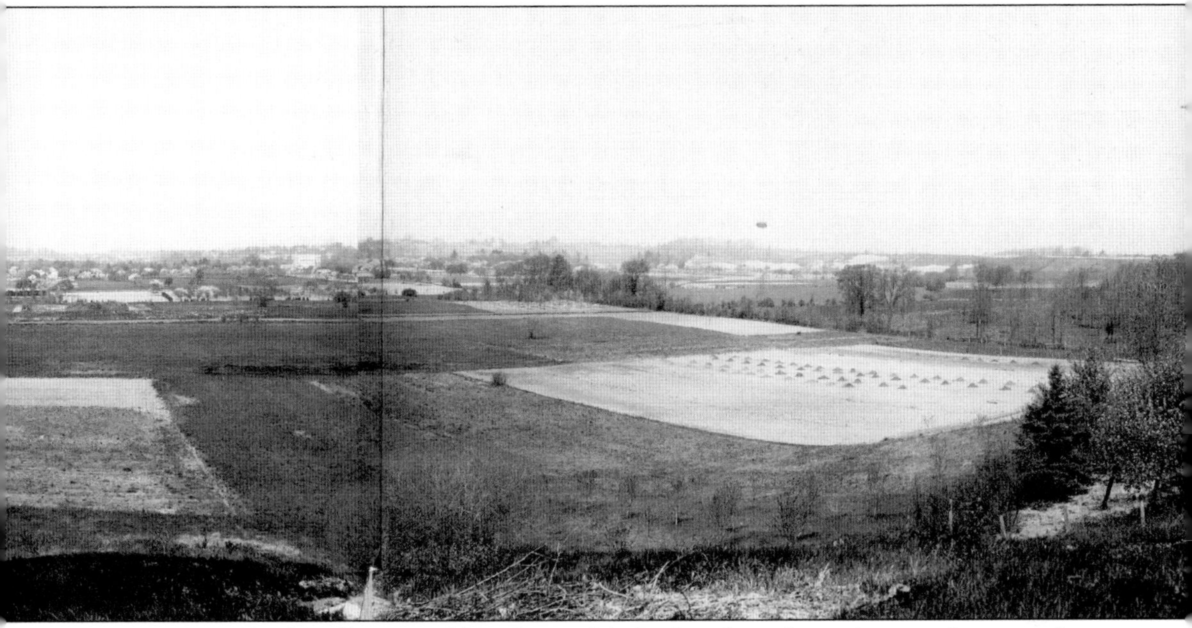

Pinegrove Ave. Chuck Miller was told by George Marks that these three photographs were taken by George Eastman, who was a friend of Herb Leary. Mrs. Marks confirms this. February 24, 1971." The photographs are presently in the possession of the Irondequoit town historian, and to the best of the authors' knowledge, this is the first time these original photographs, taken by George Eastman, the founder of Eastman Kodak, have been made available to the general public.

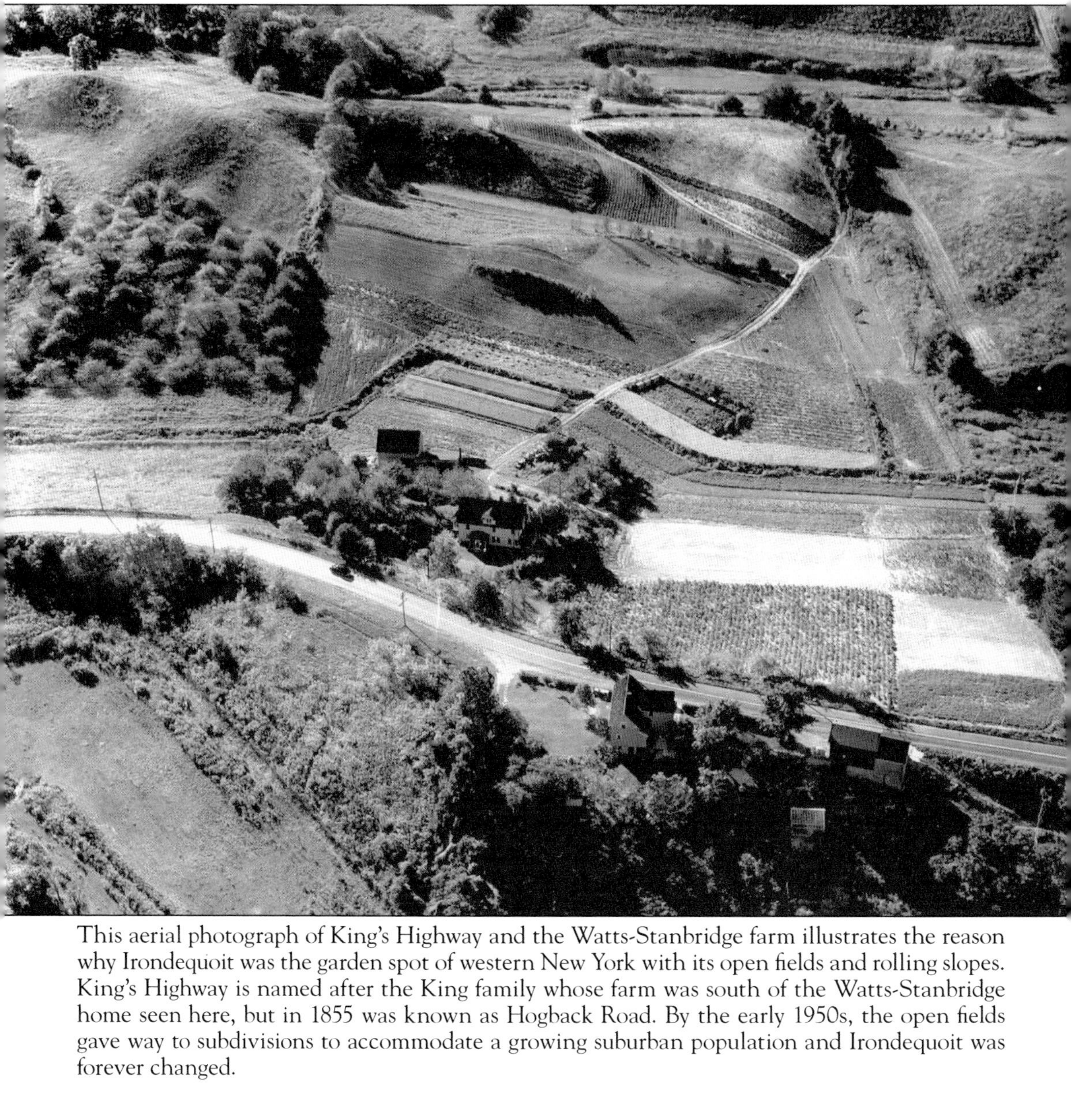

This aerial photograph of King's Highway and the Watts-Stanbridge farm illustrates the reason why Irondequoit was the garden spot of western New York with its open fields and rolling slopes. King's Highway is named after the King family whose farm was south of the Watts-Stanbridge home seen here, but in 1855 was known as Hogback Road. By the early 1950s, the open fields gave way to subdivisions to accommodate a growing suburban population and Irondequoit was forever changed.

Four

From Swamps to Sea Breeze

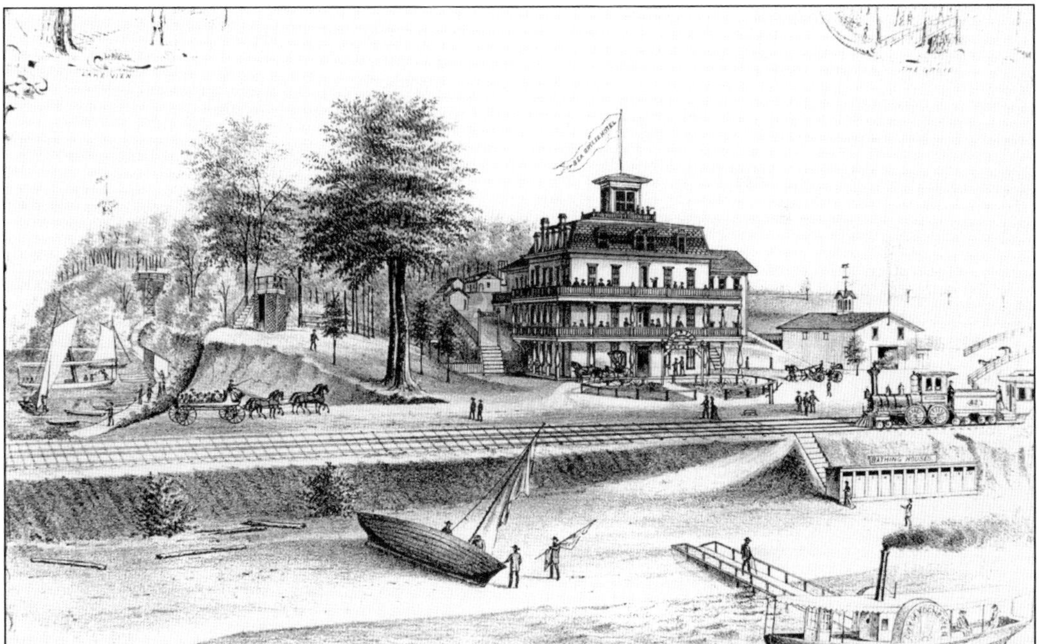

"The new company has obtained considerably more land than the old company held, making forty acres, and when those extra groves have been laid out for the pleasure of the people, which is soon to be done, there will be room at the Sea breeze for thousands of people without being kept off the grass or forced to eat lunches while standing. Evidently there is a bright future for this famous outing spot and the right policy-to make it more attractive than ever-has been adopted." This excerpt is from the *Rochester Union Advertiser* from June 26, 1893.

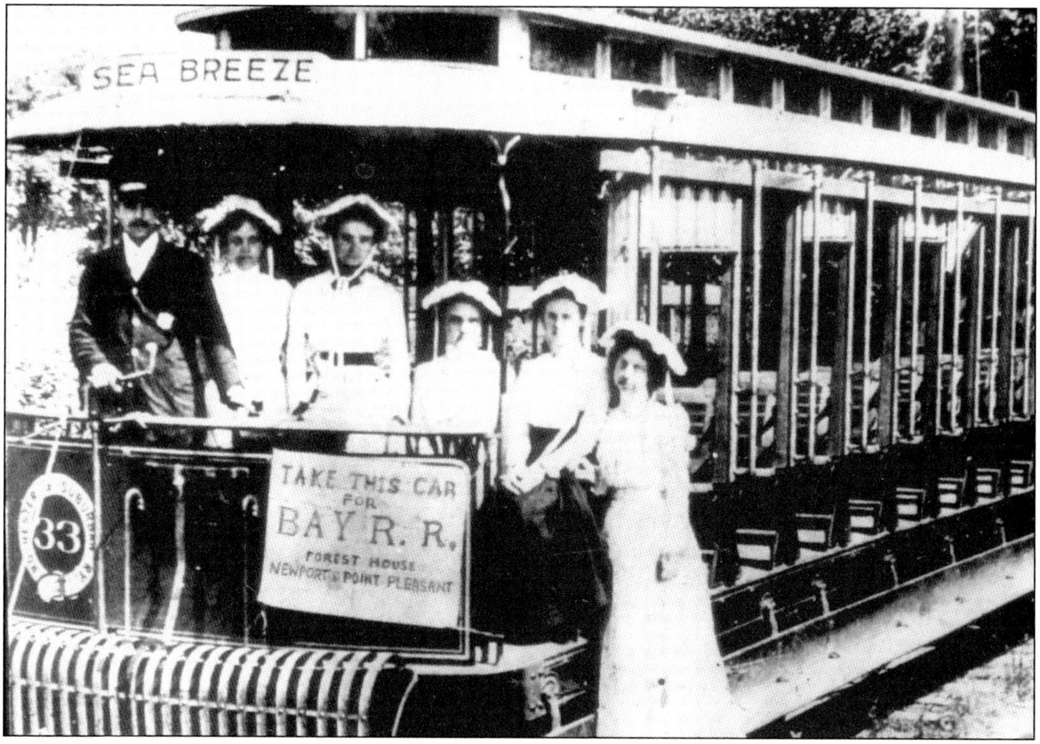

In 1865, George Allen purchased a house and five acres of land from Mary Shaw at the end of Culver Road with a view of both Irondequoit Bay and Lake Ontario. Allen converted the house into a three-story hotel. The building had three balconies, and many residents of the area patronized the facility in order to enjoy the sea breeze.

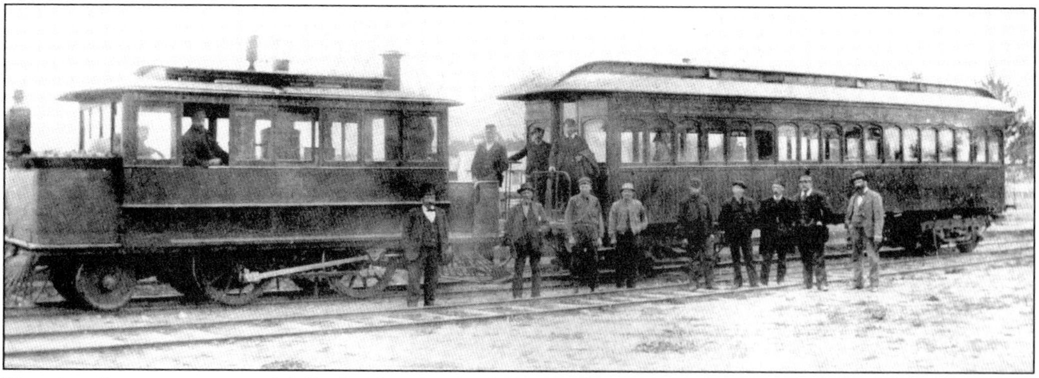

Despite the attractions of Allen's Hotel, which burned in 1885, Sea Breeze did not develop into a resort area until the coming of the train that ran along the edge of the bay. The trolley line had been introduced by former Rochester mayor Michael Filon, who visited the Philadelphia Exposition in 1876 and purchased the train that carried passengers around the exposition grounds. He formed a corporation that obtained a state charter to run the line from Portland Avenue, along Ridge Road, then to the shore opening the bay up to resort development. The first train began its run on the morning of August 5, 1879.

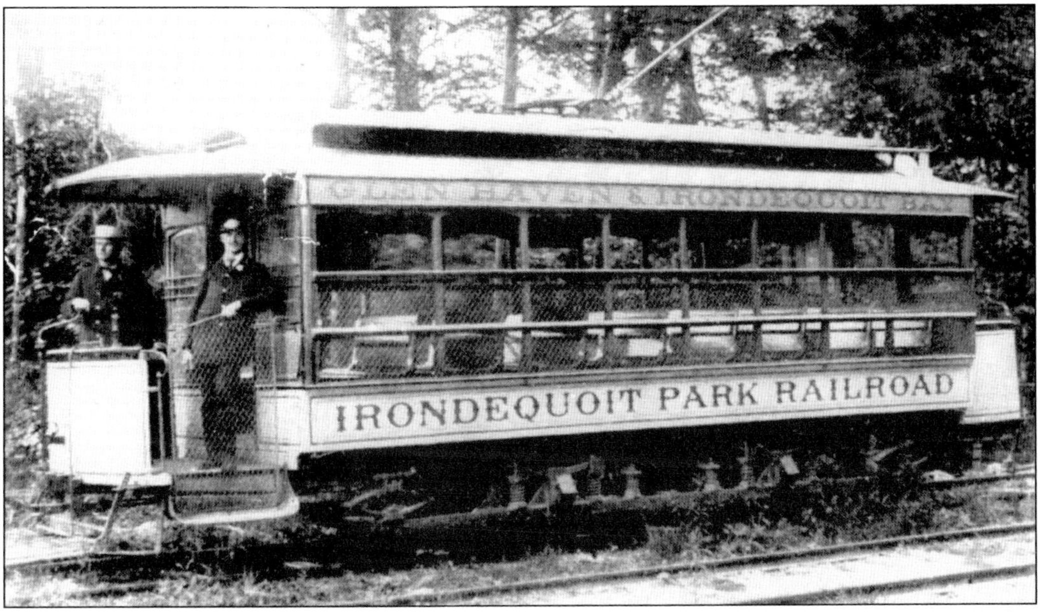

Sea Breeze was not the only resort that developed because of the train. In 1887, the Rochester-Glen Haven Railroad planned a three-foot-gauge system steam railroad from East Main and Chamberlain Streets to the new resort of Glen Haven. The line finally began operating in June 1889, and after August, trains ran every hour to the new resort. By 1890, a total of 115,582 passengers had ridden the Rochester-Glen Haven line.

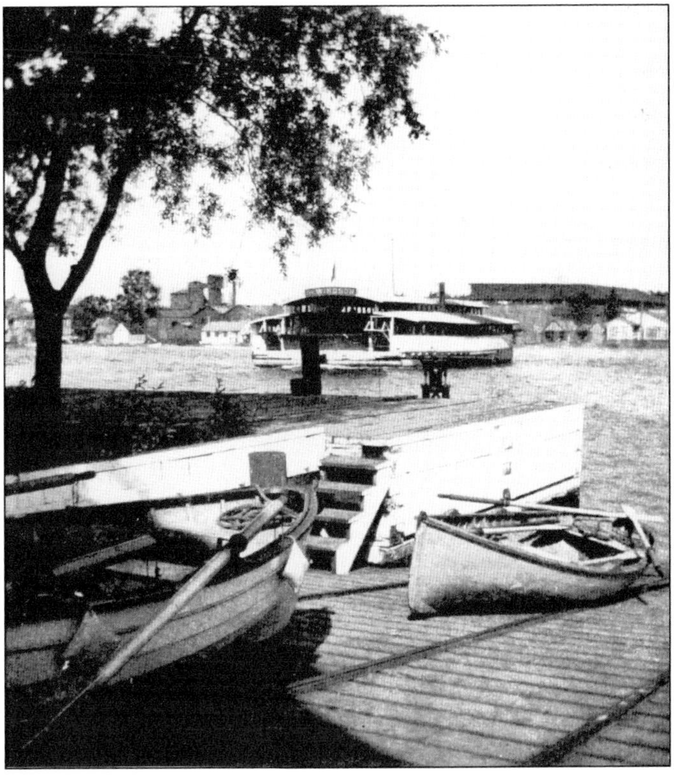

Patrons of Sea Breeze, Glen Haven, and other resorts on the bay who lived on the western side of the Genesee River could make a connection with the trains by crossing the river by ferry. The first ferryboat began operation in 1851, but in 1893, with increased traffic between the lake resorts at Charlotte and the growing summer communities in Irondequoit, the Charlotte-Summerville Ferry Company launched a new ferry, the *Windsor*, which began its run in 1894. The ferry, built by Joseph Doyle, was 75 feet long, had a beam deck 50 feet wide, 22 feet reserved for vehicles, and a space on both sides for pedestrians only. It was licensed to carry 200 passengers for the seven-minute trip across the river.

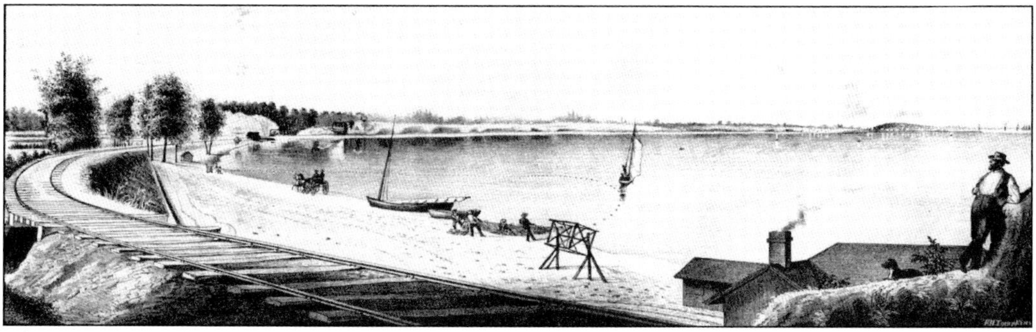

This artist's rendition of the Lake Ontario shore features a railroad track circling the shoreline emphasizing the rather bucolic nature of the landscape, which would soon change with developments around the lake.

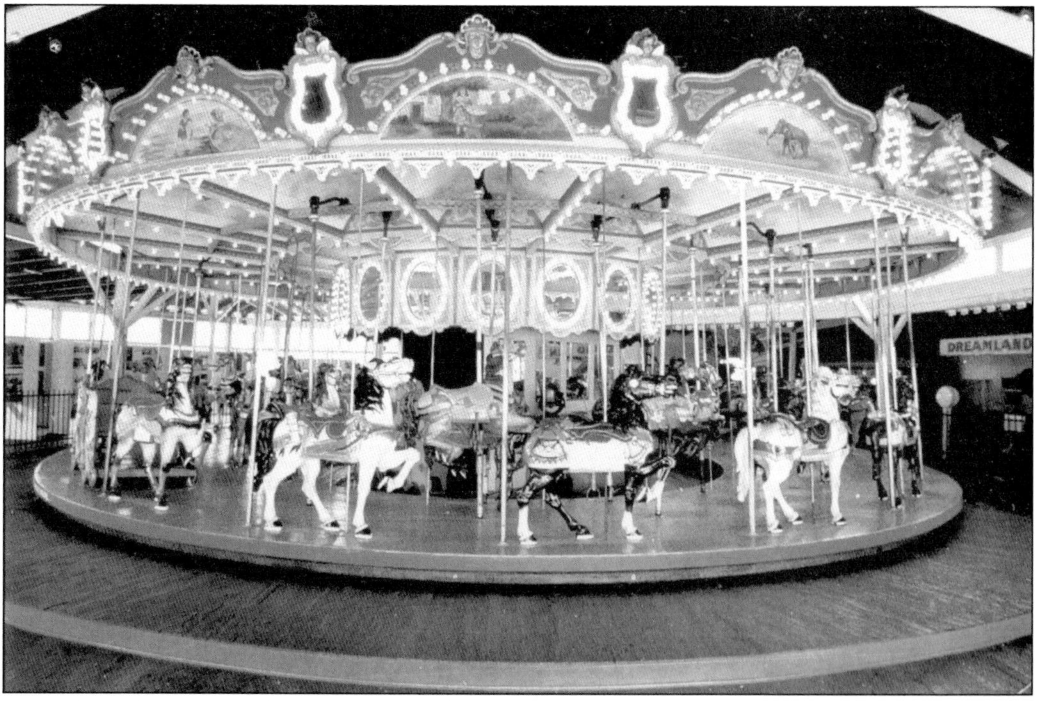

One of the hallmarks of Sea Breeze Park was the carousel, first introduced by George Long and his family. For most residents of Irondequoit, the carousel has always been the jewel of the park. This picture was taken from a postcard by Bob Sterrett in April 1999, and donated by Lois Jenkins. The Philadelphia Toboggan Company built the merry-go-round in 1915, and it was brought to Sea Breeze by George Long in 1926. It had 48 horses that included two chariots, 20 posing mares, and 28 prancers. On April 6, 1994, the beautiful carousel was destroyed by fire.

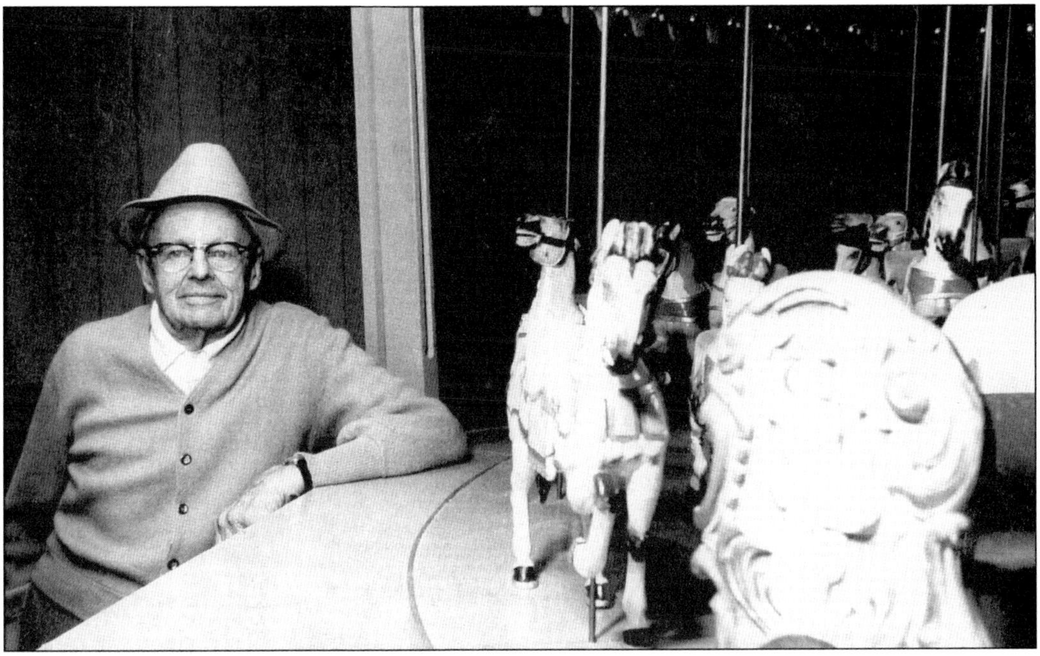

George Long carved hundreds of carousel horses. He had rented the park from 1935 to 1946, when he purchased the park outright. Until his death on September 27, 1988, he enjoyed greeting patrons of his park. His descendents still run this "jewel by the sea."

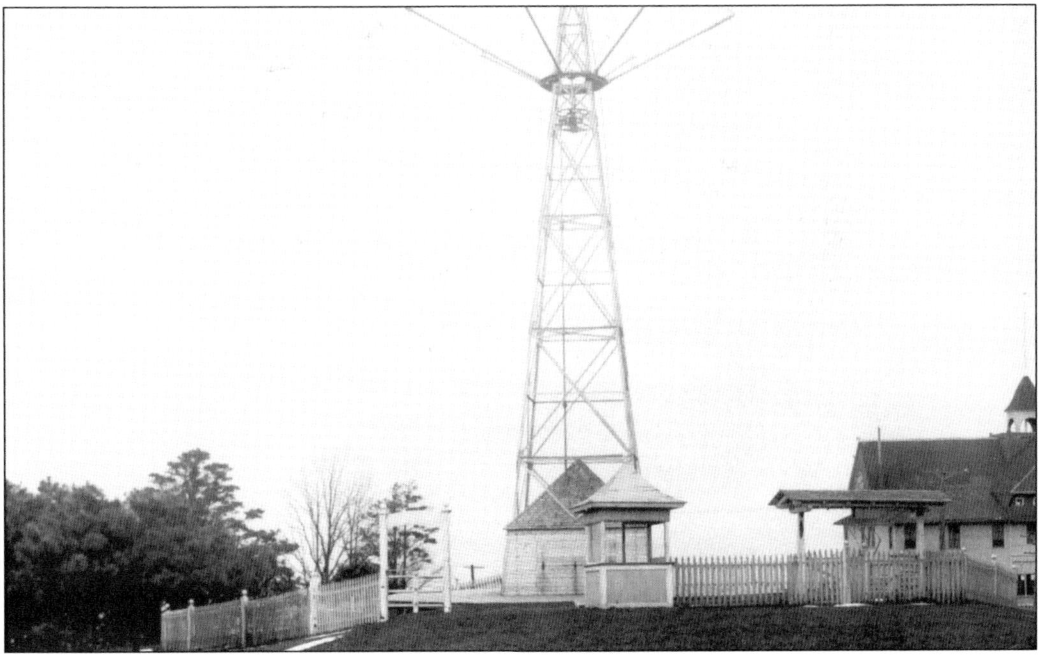

The railroad delivering patrons to Sea Breeze wished to increase the attraction in order encourage more riders. First, they built an eight-figure roller coaster, and then added a carousel. The third ride was an enormous circle swing, the first of its type in western New York. It was built on a high bluff and the long cables holding the cars swung the riders far out over the park. What attracted visitors most were the electric lights that illuminated the ride after dark.

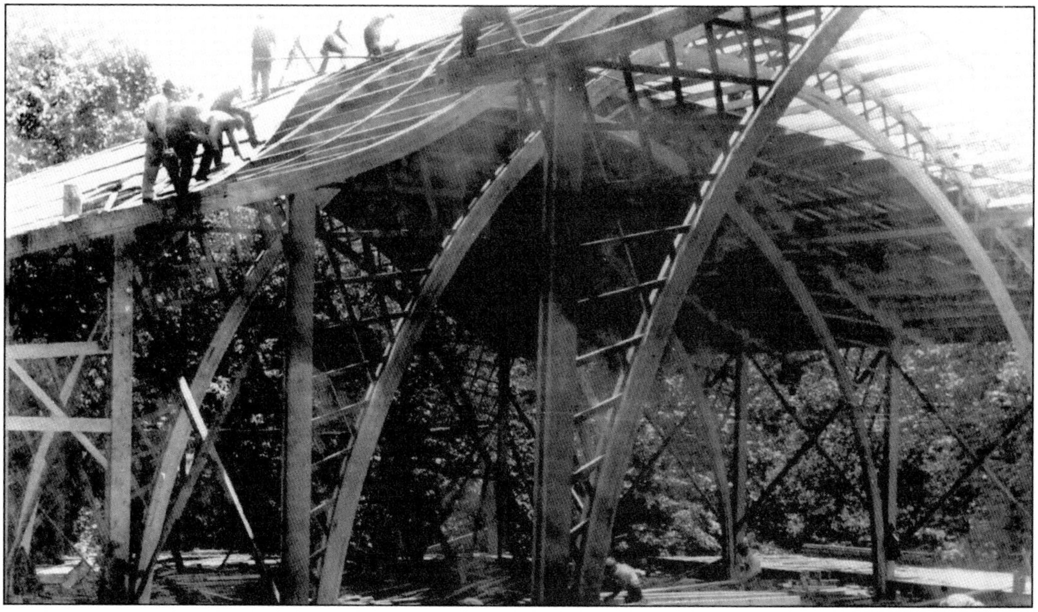

In the early 1920s, dancing was a national pastime. The owners of Sea Breeze responded by building Danceland in 1924. This picture shows the crew at work on the roof and the floor. The ballroom proved to be extremely popular and became the site of county-wide dance contests. The popular spot burned on October 6, 1933, and almost took the Jack Rabbit roller coaster with it. The dance hall was subsequently rebuilt but burned again on May 1, 1940. With World War II on the horizon and other issues taking priority for the public, the dance hall was never rebuilt.

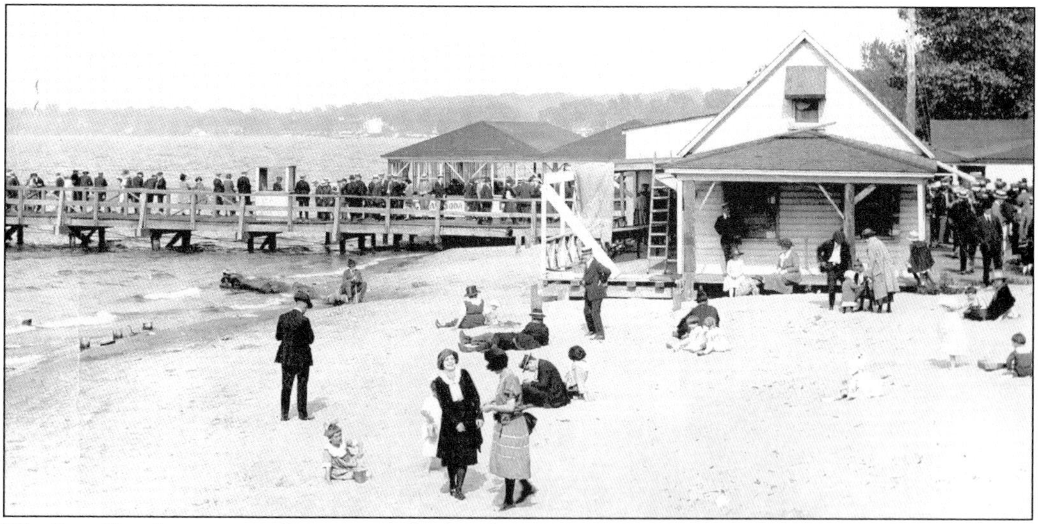

The Pier Hotel was a popular spot on the beach at Sea Breeze. This photograph was taken in the early 1900s. The little building in the front with ladies on the porch was Paul Scarlot's candy stand. The Pier Hotel is behind it, but the spacious screen enclosing the wine garden can be seen. On a busy weekend, such as this one was, the hotel employed 50 to 60 waiters who would serve a half a ton of hot dogs, two wagonloads of rolls and bread, 100 barrels of beer, and a half a ton of fish. Louis Geisler, the hotel's proprietor, also entertained his customers with his unique skill. He was a world-champion bag-puncher, and on off-seasons he toured the vaudeville circuit demonstrating his ability.

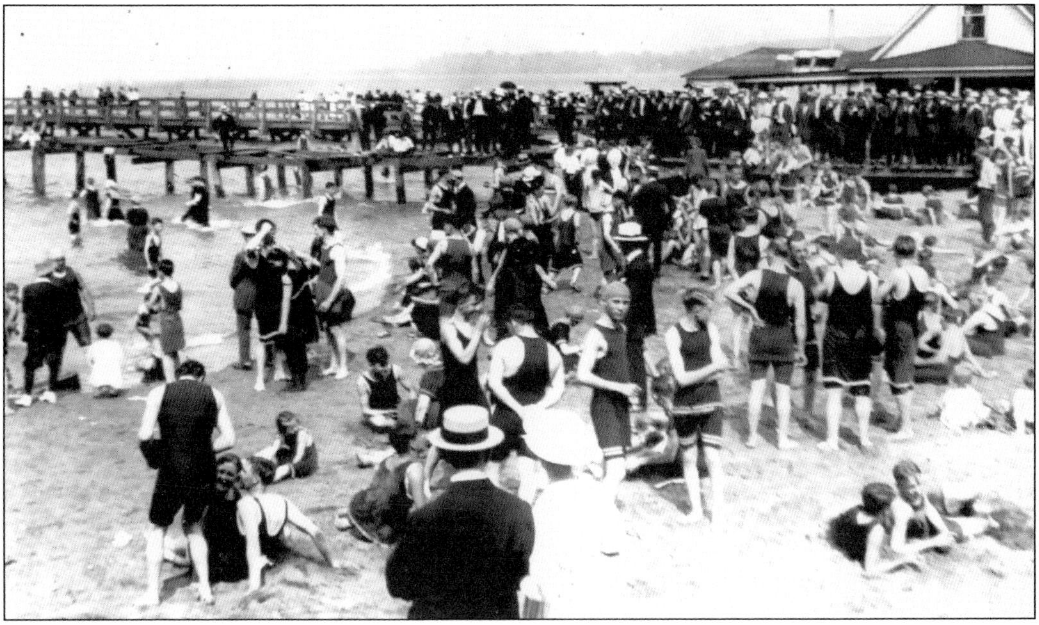

This photograph of Sea Breeze beach in the early 1920s illustrates the evolution in beach wear in the 20th century. While the suits are uniformly black and made of wool, men no longer had to cover their legs. Even women have given up the long black stockings of the 19th century or the rubber shoes and bathing caps. The crowd on the pier were not ogling the bathers but waiting for a steamer to ferry them farther down the bay to other resort hotels.

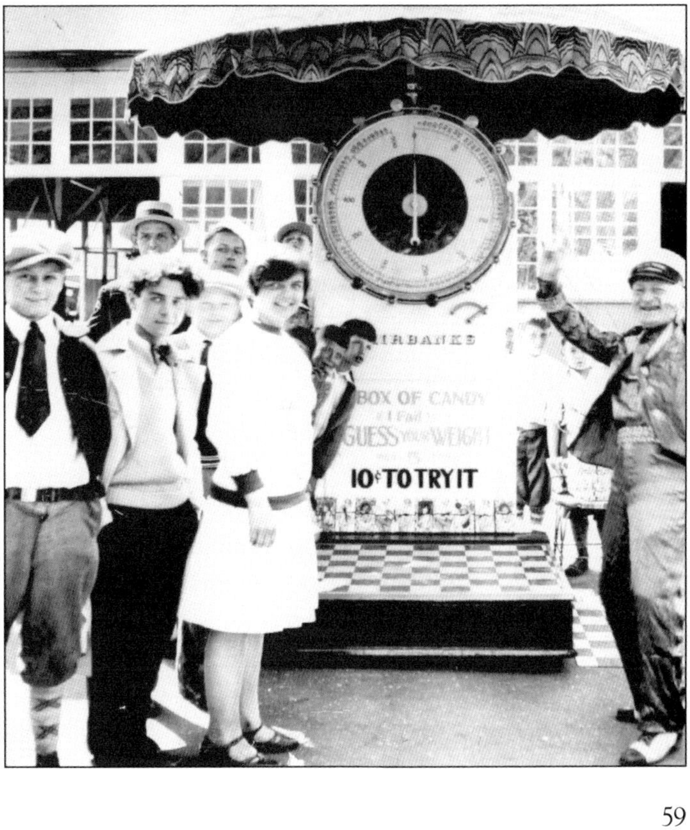

"Guess your weight, lady, guess your age. I make a mistake and the candy is yours." Smilin' Pete Conners was a brave man. If he guessed the lady's weight as more than the scales registered, he was to pay her off with a box of candy. Presumably the candy was worth less that the dime it cost to outsmart Pete. How many women would get on a scale in public to prove him wrong? Pete was part of the scene at Sea Breeze Park in the 1930s, delighting customers with his patter and jokes. His place of business was right in front of the popular carousel and, of course, in business "location is everything." His young patrons seem to be delighted to have their pictures taken with him.

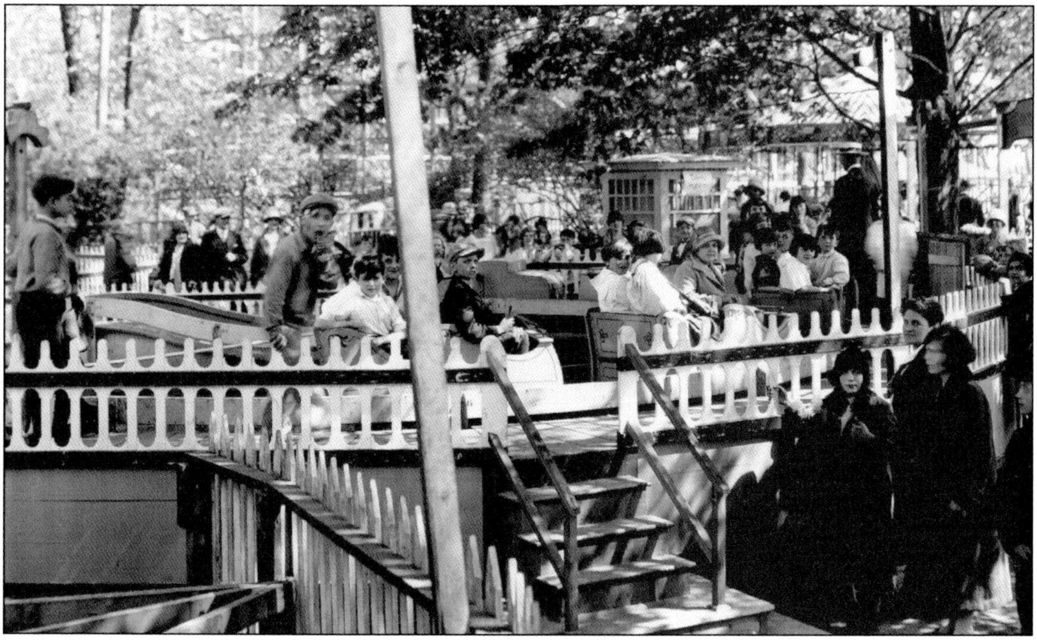

The crowds at Sea Breeze in the early 1930s enjoyed the rides built for young and old alike, but the Depression caused business to fall off. By 1937, George Long decided the Depression was ending and he leased the park from the railroad and changed the name to Dreamland Park to give it a fresh start. To residents of Irondequoit, it remained Sea Breeze in their vocabulary.

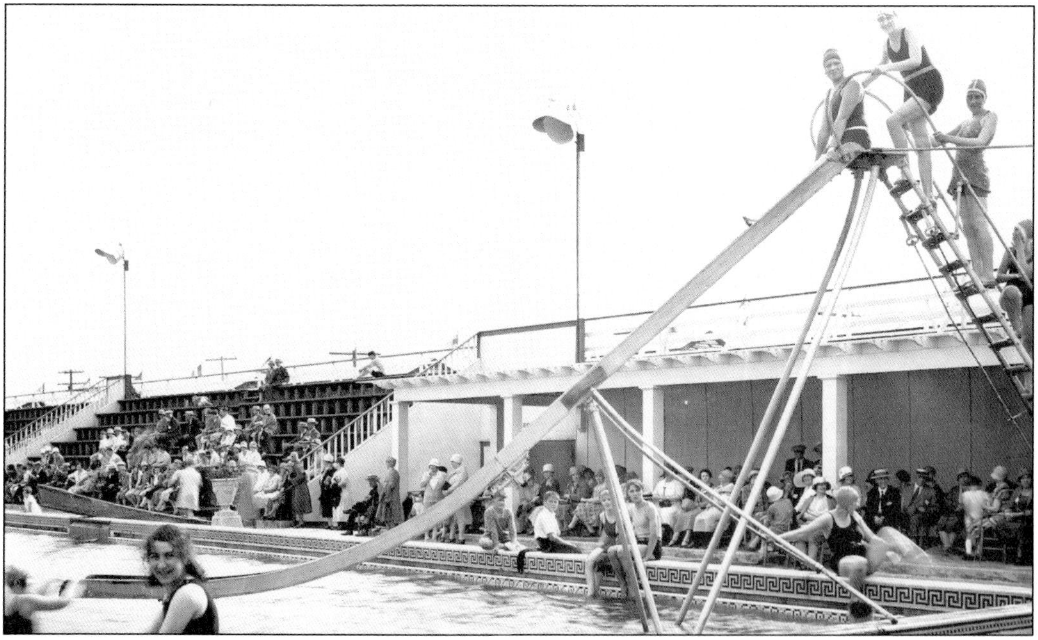

In the roaring 1920s, when the American economy seemed to be on a permanent high, a huge aquatic center known as the Natatorium was built in 1925 at a cost of $300,000. Part of Sea Breeze, the Natatorium had a saltwater pool, the largest in the world, that measured 150 feet by 300 feet. It had all kinds of attractions including several waterslides, a water wheel, bathhouse, and promenade.

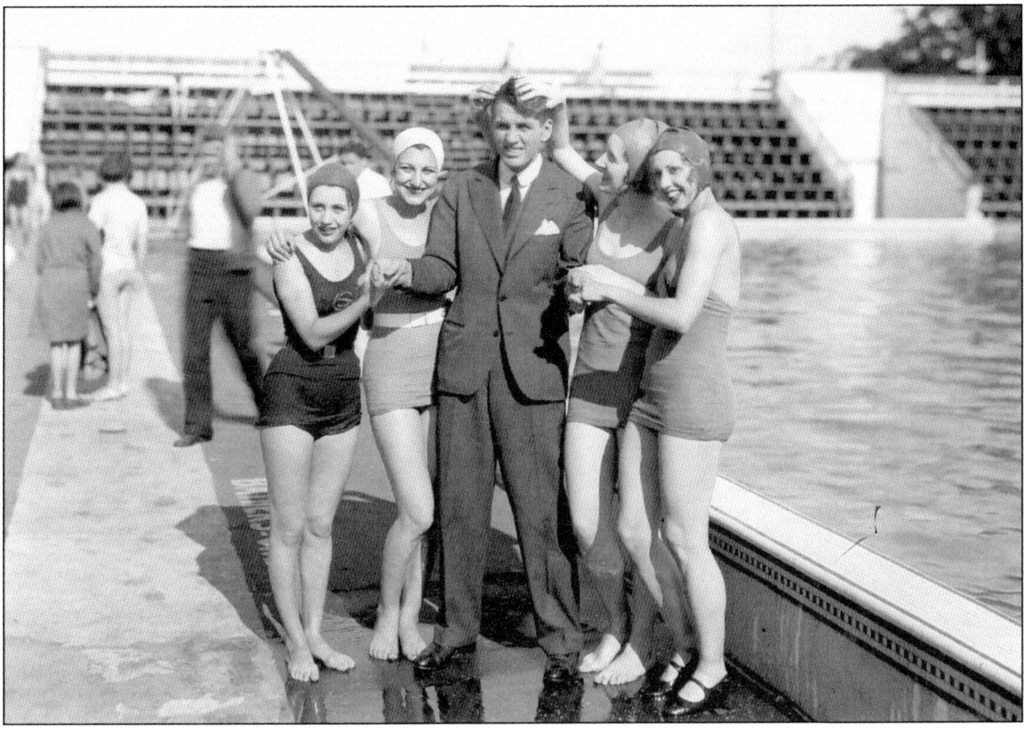

This publicity shot to advertise the Natatorium featured bathing beauties teasing one of the pool's managers. The gals modeled much more leg than their mothers ever did on the beach, and suits came in a variety of colors. The Natatorium ran up enormous costs for maintenance and fell victim to the decline of business during the Depression, closing after only 10 years of operation.

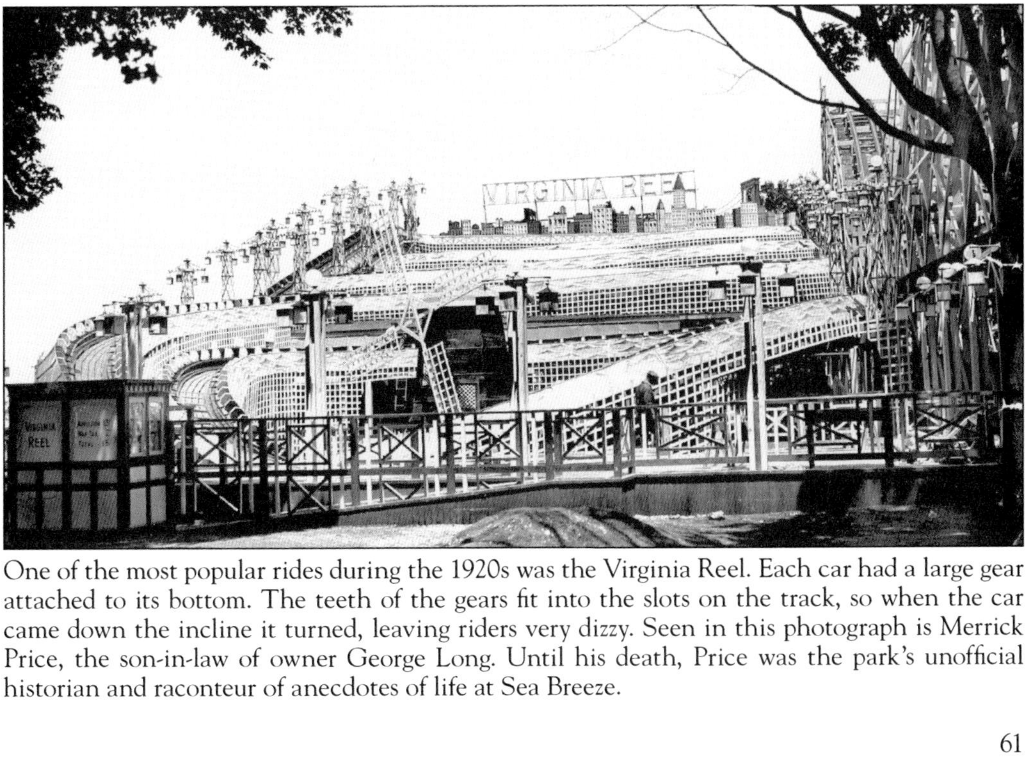

One of the most popular rides during the 1920s was the Virginia Reel. Each car had a large gear attached to its bottom. The teeth of the gears fit into the slots on the track, so when the car came down the incline it turned, leaving riders very dizzy. Seen in this photograph is Merrick Price, the son-in-law of owner George Long. Until his death, Price was the park's unofficial historian and raconteur of anecdotes of life at Sea Breeze.

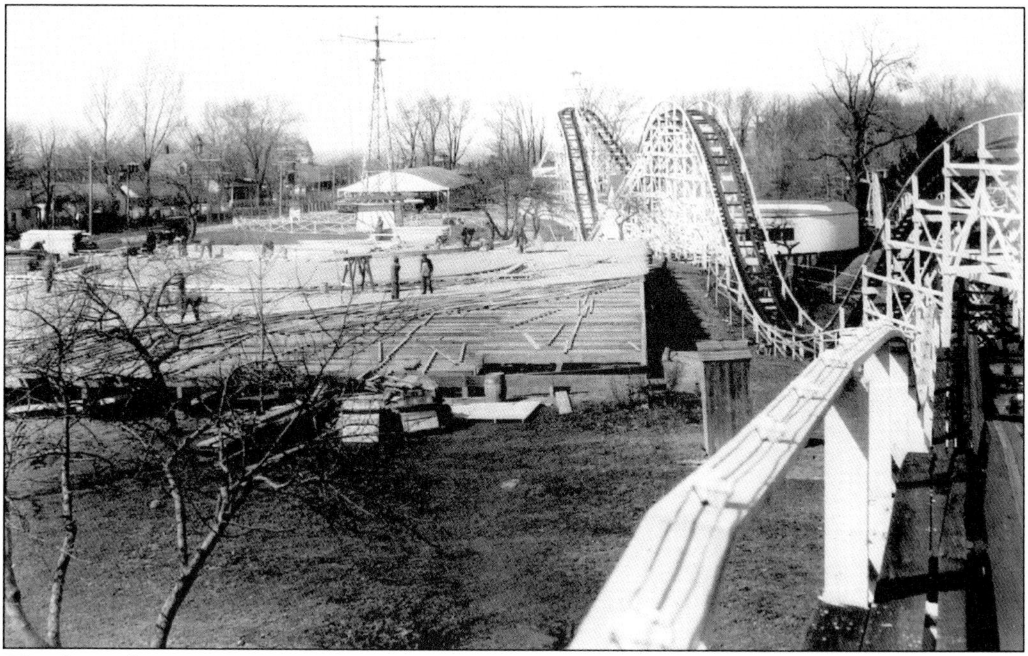

The first ride at Sea Breeze Park was a roller coaster called the Figure Eight, but in 1920 the Miller Baker Company came to the park and replaced it with a roller coaster that became known as the Jack Rabbit. It had wheels underneath the track that caused under-friction, so when it went over a hill, it would not come off the track. It is now the third oldest operating wooden roller coaster in the United States.

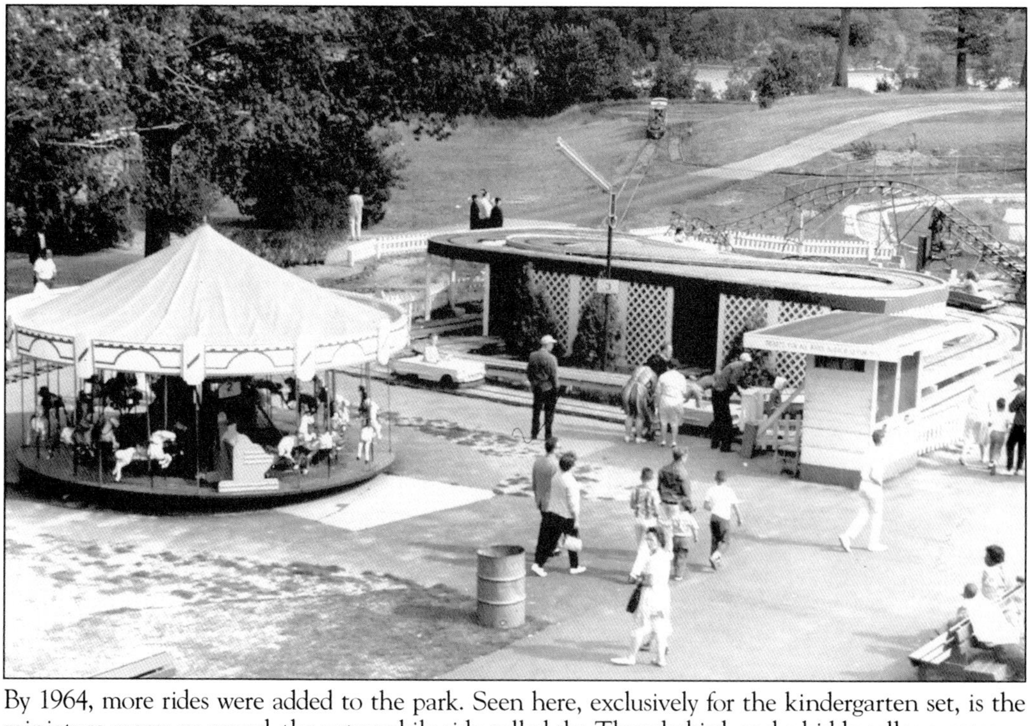

By 1964, more rides were added to the park. Seen here, exclusively for the kindergarten set, is the miniature merry-go-round, the automobile ride called the Thunderbird, and a kiddy roller coaster.

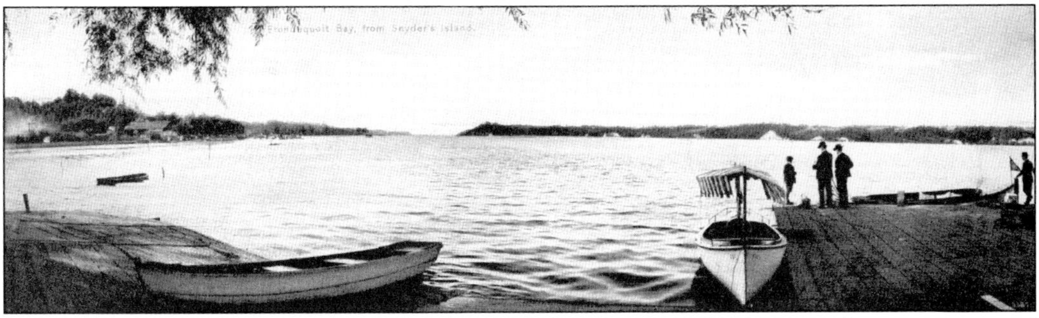

This 1905 postcard of Irondequoit Bay illustrates how inviting the bay was for sportsmen and vacationers who came by rail to the various hotels. The bay was a primary destination for the patrons of the railroads that ran from the city along the shore.

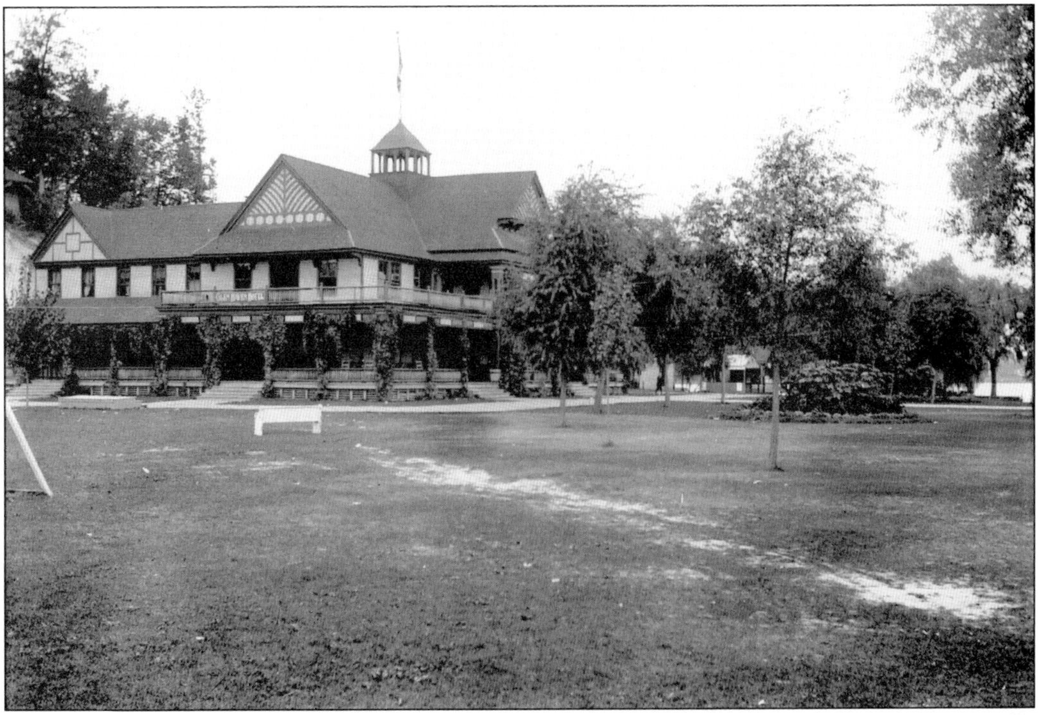

The Glen Haven resort on the bay was the only one built by the railroad to encourage traffic on the Glen Haven Line. It was built in 1899 and was a mecca for vacationers until 1929. The hotel could seat over 400 patrons in its dining rooms and its large verandas. It was surrounded by beautifully landscaped gardens and the grounds were crisscrossed with walkways shaded by trees. When the Rochester Street Railway purchased Glen Haven, they sought to increase patronage by adding a Ferris wheel, roller coaster, and miniature railway.

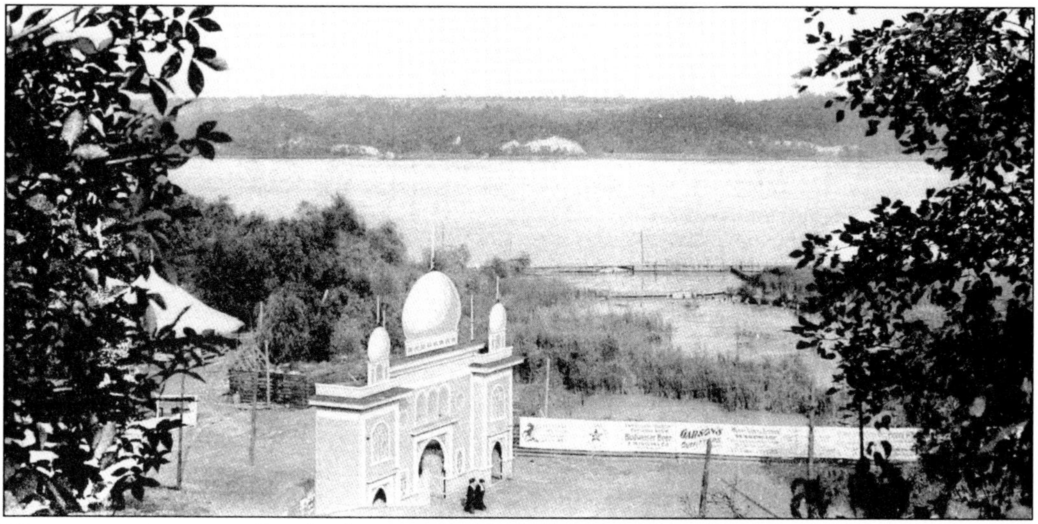

This postcard, sent to Eva Rudman in 1905, shows the entrance to the Glen Haven resort. Between 1900 and 1910, thousands of people visited the resort but, according to Raines Law, no one could be served alcohol unless they actually had a room at the hotel. It would be interesting to know how many guests rented rooms and never occupied them. No doubt many of the patrons developed ingenious ways of circumventing the law for a cold beer.

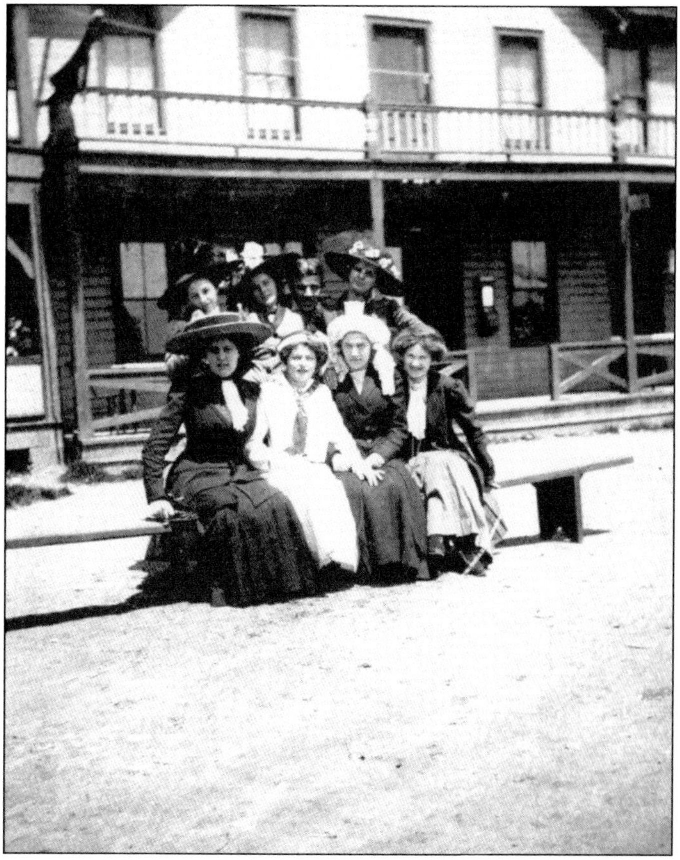

These ladies posed on the lawn of Glen Haven during a 1908 visit. The lady in the back row on the left is identified as Nora McBride. She and her friends probably enjoyed the very large dance hall, for under the balcony was a complete stage used for bands, vaudeville shows, and concerts.

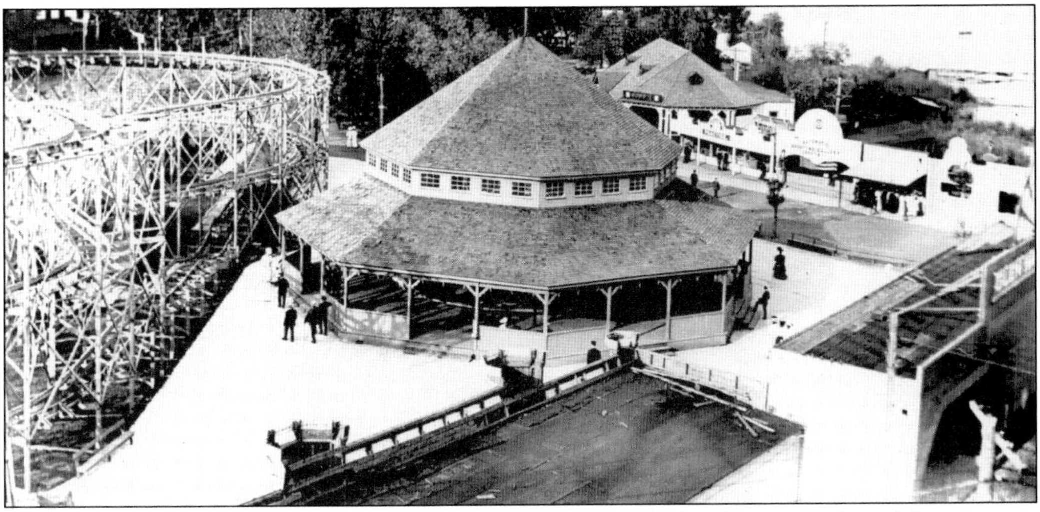

This photograph, taken around 1910, shows the extent of Glen Haven Park and Irondequoit Bay. The park was the site of a large crowd when, in 1904, the Shriners and Masons held their carnival there for a week. Twenty-five thousand people, including some of the most prominent in Rochester, flocked to the grounds to witness the reenactment of the Battle of San Juan Hill from the Spanish-American War. The 34th Separate Company of Geneva, the Naval Reserves, the First Separate Company Fife and Drum and Bugle Corps of Rochester, and the 54th Regiment participated in this spectacular event. For 40 minutes muskets cracked, cannons roared, and bombs burst in the air. As a climax, the regimental band played "The Star-Spangled Banner" while two aerial bombs exploded, displaying two 18-by-20-foot American flags.

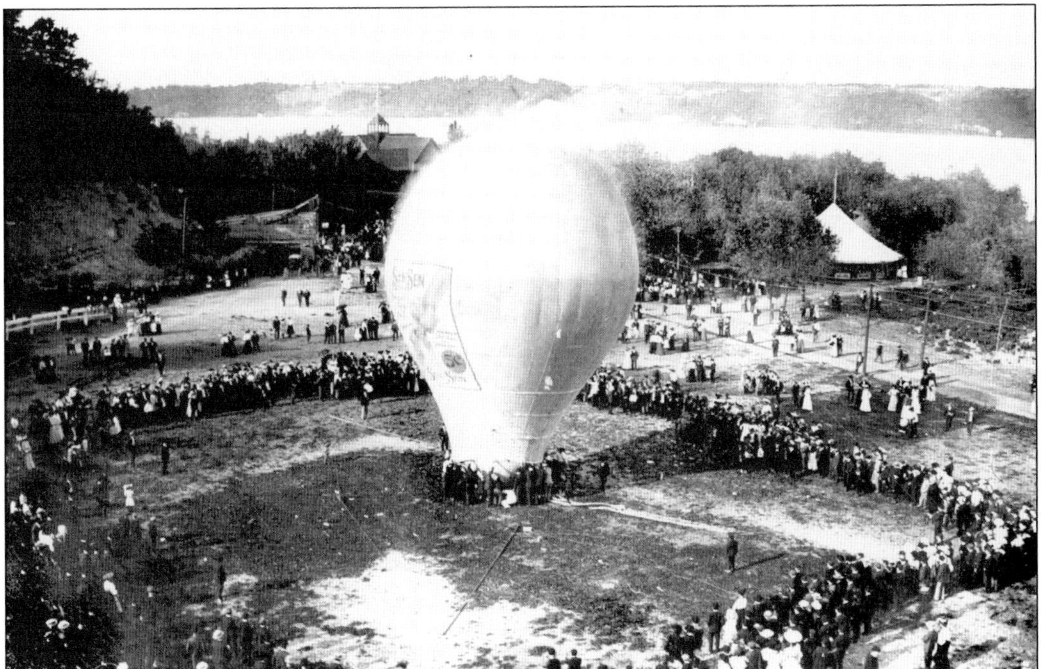

Mock battles were not the only attractions for patrons of Glen Haven. In 1904, crowds witnessed a successful balloon ascension from the ground. A careful examination of the balloon reveals an advertisement on the side for Sen-Sen, a popular licorice-flavored breath lozenge.

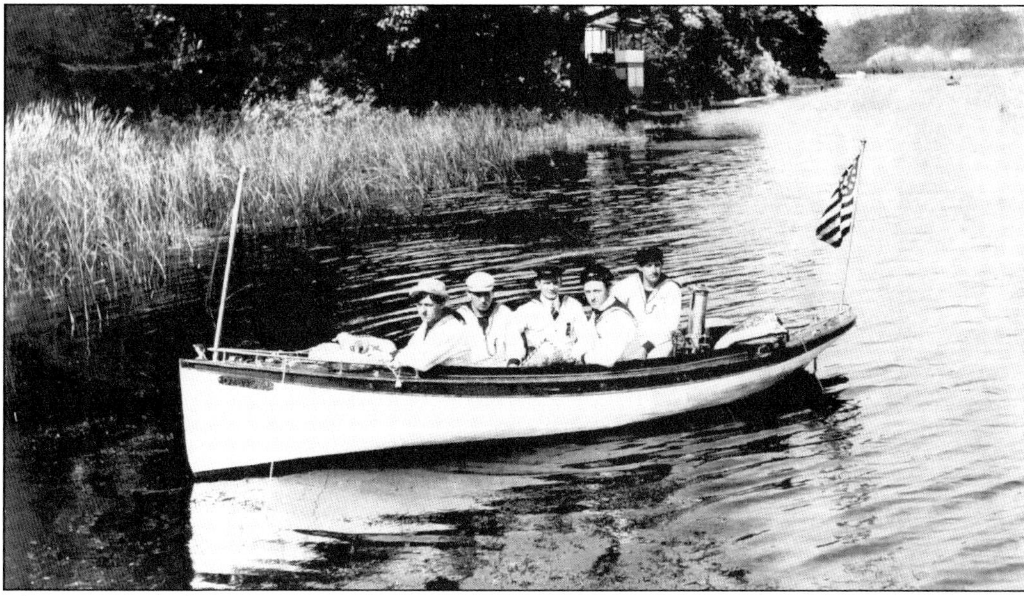

The resorts on the bay were magnets for young people and private boaters. One of the most popular groups was the Unique Social Club who had their own clubhouse on the bay but also frequented Glen Haven. In 1906, the members posed in the first gasoline motor launched on the bay. They christened it the *Otetiani* and it won the first prize in the Carnival of Damascus Shrine Patrol in 1904. In the picture, from left to right, are Charles Peiffer, Albert Picole, Fren Herman, Fred Peiffer, and Henry Peiffer.

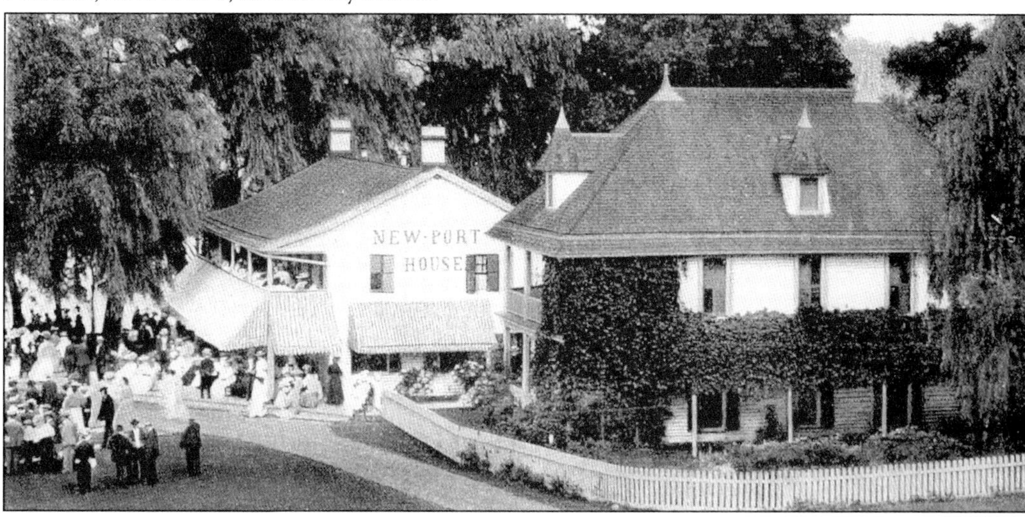

In 1840, Joseph Vinton converted his sawmill to an inn. The Newport House became the first hotel on the bay and it is the last remaining today. Later he sold the property to the Walzer family who increased the patronage of the hotel by offering a menu of fine dinners that attracted a large following among well-to-do clientele. After Orlo Walzer's death in 1880, William Sours, an employee, took over management of the hotel. He built additional rooms, a pavilion, large docks, and also added a road. For many youngsters in town the high point of the summer was the annual Sunday school picnic. Young people enjoyed the boat rides on the bay and dancing in the hall. During the height of the season, the Newport House could serve between 300 to 500 patrons a day.

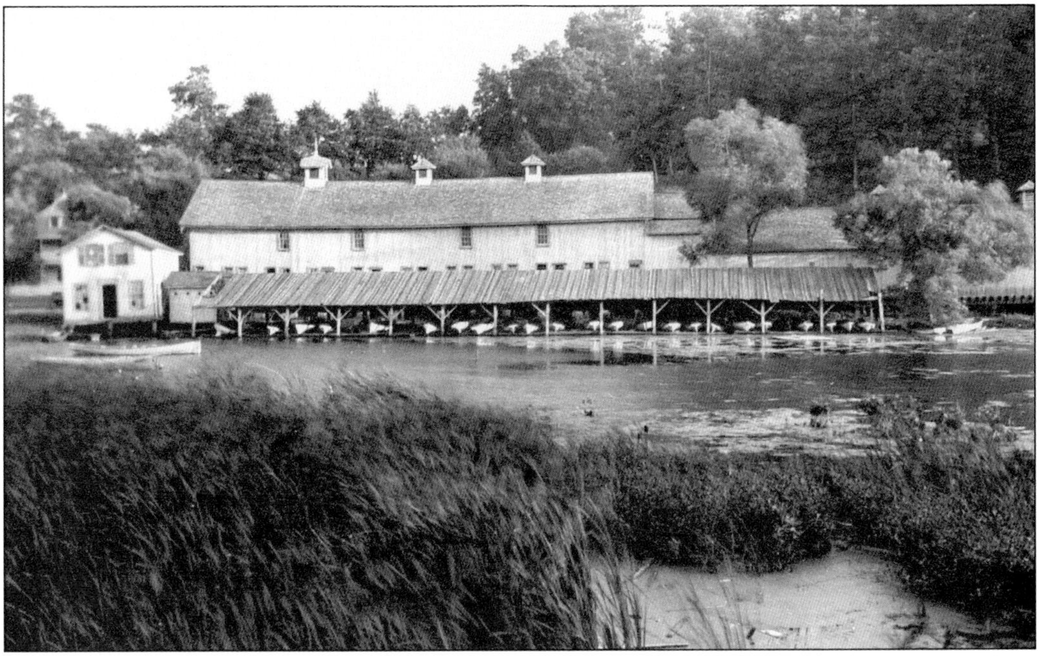

The Newport House also attracted fishermen from all over the state. The boat livery shown here offered both boats and fishing tackle for rent. Boats cost 50¢ a day, and bait, primarily minnows, was also sold. Before 1890, there were plenty of bass, pike, pickerel, and trout in Irondequoit Bay waters.

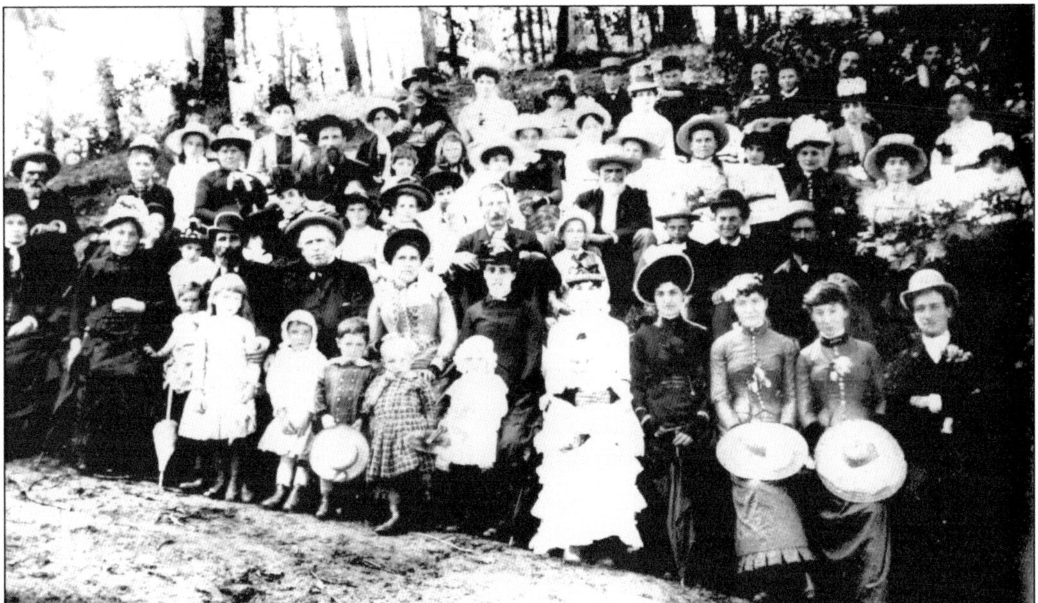

In August 1888, the Who-So-Ever Society enjoyed a picnic at the Newport House. The day of the town picnic, the north pavilion, which was the largest, was reserved by the Sunday school from the Women's Christian Temperance Union on Titus Avenue and the south pavilion by the members of the Culver Road Presbyterian church. Each family brought food for both lunch and dinner, and children who had managed to be on their best behavior were treated to a free ride aboard the *Galusha*, a steamboat.

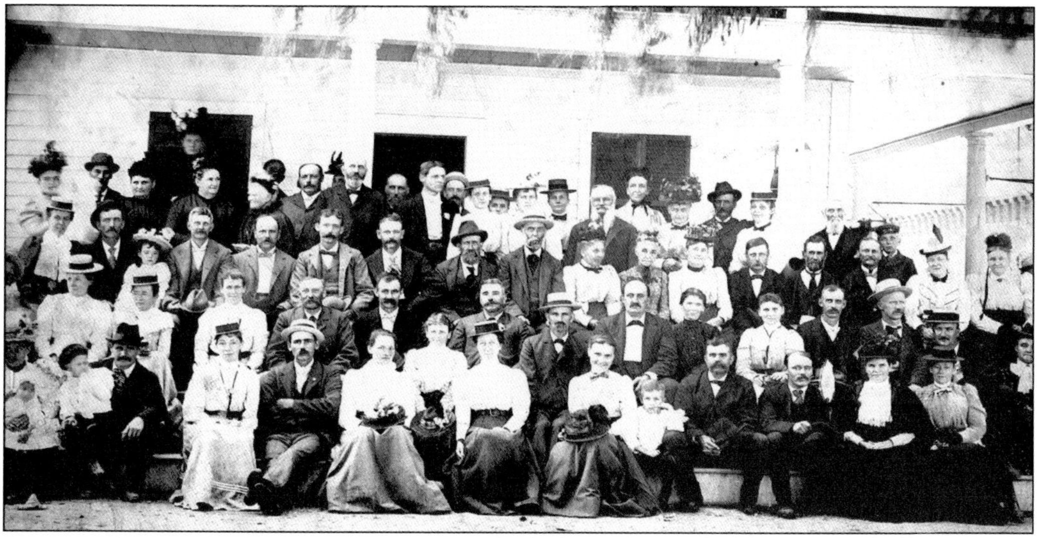

In 1890, most of the families on the west side of town were represented at the Women's Christian Temperance Union picnic at the Newport House. Identified here are Susie Porter; Chauncey Porter; Mary Hallauer, wife of William Hallauer; Jennie Pammenter; Stella Metcalf, wife of Henry Metcalf; Sarah Hill Killick; Elmer Pammenter; Charles Heffer; Mrs. Alfred Metcalfe; Sarah Marsh; Delia List; Mrs. Charles Hodges; Nellie Sutton; Agnes Anderson; Joseph Rayton; James Pammenter; George Heffer; James Howard; Frank Daggs; Mary Daggs; Mrs. Stephen Warren; Stephen Warren; Frank Callister; Walter Colt; Ellen Raynor, wife of William Raynor; Ella Burling, wife of John Burling; William Hill; Elva Hill; Charles Hodges; James B. Porter; John Burling; Charles South; Joshua Bridgeman; Reuben Dake; Mrs. Reuben Dake; Phoebe Cooper; Mary Heffer; John Heffer; William Sutton; Abram Franke; Ruth Franke; Louise Heffer with her baby; Fred Heffer; Hattie Rudman; Mrs. George H. Rudman; Mrs. Henry Killick; Henry Metcalfe; George H. Rudman; Rev. Pleasant Lee Powell; Lottie Rayton, wife of Albert Rayton; Laura Heffer; George Cooper; Mrs. Harrison Stanton; William Leake; Abbie Benson; Frank Dake; Harrison Stanton; Benjamin Franke; Nellie Franke; and Beatrice West.

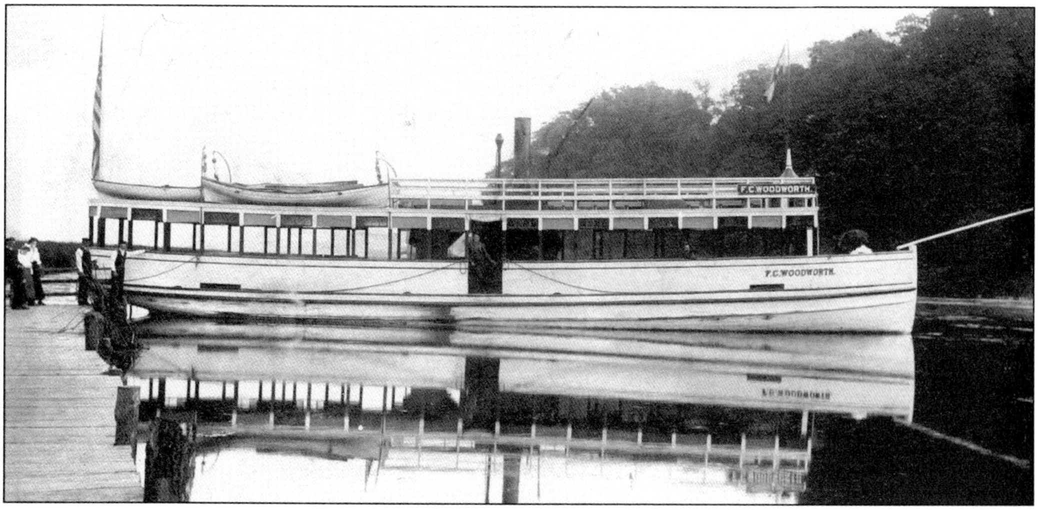

The Steamboat *NH Galusha* was the first side-wheeler on Irondequoit Bay, but Orlo Walzer replaced it with the *F. C. Woodworth* in 1885. It seated 200 and was one of several boats owned by F. C. Woodworth. The propeller-driven steamboat operated from 1885 to 1910.

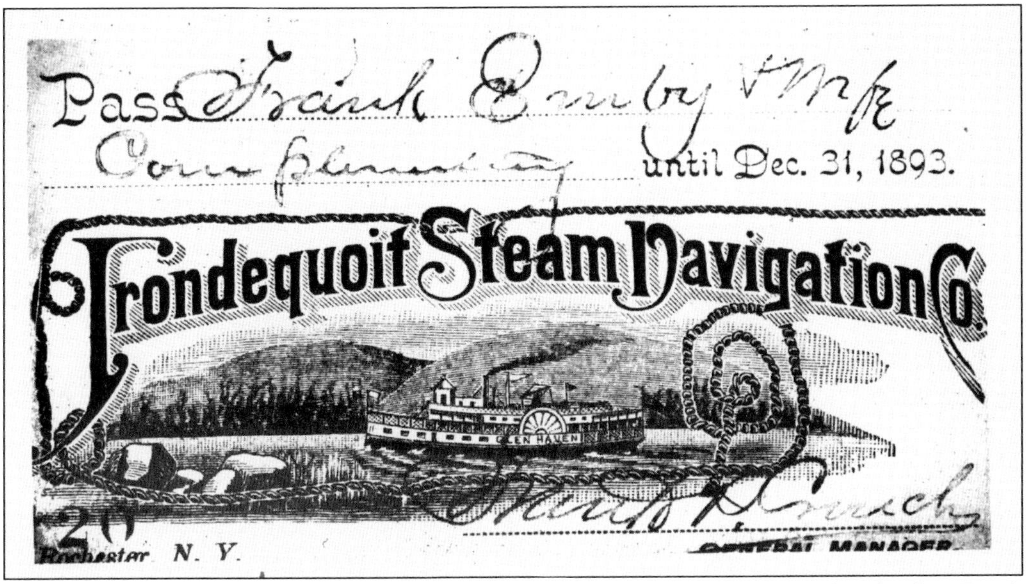

There is an old saying that "there is no such thing as a free ride or a free lunch," but Frank Owby and his wife were the exception to the rule for they enjoyed free rides on the *Glen Haven*, formerly the *Galusha*, on Irondequoit Bay until December 31, 1893.

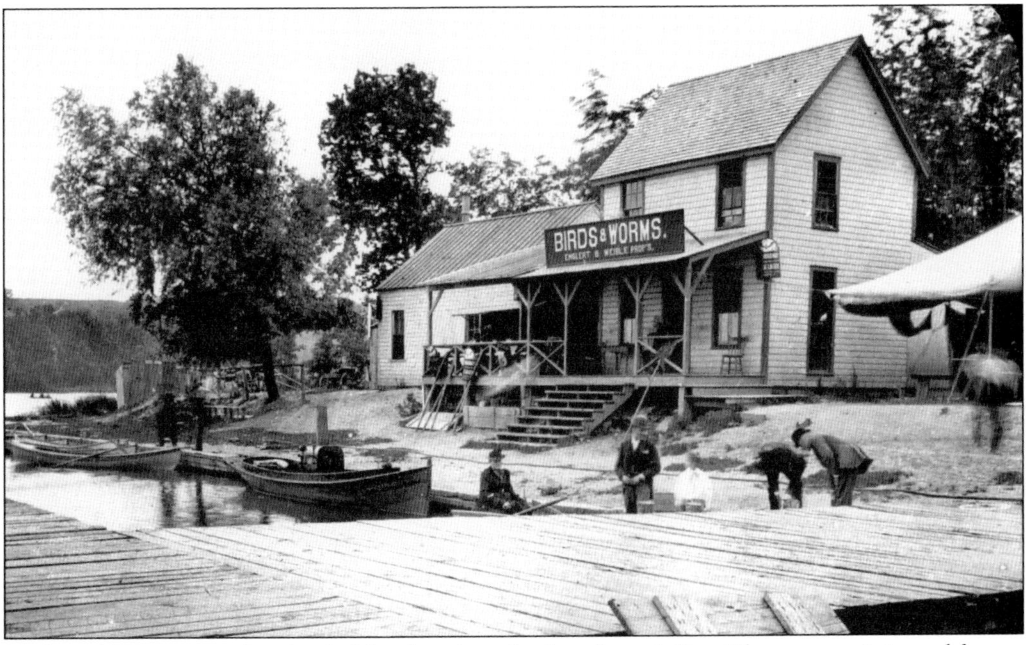

Birds and Worms was the third oldest hotel on the Irondequoit Bay. The name originated from a fishing and hunting organization started in 1870. The "birds" were the hunters in the group and the "worms" were the fisherman. In 1872, they built a clubhouse near the deepest part of the bay north of little and big Massauga coves. In 1877, James and Dennis Vanderlinde built a resort on the spot and operated it until it burned in 1890. That year, another hotel was built near the shore and run by two men named Englert and Weible until 1893. In April 1941, Val Weber reopened the hotel, remodeled it, and enlarged it for overnight guests. The building was sold in 1946 to the Newport Yacht Club.

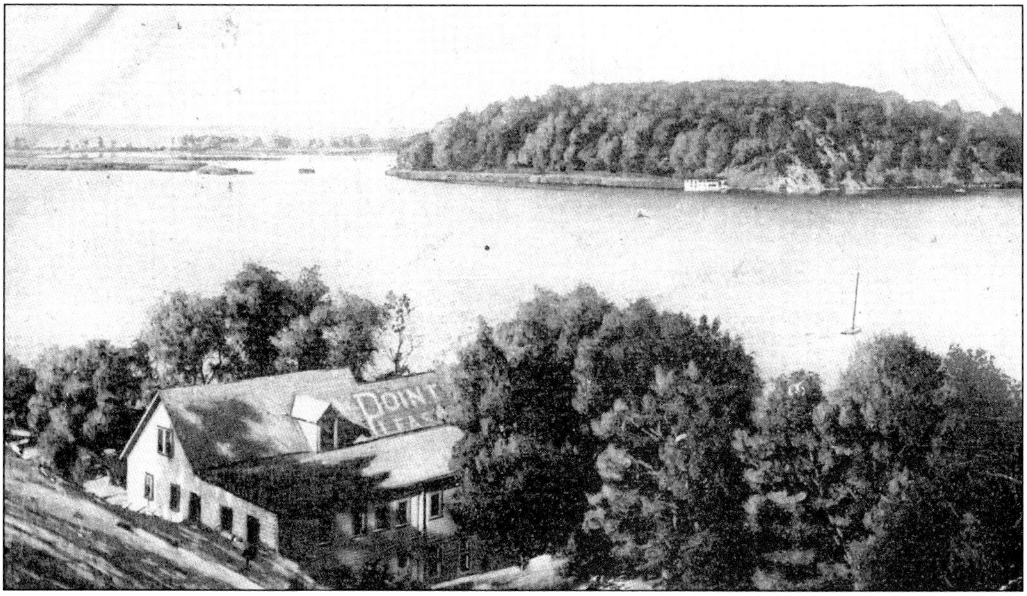

This 1917 postcard shows one of the most popular recreation spots on the bay. First known as Woodchuck Point, it became more familiar to vacationers as Point Pleasant. Whatever name they used, grouse hunters and fisherman in the late 1800s favored the area. The hotel was built in 1900 and the photograph for this postcard was taken in 1906. On December 21, 1954, patrons celebrated the coming New Year at the popular spot. That party was the hotel's swan song, for, like others before it, the building on the bay burned to the ground, leaving just ashes and fond memories.

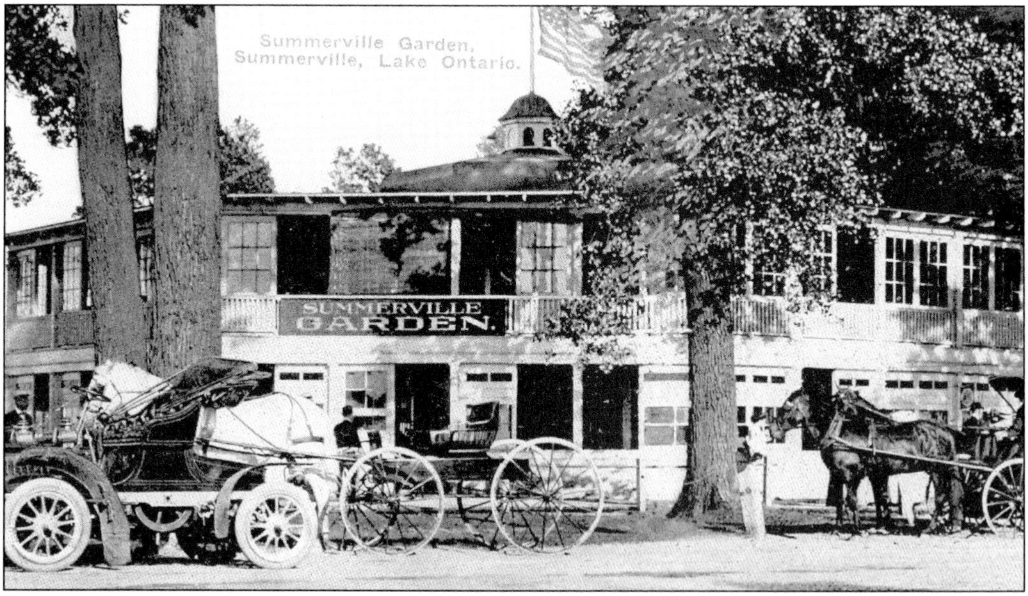

On the west side of Irondequoit at the end of St. Paul Boulevard stood another famous eatery and gathering spot. This was the Summerville Garden Pavilion built next to the trolley loop at the end of the boulevard. The Rochester and Irondequoit Railway actually planned the development which included not only the trolley loop, but facilities for the Windsor Ferry, a bathing pavilion, a park on the river, and this unique octagonal building which was quickly named by patrons as the Roundhouse. It became famous for its fish fries and cold beer.

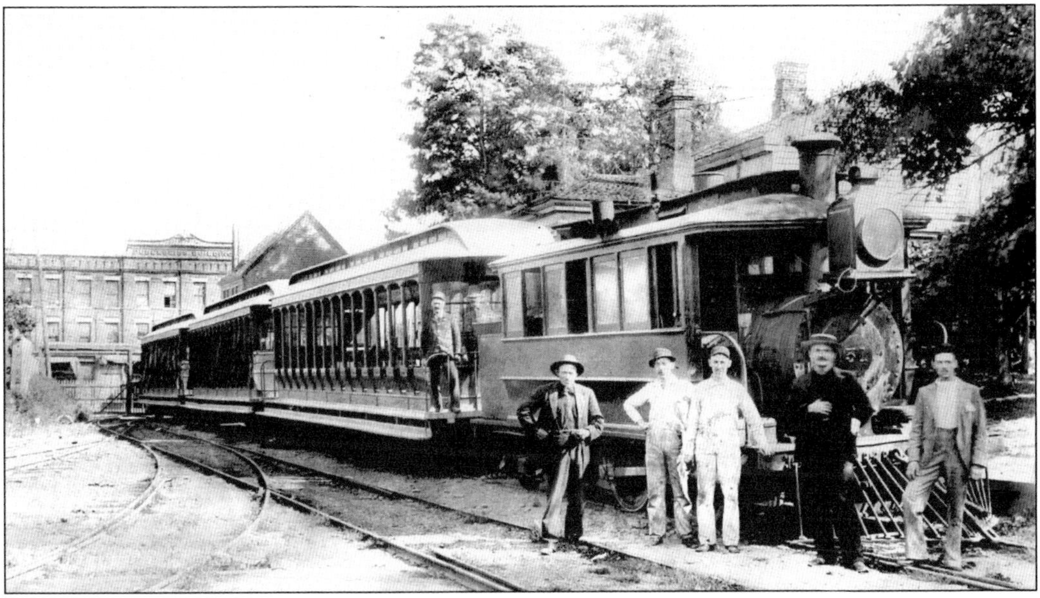

The small railroad purchased by Michael Filon at the Philadelphia Exposition was nicknamed the dummy line because the boiler was enclosed for its entire length so that the engineer and fireman could walk on either side of the locomotive while it was in motion. Whether the word dummy was directed towards the engineer or passengers is still a bit of a mystery. The locomotive pictured here at the Portland Street Station, Number 31, was purchased 10 years after the line first began operation. It weighed 35 tons and proved to be too heavy for the tracks.

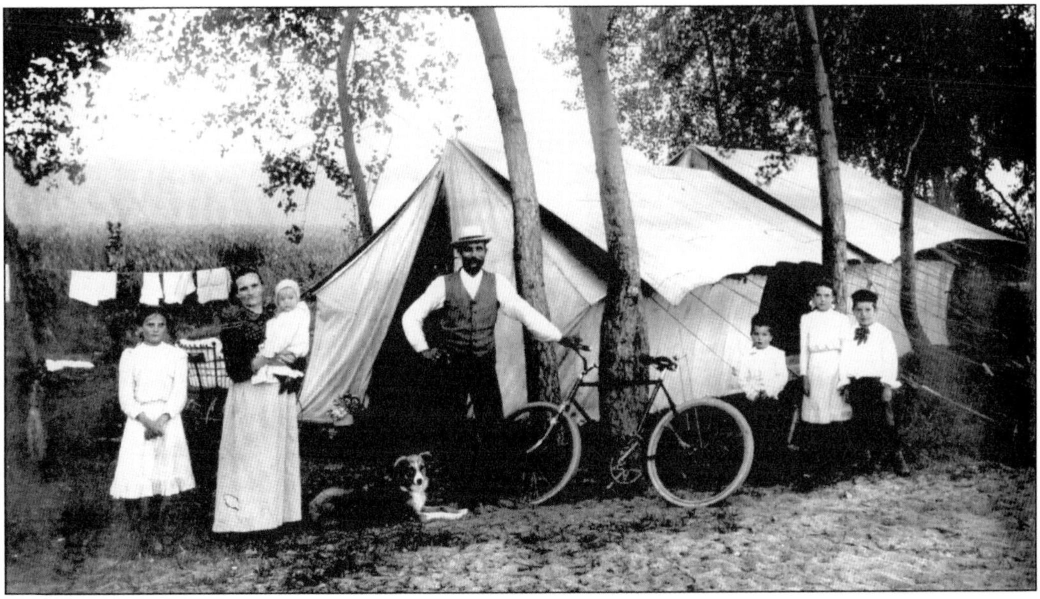

While many vacationers gravitated to the White City resort on Lake Ontario because of the white canvas tents erected on the platforms rented to them by the railroad, other campers preferred more simple accommodations. This is the Schlageter family camping on the west side of Irondequoit Bay near the outlets in the summer of 1902. From left to right are Carolyn, mother Carrie holding baby Andres, Shep (the pet dog), Ferdinand Sr., Ferdinand Jr., Mary, and Leo. Ferdinand Sr. rode his bike to Rochester every day where he worked as a builder.

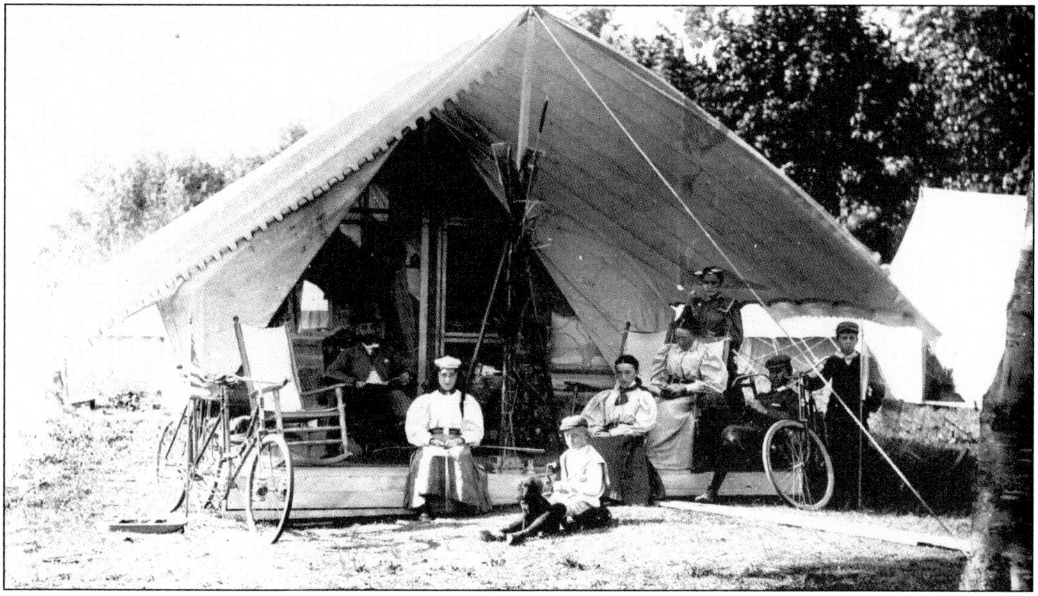

In 1897, the Chapin family posed outside their tent at White City. Mr. Chapin, perhaps having just arrived by trolley from his office in the city, is still wearing his suit and derby hat while relaxing in the shade of the tent overhang while his wife, dressed for the picture, is reading in her rocker. The children, who are not identified, do not look as though they were ready for a romp on the beach, and even the dog seems very sedate in honor of having been included in the family picture.

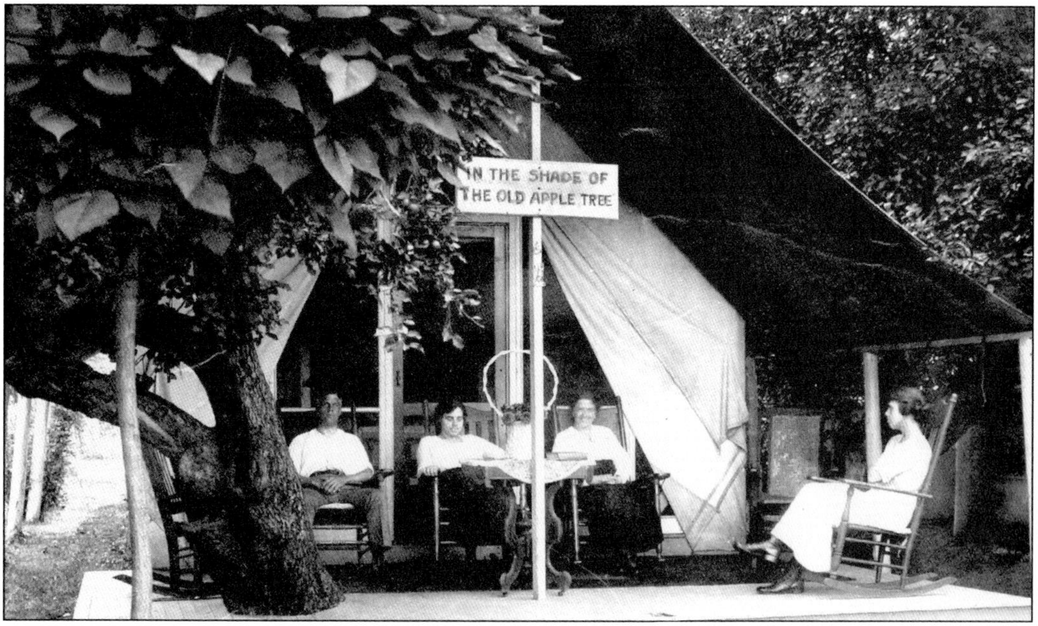

The Avery tent at 9 East Lake Front was the only tent that could boast a tree on their porch. The Avery platform was built around the tree so that porch sitters were, as the sign says, "in the shade of the old apple tree." Relaxing in the rockers are, from left to right, Philip Avery, Marian Mosher, Florence Mosher, and Lucy Avery. Marion and Florence were both great-nieces of Susan B. Anthony.

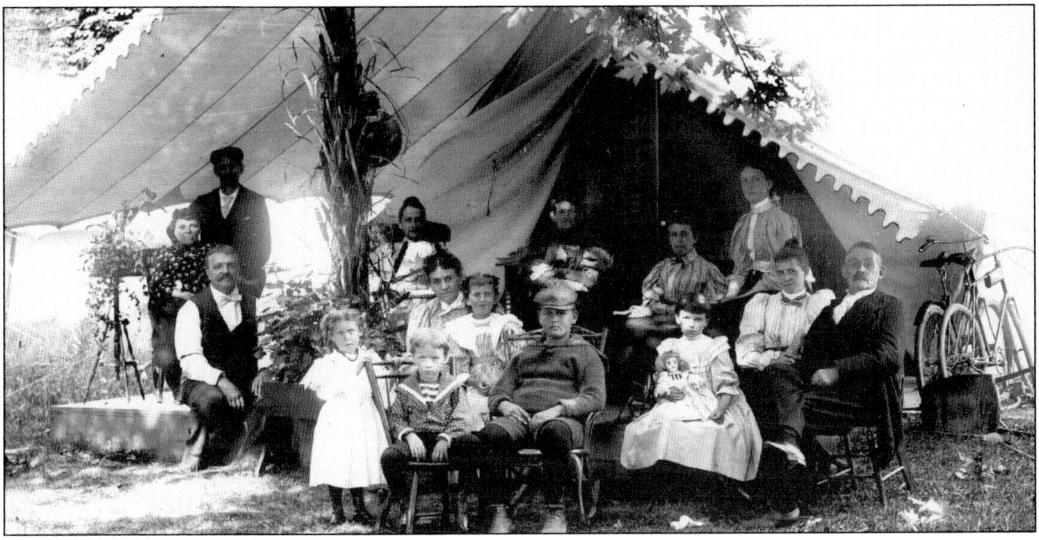

This tent retreat was the summer home of Professor Wilkinson, a piano teacher. His family and friends also posed on their front porch. The first girl on the left is Gladys Wilkinson, the professor's daughter. The tent resort known as White City began in 1870, when Joseph Tone laid out five streets in anticipation of the railroad line coming to Irondequoit. In 1893, his foresight was justified when a railroad syndicate bought his land, built wooden platforms, and began to rent the lots out to vacationers for $40 a season. Gladys later married Doctor Musselman, the man on the extreme right, who was an herb doctor. They lived on St. Paul Boulevard just above Cole (now Colebrook) Road.

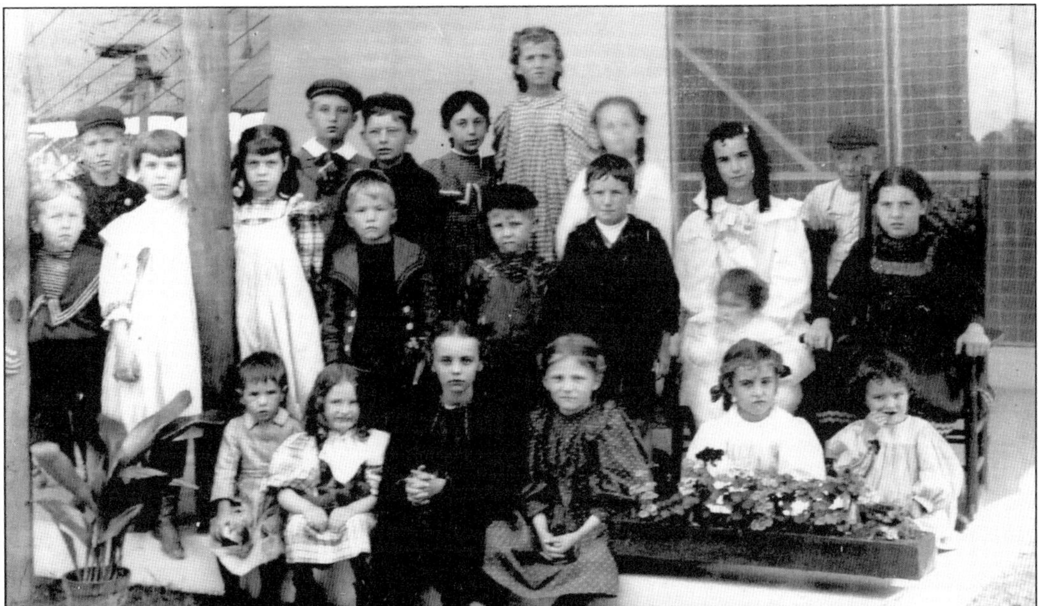

On July 30, 1897, a group of children gathered on the porch of the Wilkinson's tent, now named Camp Gladys. Although the tents were elaborate with screens over the entry, the occupants still had to haul water from a faucet at the end of each street. The water, supplied by the Rochester and Irondequoit Railway, came from springs on a farm a mile and a half away through an iron conduit which was turned on May first and turned off on September 1.

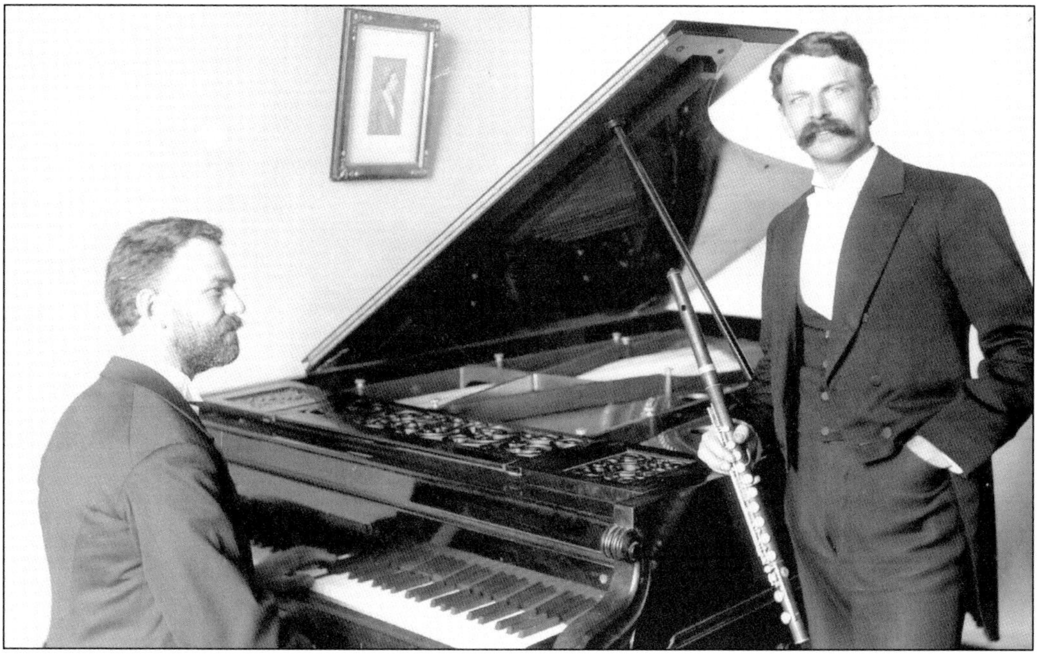

Professor Wilkinson, seated at the piano, is an unknown quantity. He was a professor of music who taught piano, but more importantly, his legacy includes two sets of glass negatives of many pictures taken at White City. These negatives were found at a garage sale and when developed, produced pictures of remarkable clarity and sharpness.

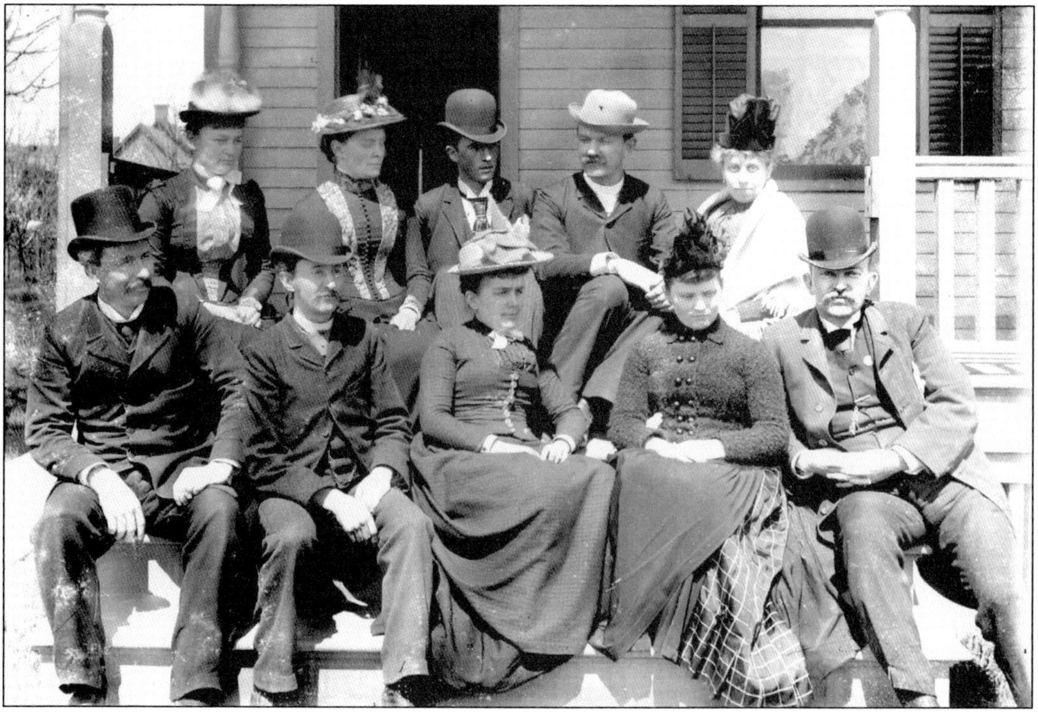

The location of the house and the occasion for which these friends of the professors posed is unknown. But the picture reflects the fashions of the first decade of the 20th century.

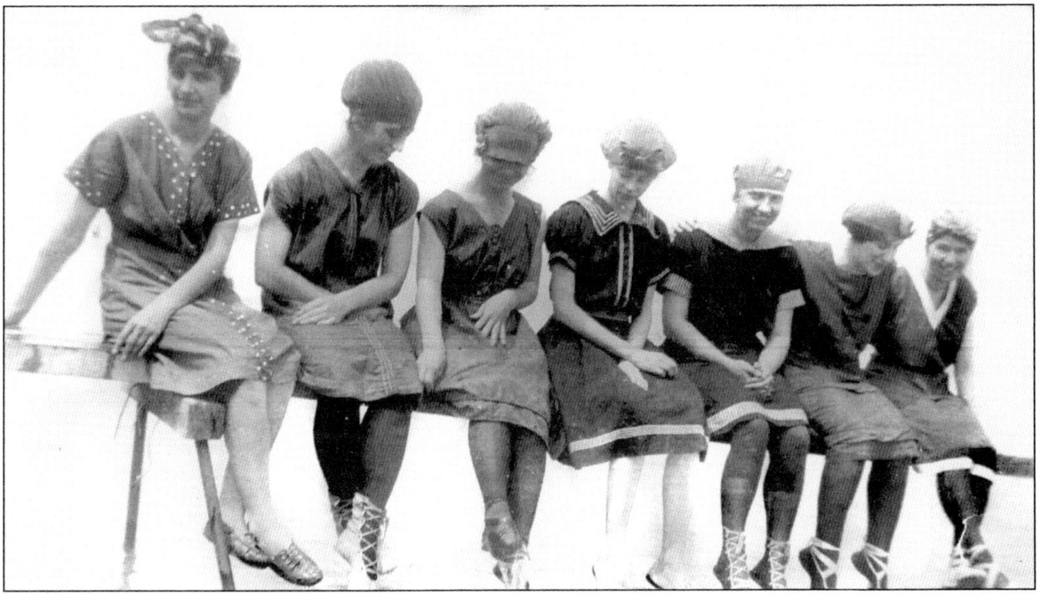

In 1916, the members of the Beta Gamma sorority posed in what was then termed as their bathing costumes, dangling their toes in the waters of Lake Ontario. Demurely clad in stockings, bathing slippers, knee-length bathing dresses, and caps, there was little danger that they would end up with sun burns. The sorority girls are, from left to right, Irene Price, Ernestine Blaw, Elsie Todd, Bessie Allen, Thelma Price, Alvaretto Green, and Gladys Meech. Imagine what they would have thought of today's swimsuits.

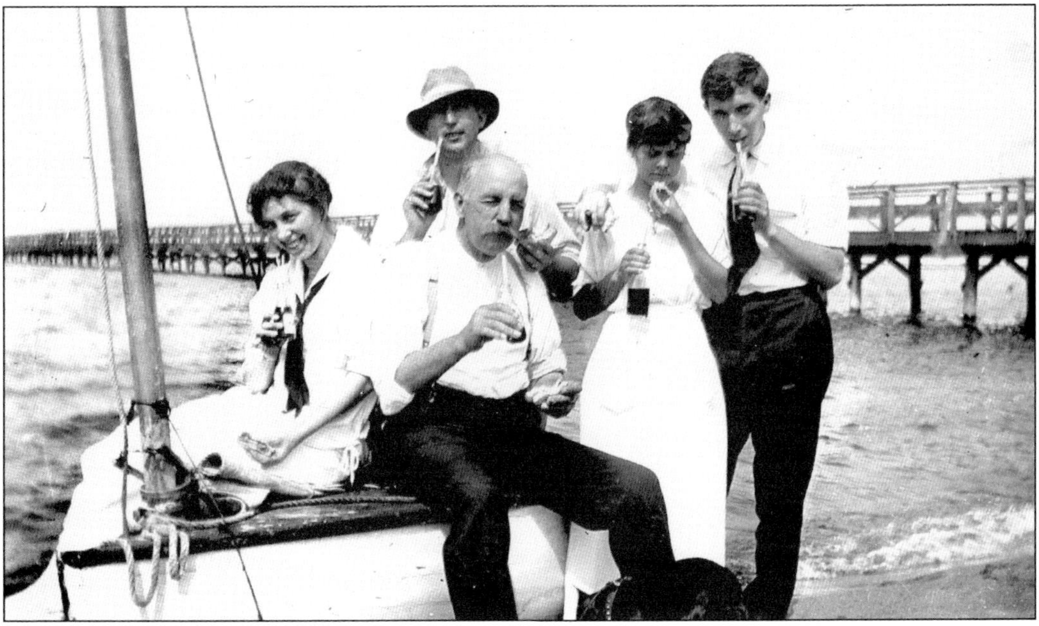

The beach at Durand-Eastman Park was also a popular spot for local residents. In 1915, this group takes time out from a sail. They are, from left to right, Mable Sharp Bortle, Albert Sharp (behind his father), Moses Sharp, Albert Sharp's girlfriend (unidentified), and Ray Fisher. Behind them was the 1,000-foot wood pier built off the beach in 1915. In the winter of 1915, a total of 400 feet of the pier was ripped off by storms.

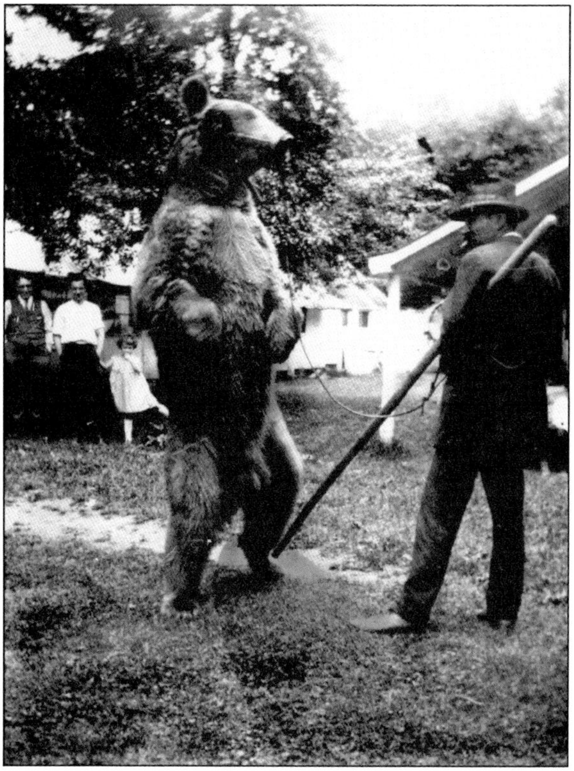

There was always something exciting going on at White City. In 1920, a band of gypsies camped on the White City ballpark ground. One member of the group delighted the children by bringing his dancing bear to Lincoln Avenue. Another man "passed the hat" and the children donated their nickels and pennies. After Fred Bortle took this picture, he filled a tub with water for the bear to have a drink.

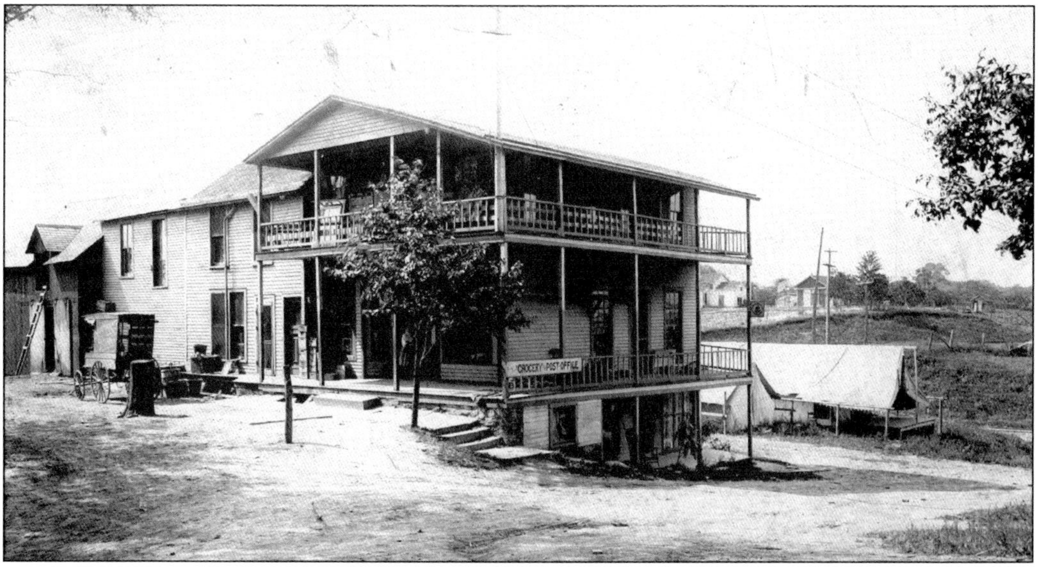

For the housewives of White City and the permanent residents of Sea Breeze the only store in town was Strickland Grocery, which opened in 1895. Before then, most of the residents were farmers who traveled into to Rochester often with their produce and, while there, did what shopping was necessary. But with the coming of the trolley and the influx of summer residents who did not want to travel back into the city, Strickland had ready made customers. The store was located on the southwest corner of Washington Avenue and Rock Beach Road. The little wagon on the left made home deliveries. Strickland's was also the post office.

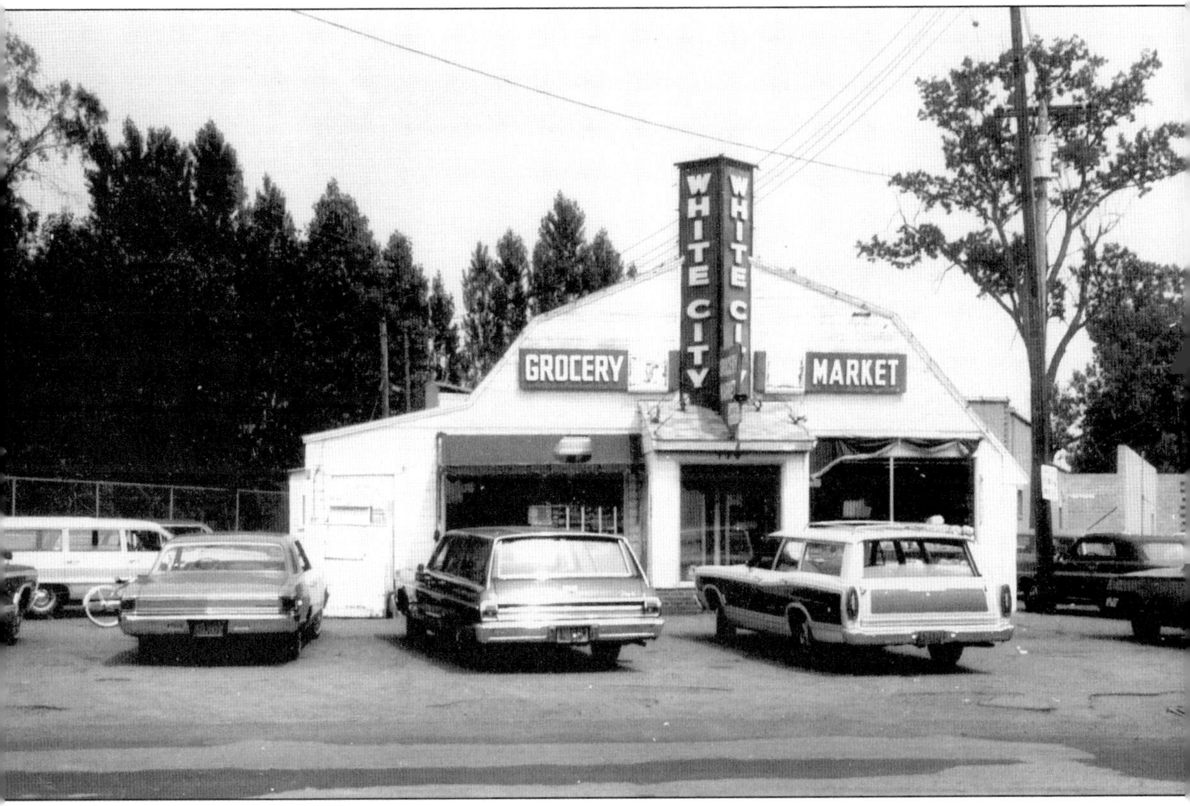

Times changed but the residents of White City still had their own grocery store. Wagons were no longer parked out front, and station wagons became the vehicle of choice in the 1950s and 1960s. The store no longer had a post office, but the sign reminded everyone that even though the tents were gone, the area's name remained.

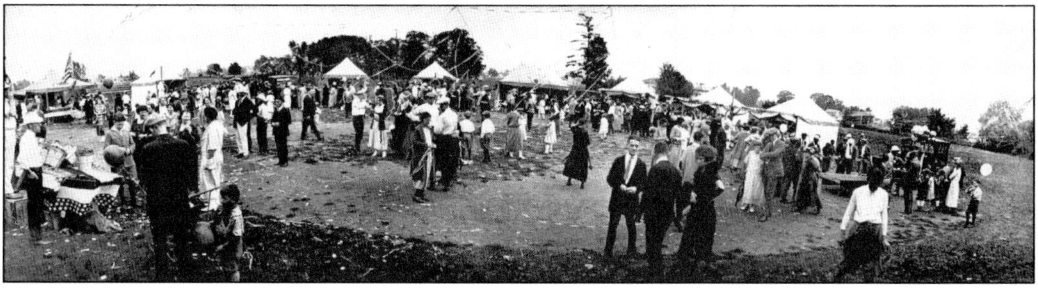

White City had its own government known as the White City, Windsor Beach, and Summerville Athletic Association. The governing board of the association not only enforced the rules of the tent city but provided a calendar of activities. In order to raise money for the annual Fourth of July fireworks display held each year on the beach in front of the Windsor Hotel, the board sponsored a carnival that was held on the ball field located on what is now Norcrest Drive. The carnivals began about 1920 and this is a photograph of one of the very first ones held. The annual carnival became a casualty of the Great Depression, but today spectacular Fourth of July fireworks at the town hall draw thousands of people from all over the county.

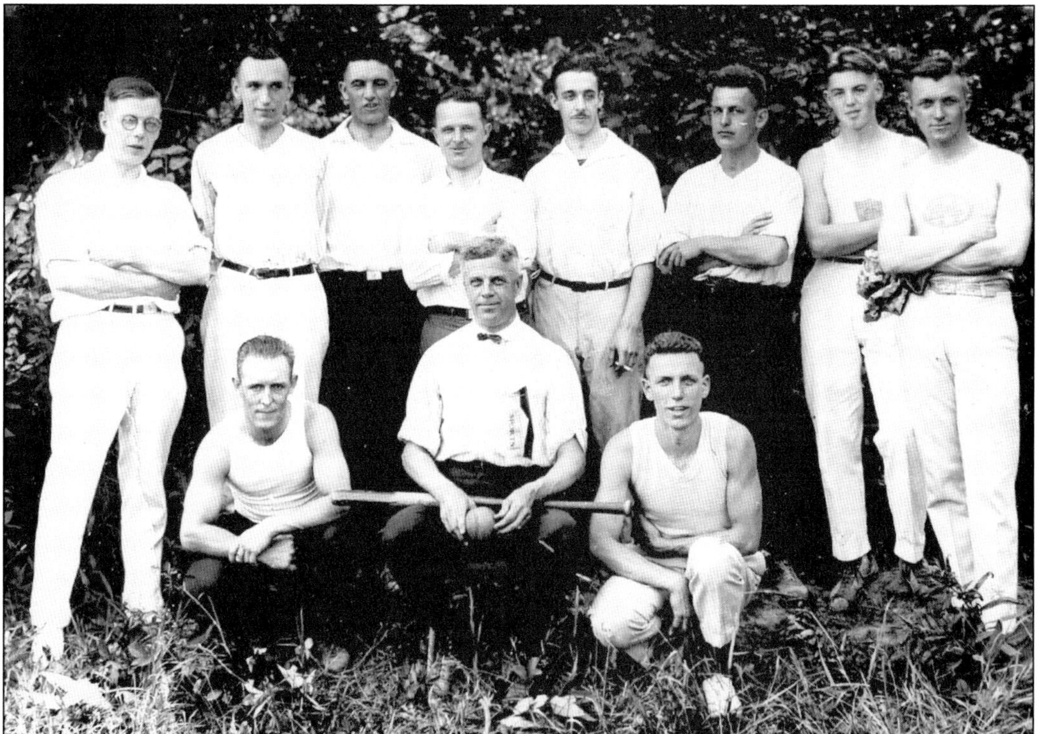

Carnivals, field days, and dances at the Windsor hotel were not the only diversions offered to White City tenters. The enclave also boasted a baseball team. At one time Sunday baseball was banned in Rochester but fans could see a game at the White City ball field. They could watch teams like the White City Oxford or this ball team from 1920. Members of this team include, from left to right, (first row) Avery Serth, Paul Avery (the manager), and Carl Schoener; (second row) Percy Dunherr, Rowland Perry (assistant manager), Rock Slattery, William Curran, Gus Zimmerman Jr., George Crastner, Floyd Bortle, and Charles Schoener. The clubhouse was located under the grandstand. The facility was dismantled in 1939.

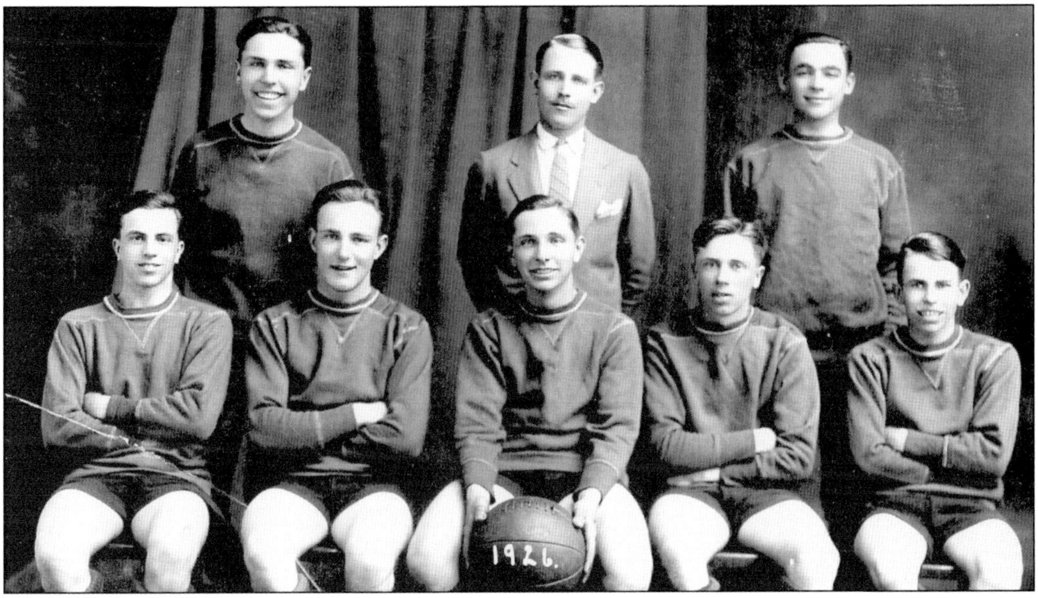

Baseball fades like the leaves of Irondequoit's oaks and maple trees, and then basketball season arrives. Irondequoit's first high school was established in 1924 and these stalwarts represented the school in 1925 and 1926. Written across the top of the picture, with nicknames, were Gordon "Bozo" Snider, coach Ira Wilson, and Chuck Loescher. In the first row are Arthur "Bud" Chappell, Robert Bristol, "Jumping Jack" Shoes, Allan "Spike" Snider, Allan "Duke" Lundahl, and "Shirt" Bundt.

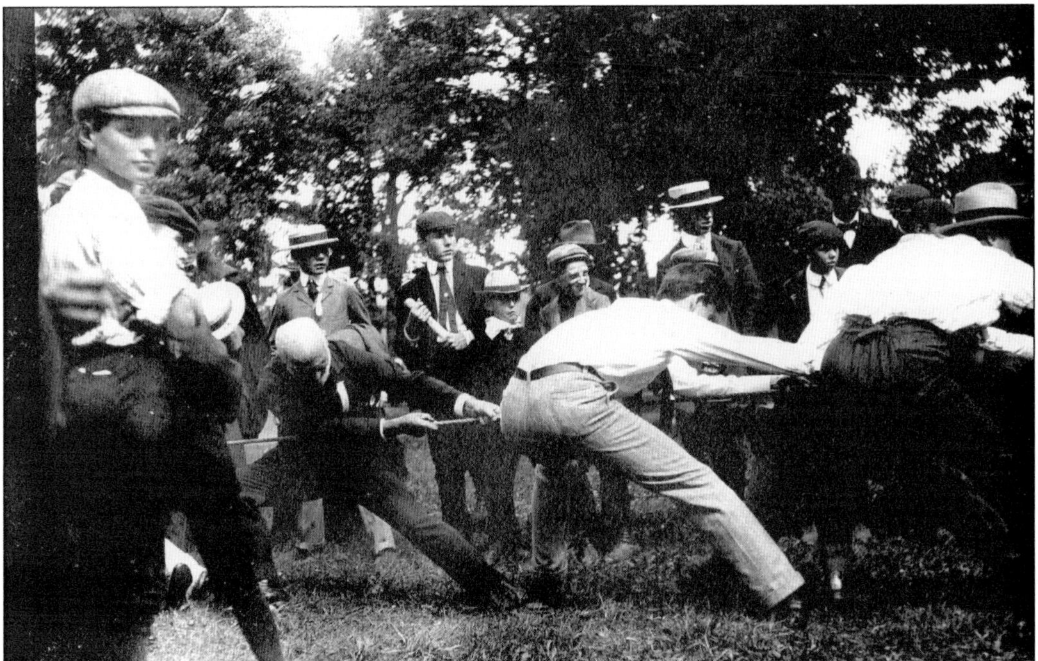

A more unconventional team sport, often the high point of "picnic athletics," was the tug-of-war. Note the spectators dressed in suits, ties, and the summer necessity, a straw hat. The young man on the left is more interested in the camera than the contest.

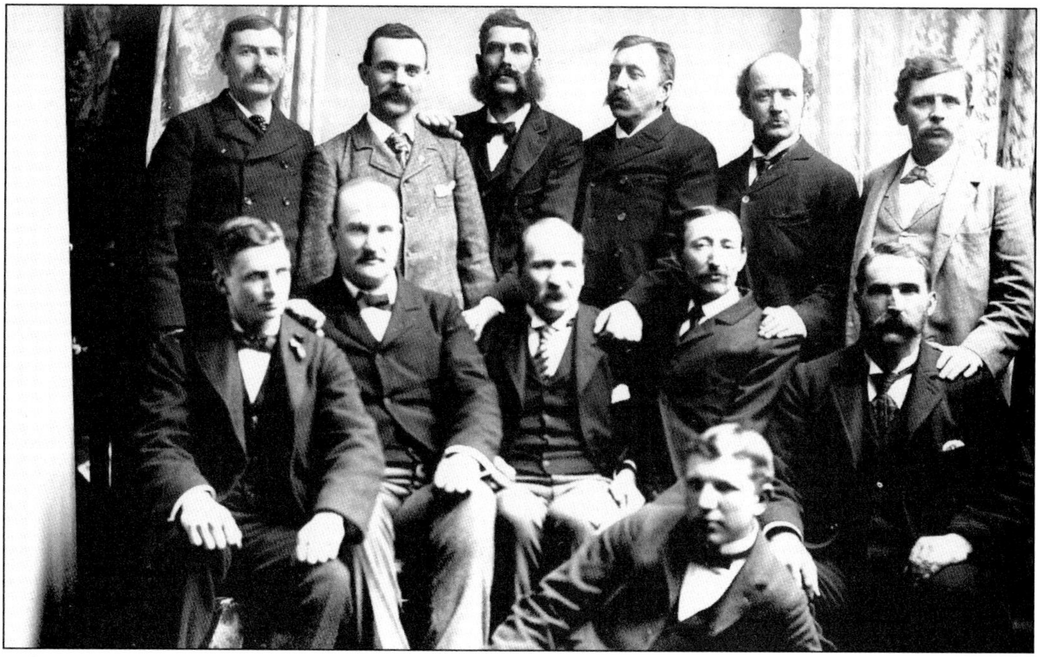

When Dr. Frank Grant, son of pioneer Sydney Grant, came to town, he was entertained by his friends who preferred to call themselves "old-timers." Most were sons of Irondequoit's pioneers. From left to right are (first row) Bert Howard, Walter Colt, Edward Colt, John Camping, and Thomas Pengelly, with Arthur Curtis stretched out on the floor; (second row) Adolph List, Seymour Titus, William Raynor, brother Theodore Grant, William Leake, and Frank Grant. Frank Grant graduated from the University of Rochester medical school and then moved to California.

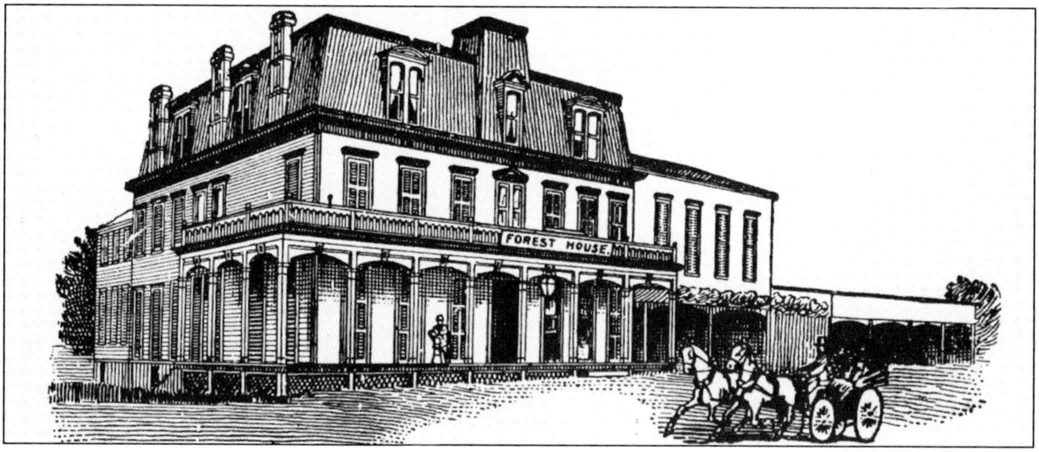

In 1860, Isaac Forest bought the old Swayne's Tavern and razed it six years later. He then built the Forest House, and for 30 years it was famous as the best-equipped hotel in the state. It was three stories of elegance with a huge basement that contained the town jail. Its slate mansard roof had a high observation tower in the center with a 50-foot flagpole. There were 30 rooms to accommodate guests and three bathhouses. The dining room could accommodate 200 guests. The hotel was furnished in the King Edward style with carpeted sitting rooms and parlors for the ladies who, in those days, were not allowed in barrooms. The second floor ballroom was large enough for 120 couples. This sketch is cut from letterhead used in the 1890s. No actual photographs exist of the impressive resort.

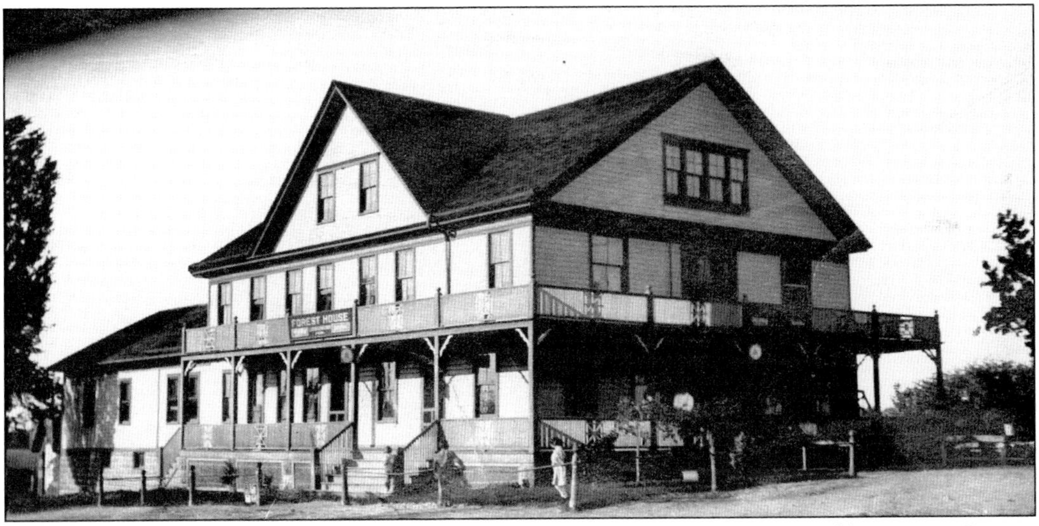

The first Forest House was destroyed by fire and Irondequoit would not see its likes again. George Fisher, who owned it at the time, did rebuild this second Forest House in 1907, but he could not duplicate the elegance of the beveled glass mirrors and floor to ceiling paintings. However, many townspeople have happy memories of it.

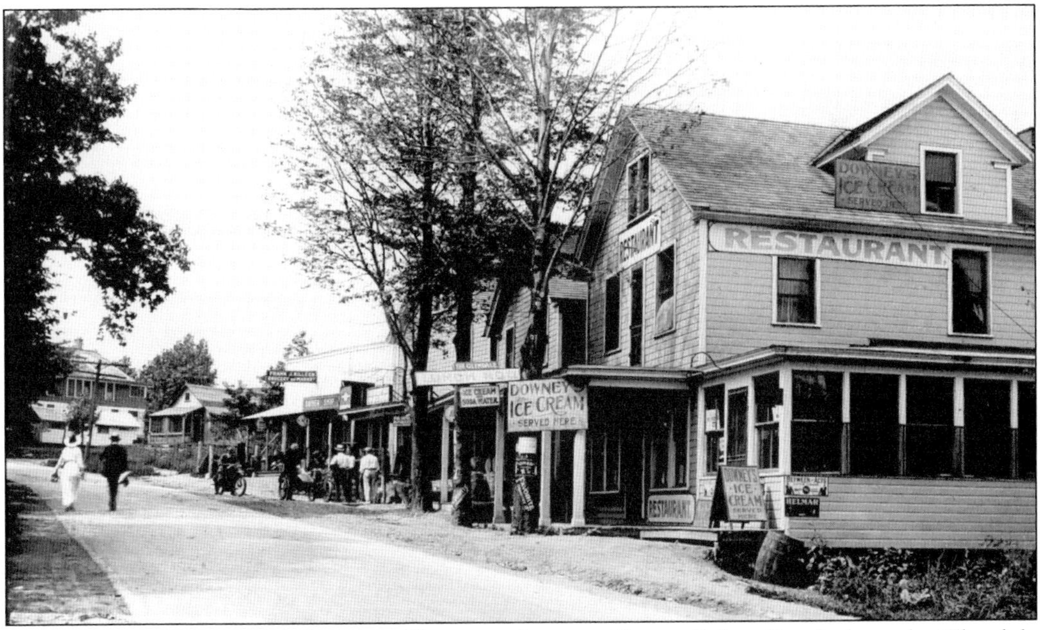

This picture taken in 1915 shows the "business district of lower Culver Road where the Glendale restaurant served two fried eggs for fifteen cents and people could stroll down the middle of the street despite Clarence Morse on his motorcycle."

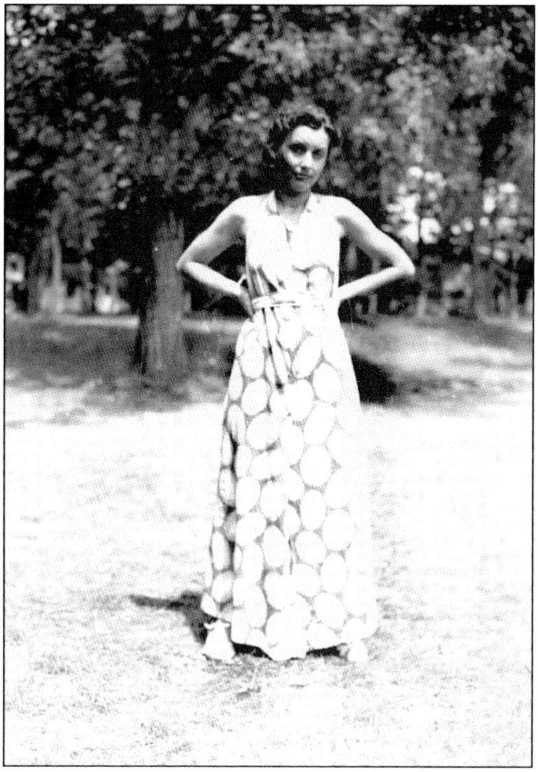

Phyllis Cole Richens models one of the favorite summertime fashions of the 1930s, the beach pajama. The full-length dress was actually billowy pants with a halter top—a cool costume for warm weather.

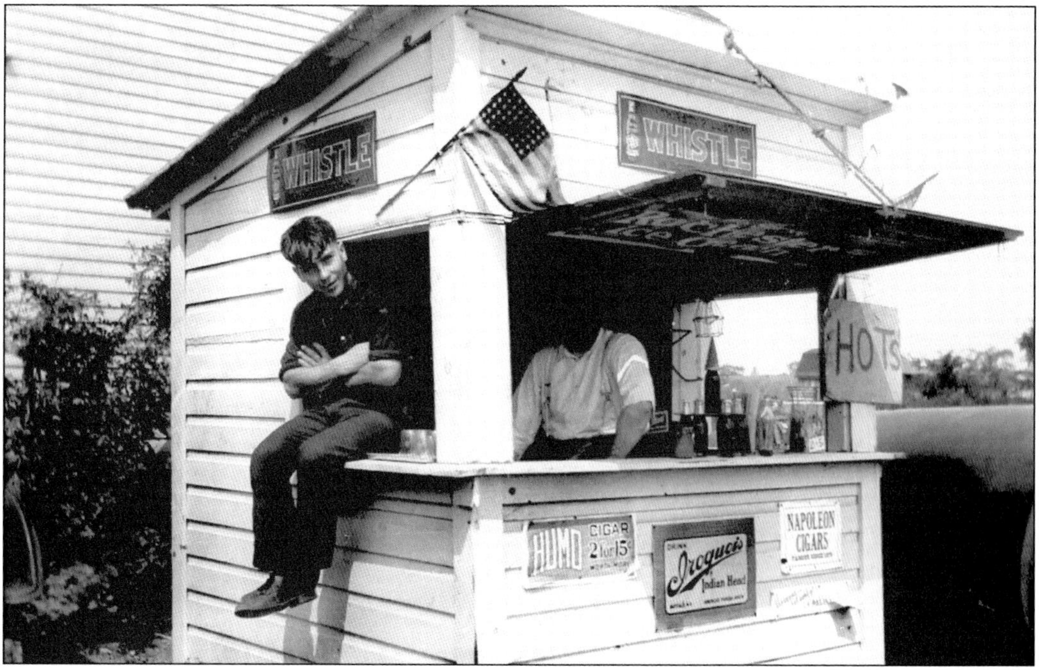

This small hotdog stand at the entrance to Durand-Eastman Park was the precursor to Vic and Irv's, Bill Gray's, and the other stands at the end of Culver Road called Hot Dog Row.

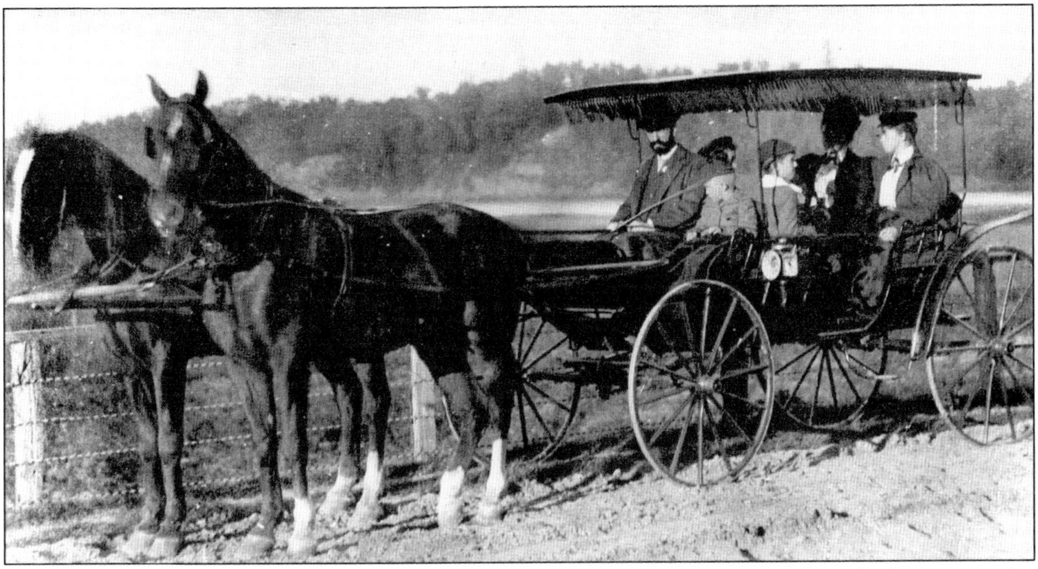

The Chapin family rented a tent platform every season at White City and made the trip to the Lake Ontario shore in their surrey with the fringe on top.

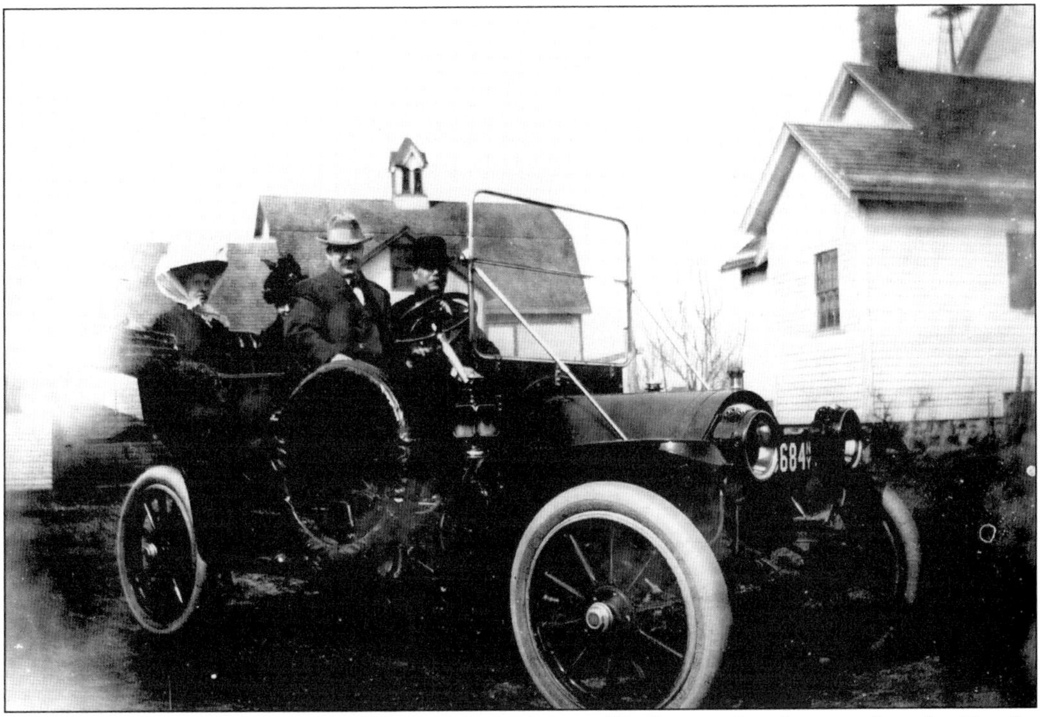

The surrey with the fringe often got stuck in the muddy dirt roads of spring, but the Franke family was more mobile with this classy car driven by Ben Franke. Next to Franke is Jim Porter, and the woman wearing a large hat secured with a net is Lottie Howard Franke.

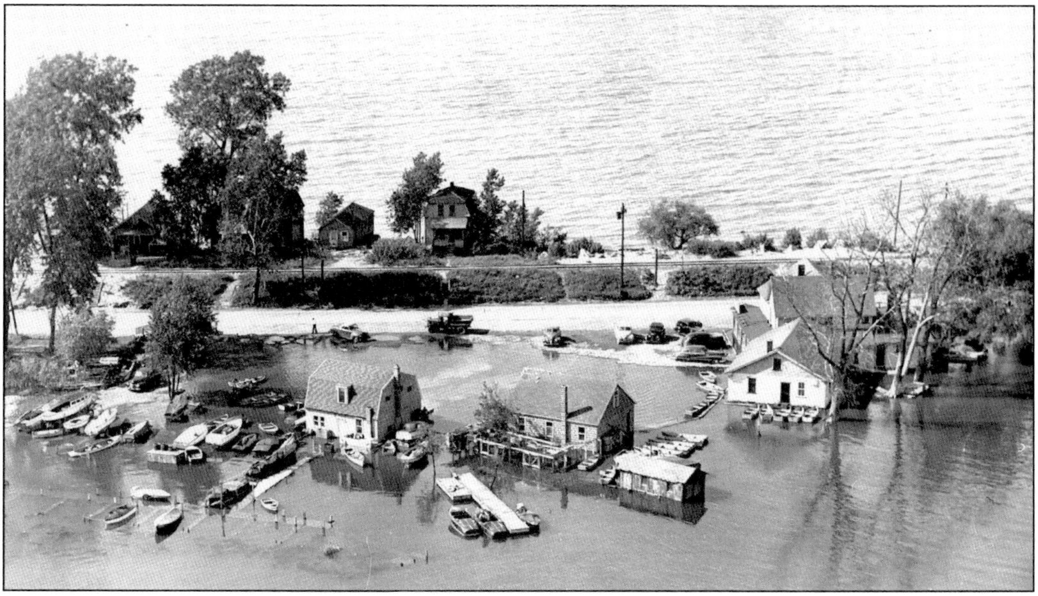

In the spring of 1953, the lakeside residents endured one of the drawbacks of living between Irondequoit Bay and Lake Ontario. The waters of the bay almost engulfed the new two-lane highway.

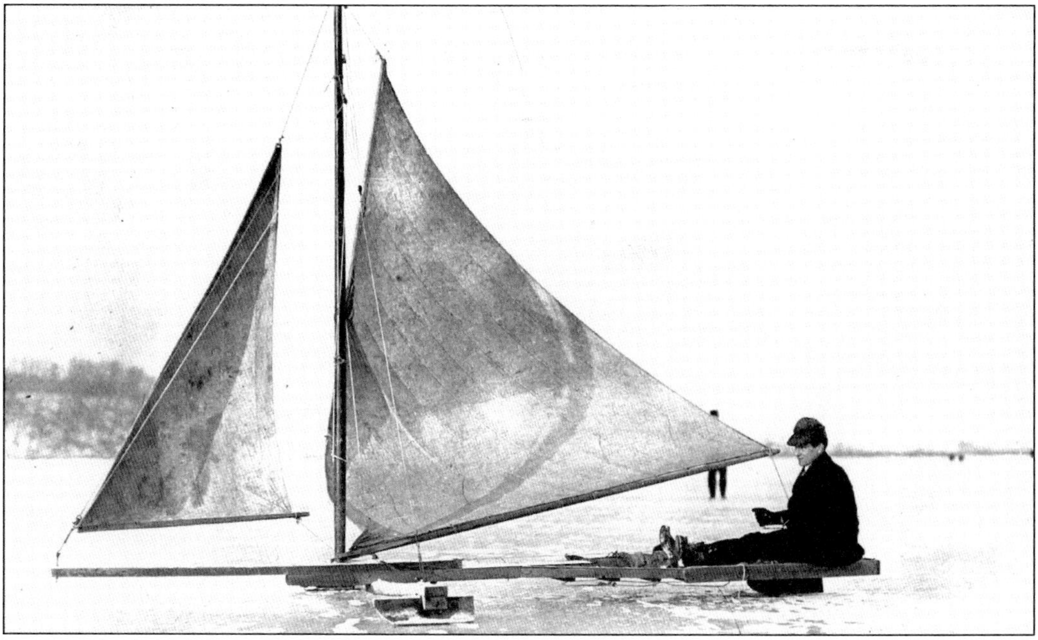

Fun on the bay did not end with the coming of winter. This Irondequoit resident sailed across the ice in 1912.

Five

THE 20TH CENTURY TRANSFORMATION

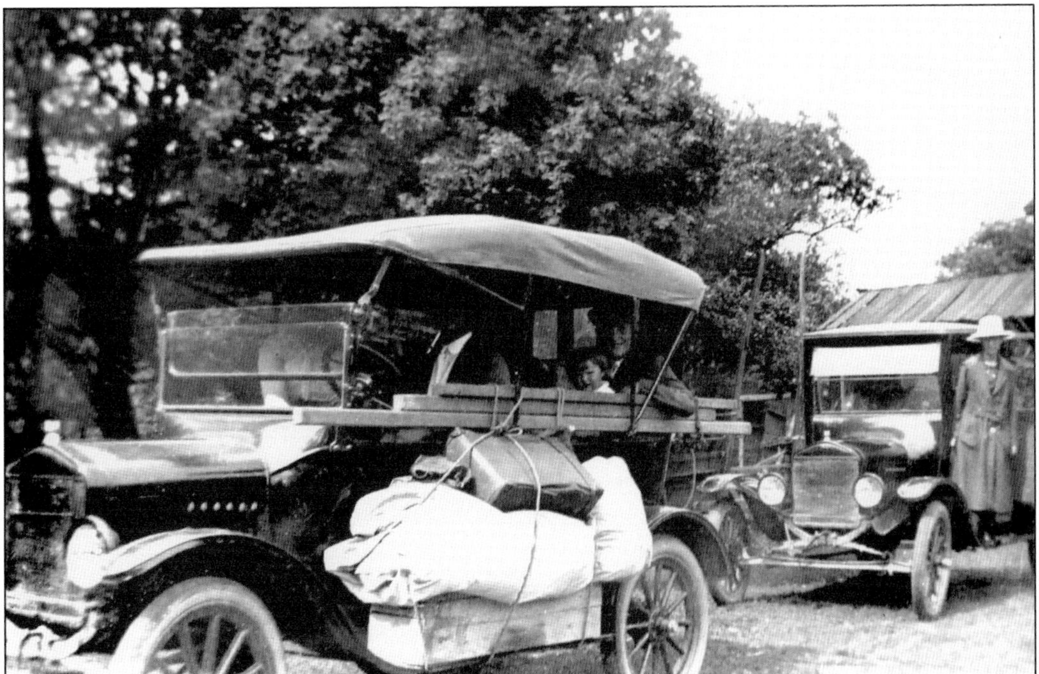

"The automobile would allow families to vacation in Florida, California or Canada instead of Sea Breeze or Glen Haven. Fathers would drive to work from the suburbs. Families would buy up farm land for housing sites and Irondequoit would change from the garden spot of western New York to a suburban town." This excerpt is from *Early Irondequoit Memories*, Irondequoit Historical Society, 1997.

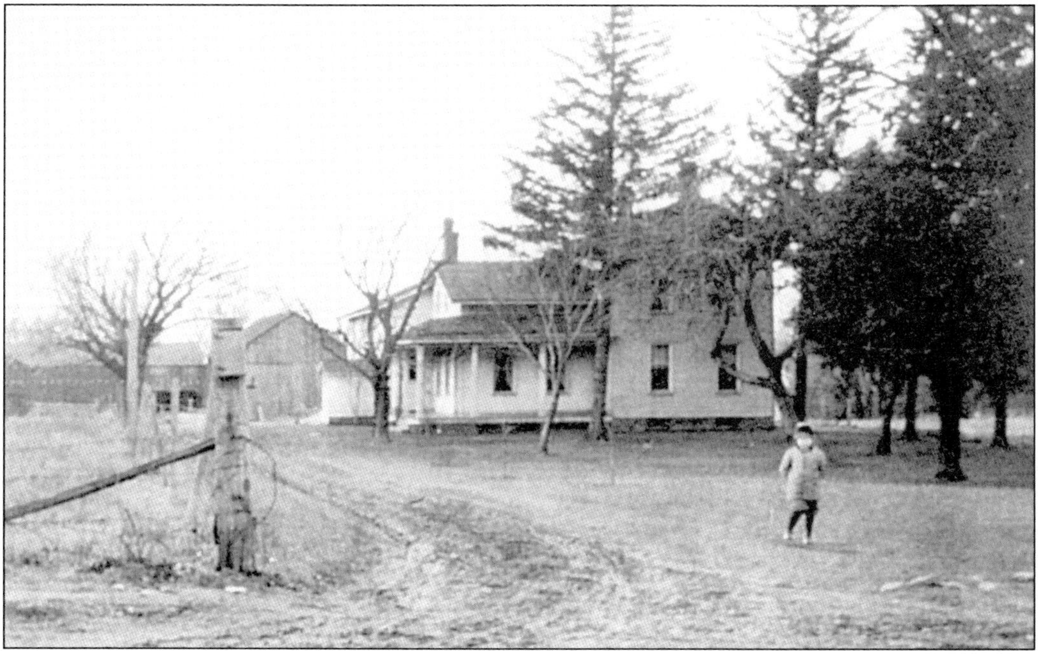

In 1912, Irondequoit was dotted with family farms such as this one on Culver Road owned by Elmer and Isabel Buckland. Starting in the 1930s, with many families able to afford automobiles, the movement of population from the city to surrounding towns began. The Buckland farmhouse still stands, but there are no farms left in town.

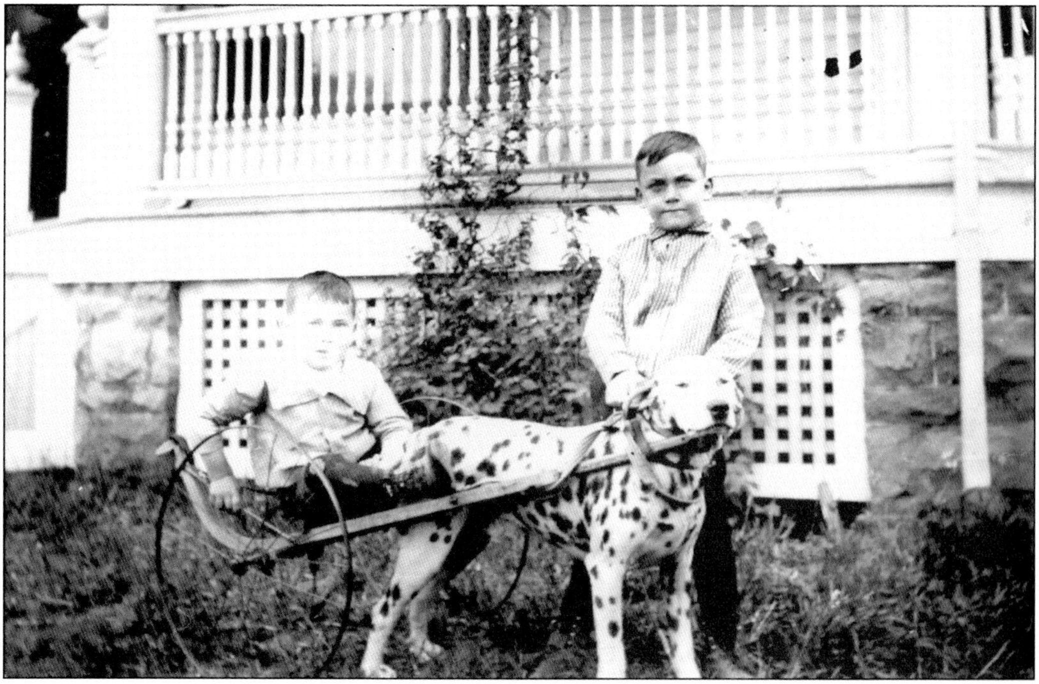

The large farmhouses that dotted the landscape often sheltered three generations of a family and certainly were "children friendly with large yards that could accommodate boys like William and Mort Hill with their Dalmatian Spot."

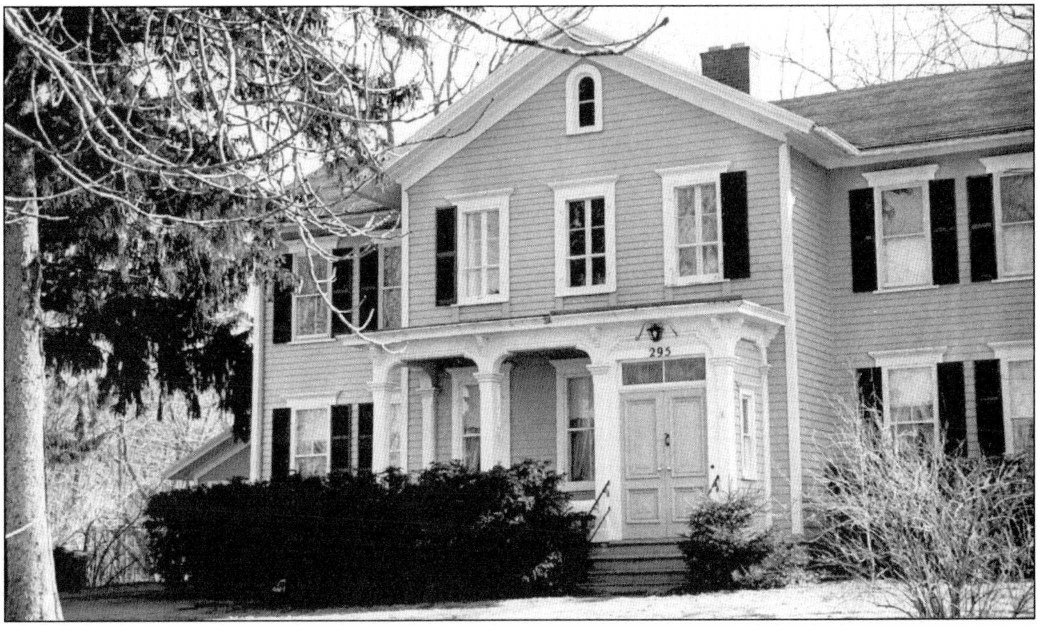

Josiah Cole built a lovely house on Cole Road with a second story porch. In 1943, Emma Shea purchased the house and felt that the porch made the rooms on the second floor too dark and gloomy; an opinion shared by two ladies who came to install new carpeting and complained that the area was very spooky. Despite the reputation for spookiness the house had no trouble finding new owners. The Specht family owns it today.

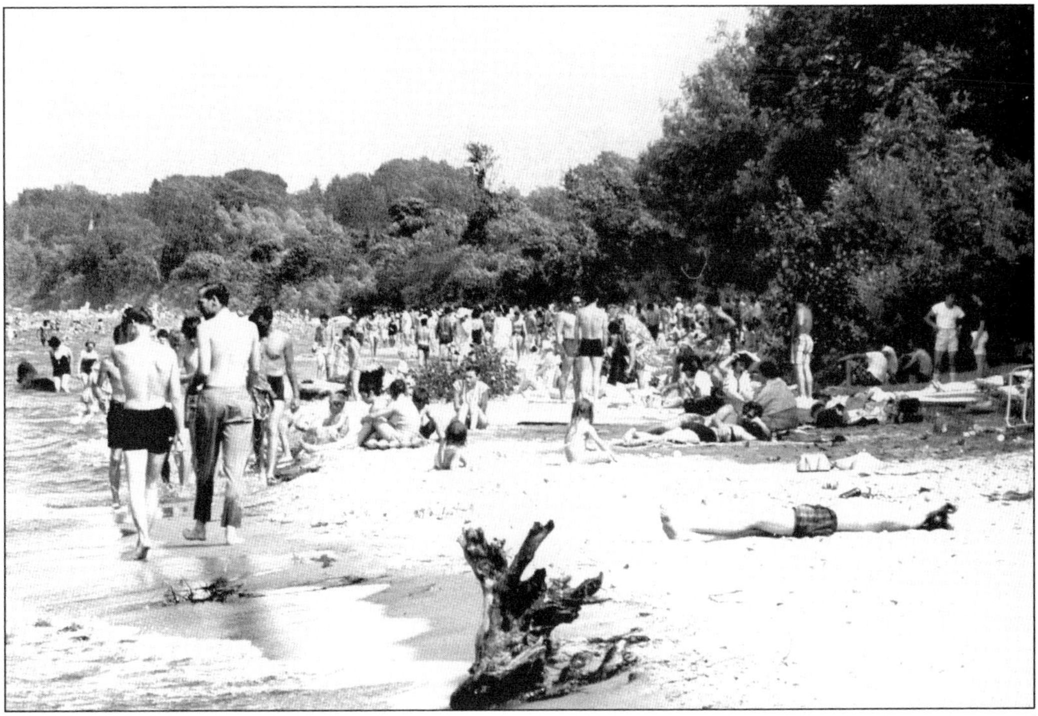

Despite the demise of White City, Lake Ontario still attracts visitors as this 1965 picture of Durand-Eastman beach shows. This section is just west of Sunset Point.

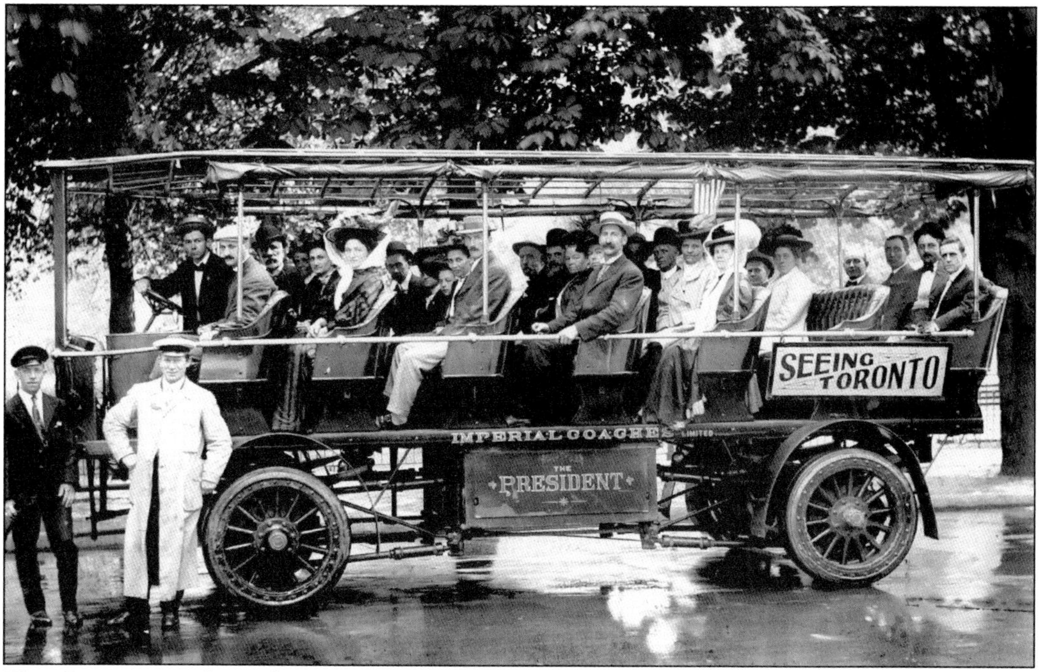

The Grange members also spread their wings. This group toured Toronto and posed for a souvenir photograph taken by the McLean Photo Company to commemorate the visit. The Imperial Coach Company not only conducted the tours, but also sold the photographs.

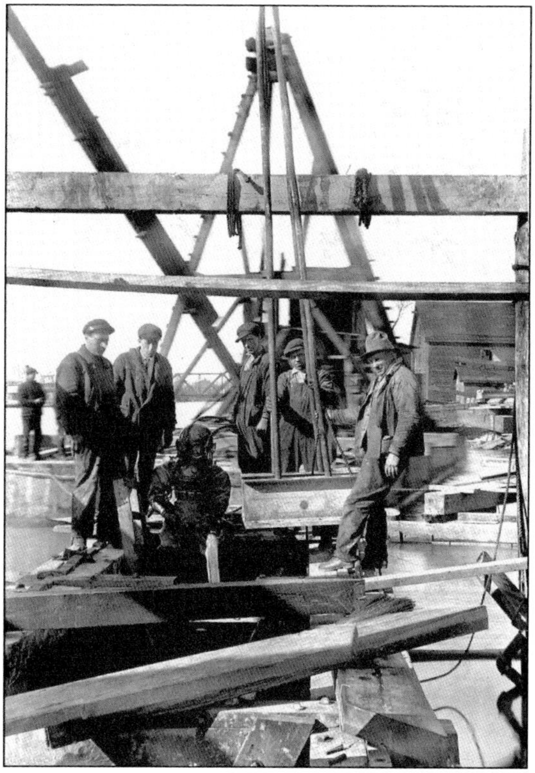

The Stutson Street Bridge, built at a cost of $386,789 opened for traffic on March 1, 1918, making the Windsor ferry obsolete. Merchants in Charlotte were delighted because their customers in Summerville no longer had to make a long drive when the ferry was not running.

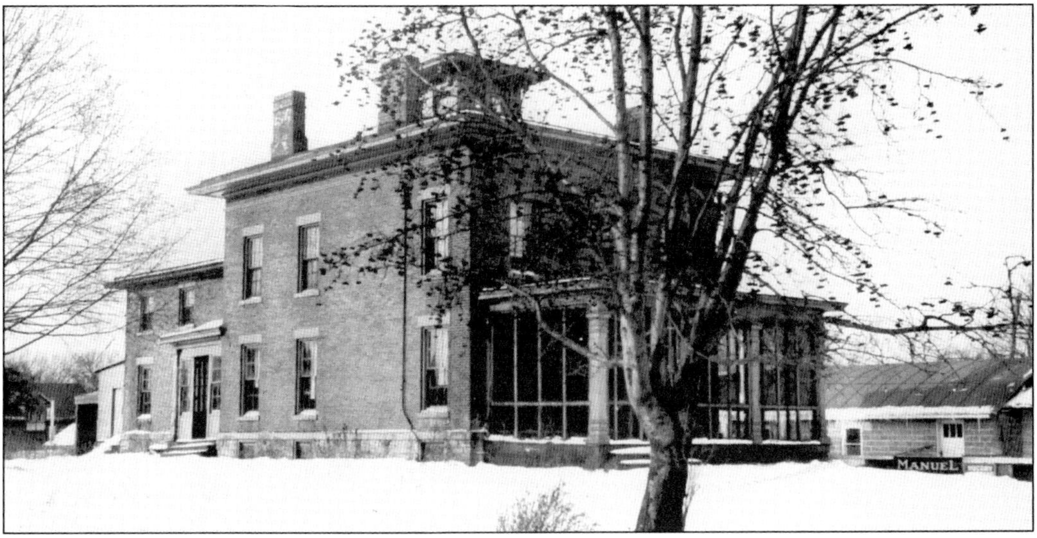

The phrase used today to encourage the use of older buildings is "adaptive reuse" and a good example is the Bradstreet mansion on Culver Road. Samuel Bradstreet bought the farm once owned by the Woodman family. Today the home is a popular restaurant.

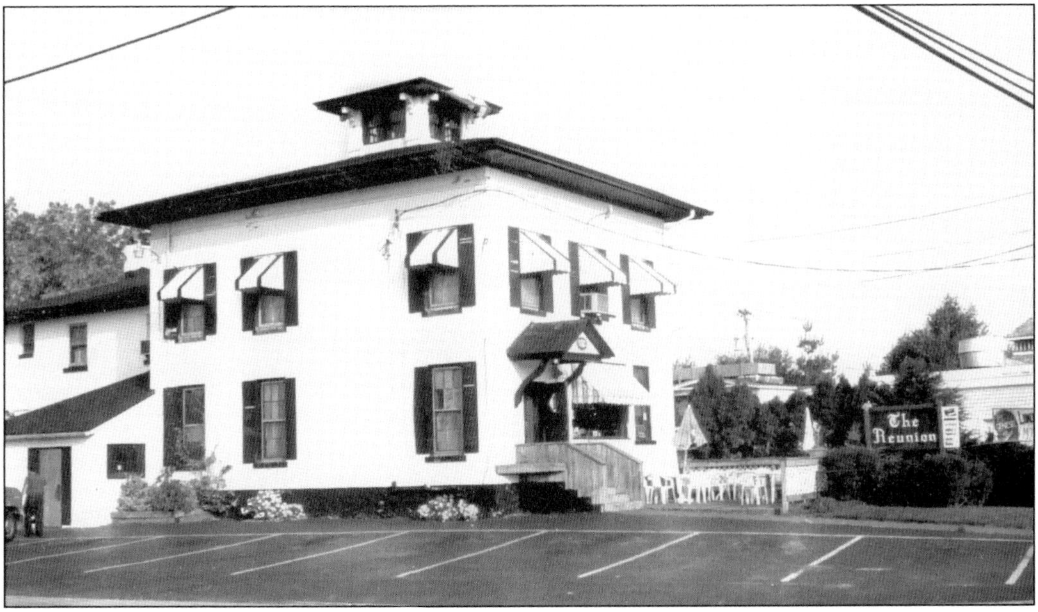

The Reunion Inn has a colorful past. The farm was once owned by an early settler, Sylvester Woodman, who was reported to have been a pirate that settled in the wilderness of Irondequoit very early in the 1800s. Some patrons to the inn have claimed that a young woman in a long skirt, old-fashioned blouse, and long hair appears and disappears to diners, adding a bit of adventure to dining out.

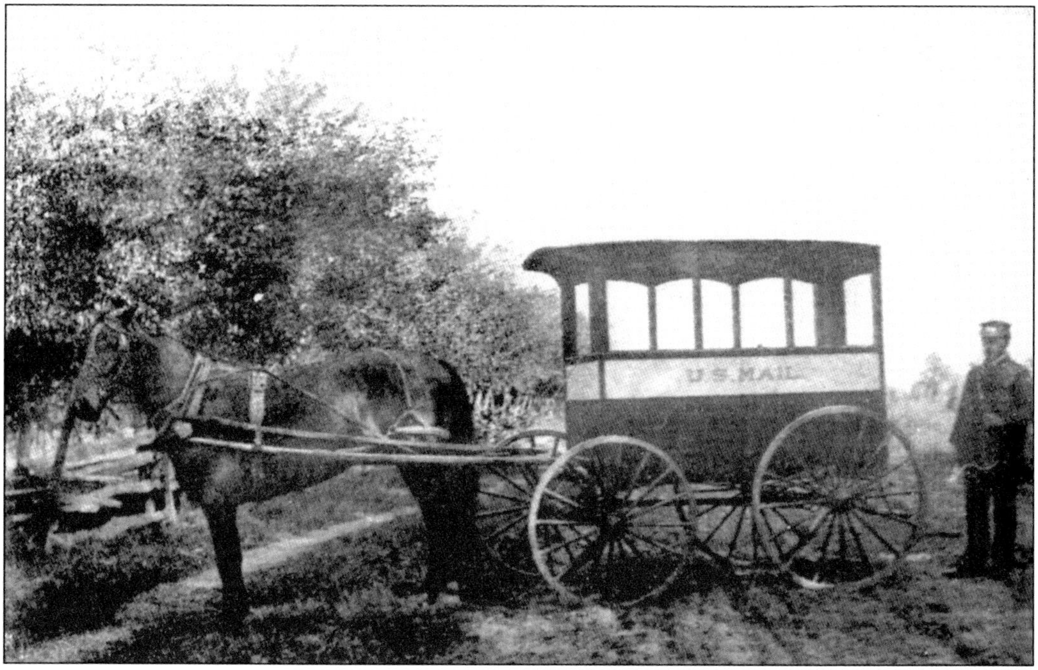

Norris Walzer was one of 14 children of Joseph and Isabel Walzer. His other claim to fame was that he served as the first rural mail delivery man in 1898.

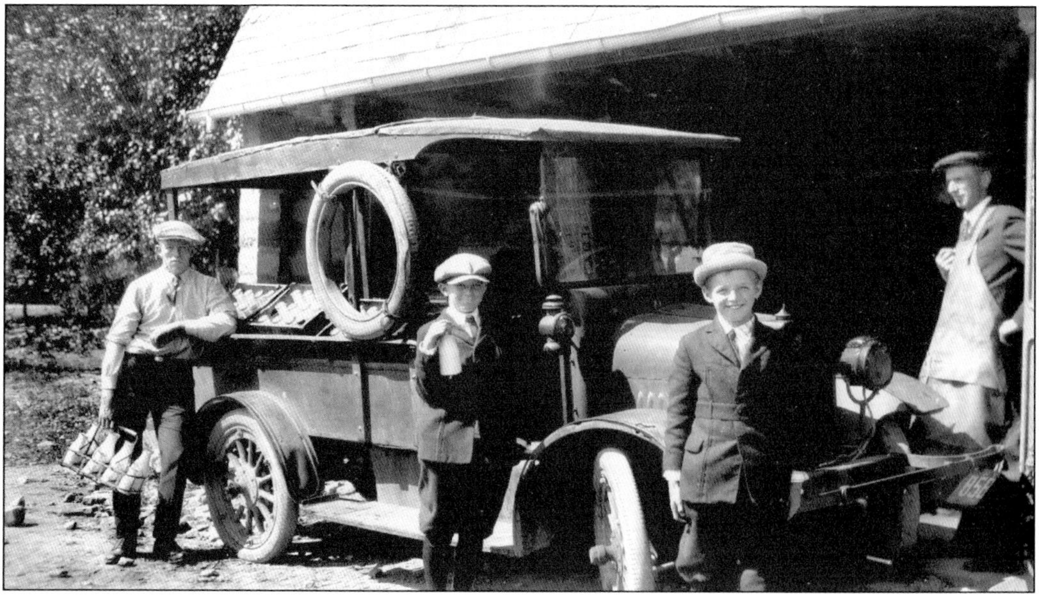

By 1923, the horse and wagon started to give way to mechanized delivery. Pete Johnson (left) delivered milk for Walter Schneeberger (right) and in between are his sons Paul and Bill. The barn was located at the corner of Bayview and Glen Haven Roads.

The late 19th century was the height of the bicycle craze. In 1897, over two million bicycles were produced in the United States. These three obviously rode their bikes into a photographer's studio.

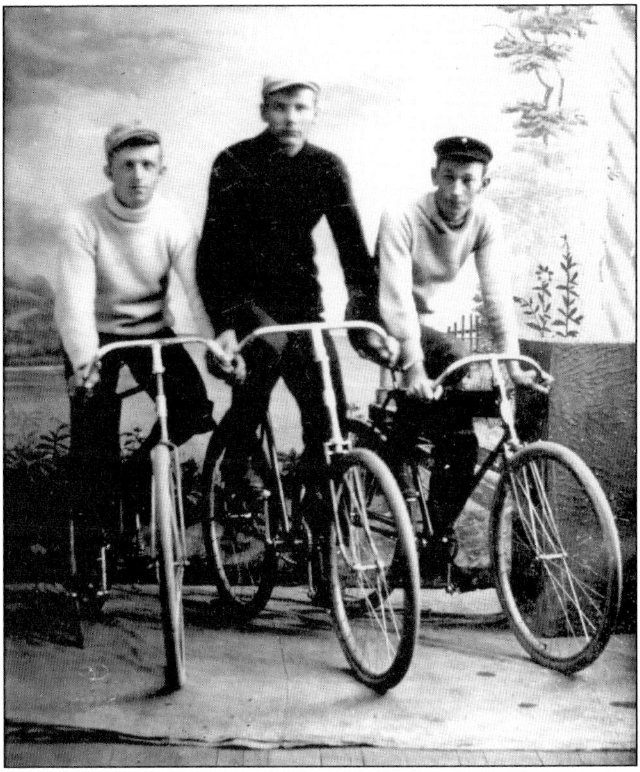

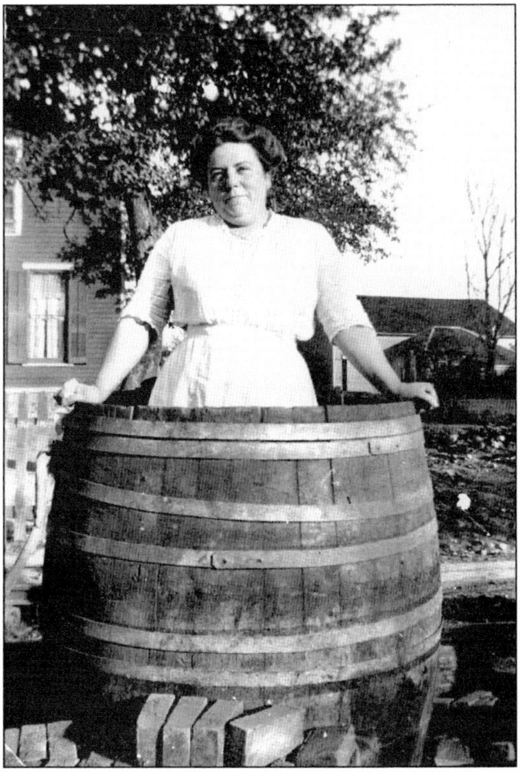

In 1916, Mrs. Bogart seemed to be having "a barrel of fun" getting ready for a family clambake in 1916. She should be; by that year clambake cooking techniques shifted from using a stone-lined pit heated by fire for several hours to homemade steamers.

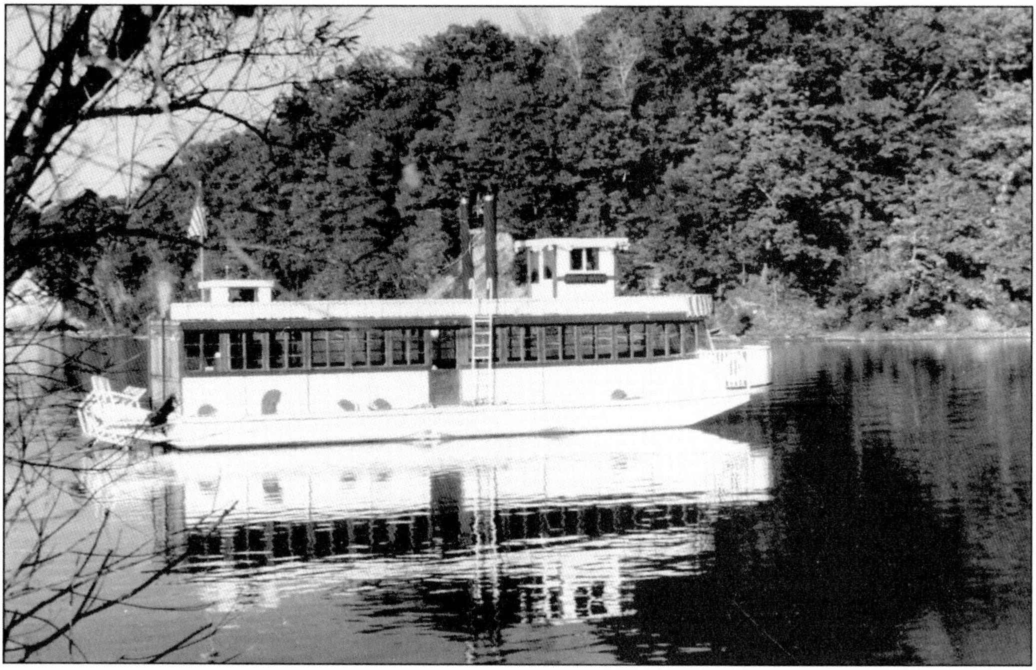

The steamboats that plied the Genesee River, Lake Ontario, and Irondequoit Bay have long since disappeared. Excursion boats like the *Bounty Queen* still take visitors up the river to view the breath-taking foliage along the banks.

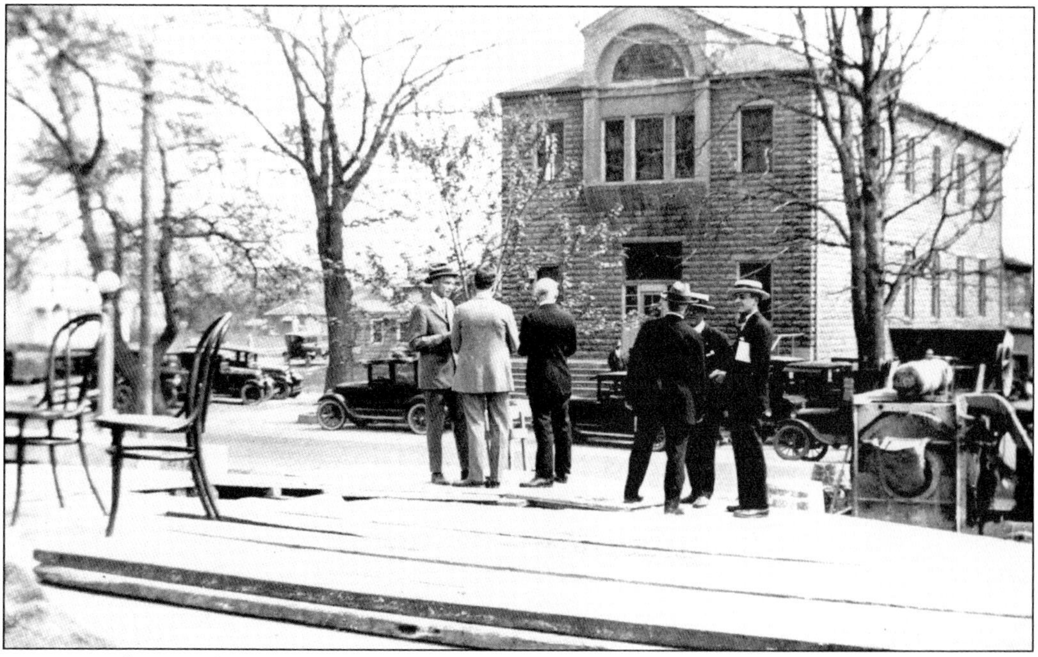

Grange Hall, once the social center of this farming community also underwent a change. As the number of farms decreased, so did the membership. Finally the building was sold, but it has had a new lease on life. The world famous House of Guitars music store now occupies the historic building.

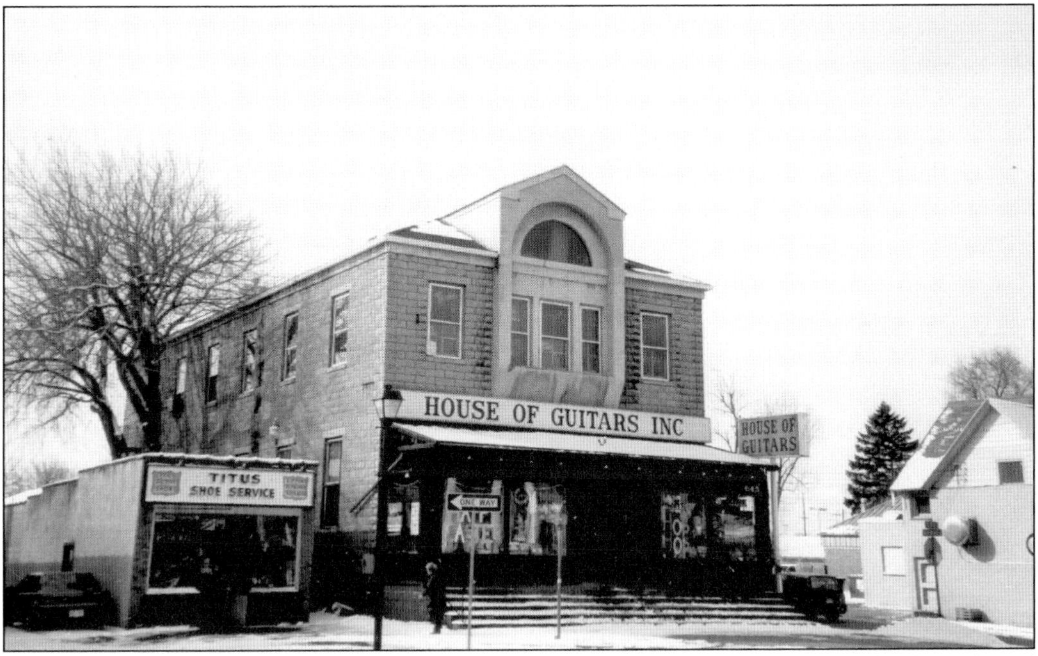

The House of Guitars is owned and operated by Armand, Bruce, and Blaine Shaubroeck and is world renowned for its collection of new, used, and vintage guitars housed in this historic building. Do the ghosts of former Grange members enjoy the sounds of rock, jazz, blues, and heavy metal?

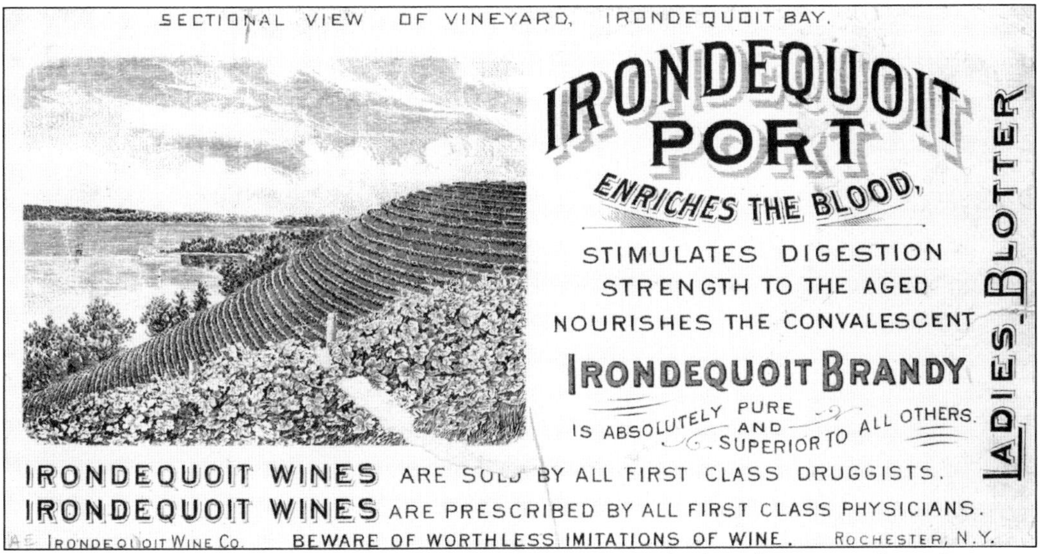

This ladies blotter extolling the virtues of Irondequoit port, which it claims stimulates digestion, strengthens the aged, and nourishes the convalescent, is another reminder of the changes that came in the late 20th century. There are no more vineyards and certainly no druggists selling the famous port wine.

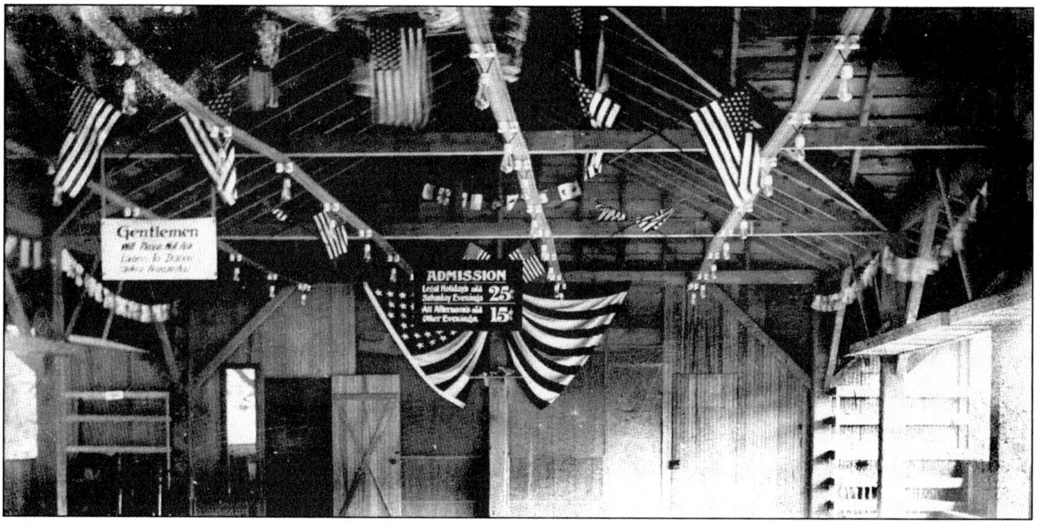

The dance hall is another relic of the past. Mrs. Lindley, who owned this picture, played piano for dancers at the hall in Sea Breeze for nine years.

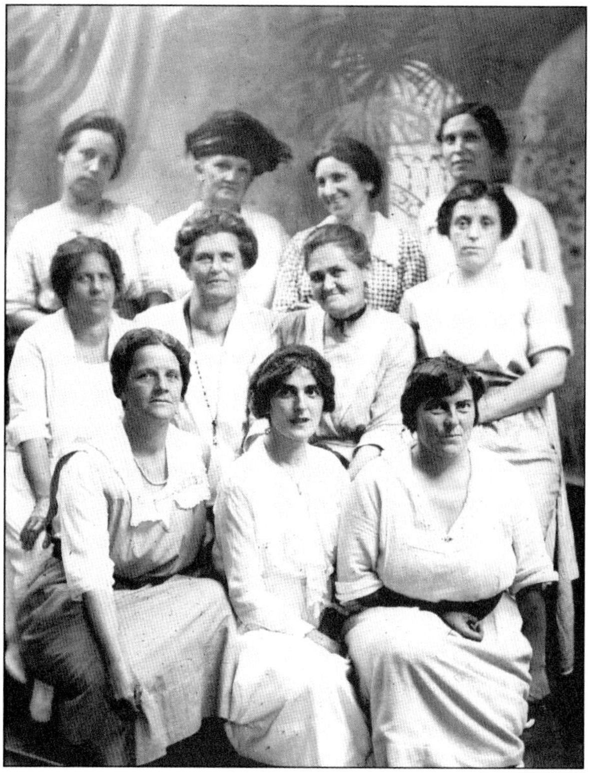

Caroline Seitz was president of the Ladies Aid in 1922 and posed with the other members, Rose Walzer, Ethel Walzer. Minnie Walzer, J. Fisher, Elsie Reese, Cornelia Evershed, C. Wittig, E. Nown, Ina Walzer and E. Kirchlake. Such church affiliated organizations flourished until women entered the work force in the late 20th century.

Not only did entry into the world of business and professions change the role of women in society, but so did the automobile. In some cases the freedom the car brought also had some liabilities. Maude West, former Irondequoit town historian, found that out when she had to change a tire on a road trip through New England in 1919.

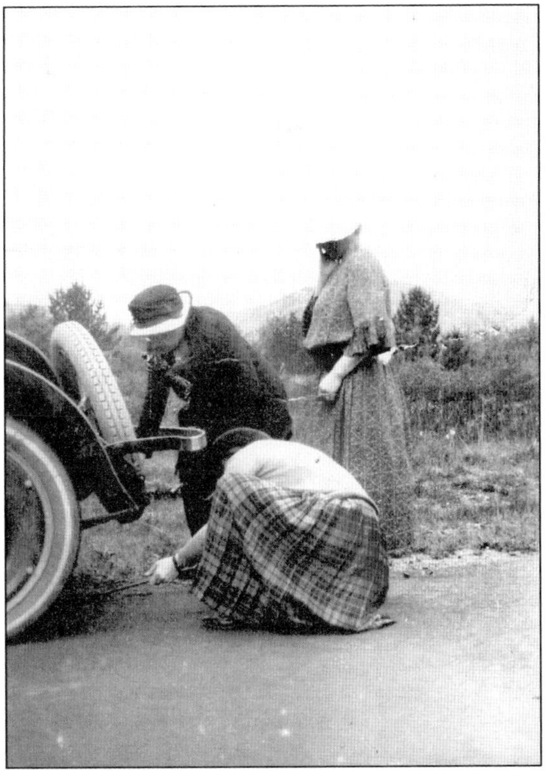

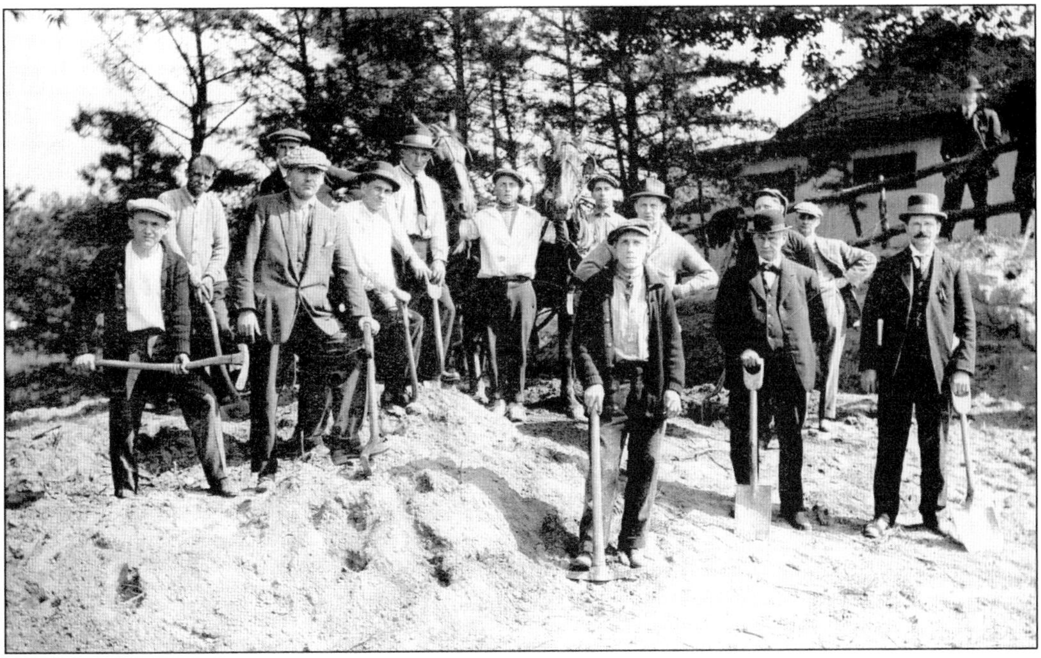

As Irondequoit grew so did the need for civic services, especially fire protection. The first volunteer fire company was formed in Sea Breeze, and these men posed while digging the foundation for the Sea Breeze firehouse. The men in three-piece suits must have arrived on the scene just in time for the picture.

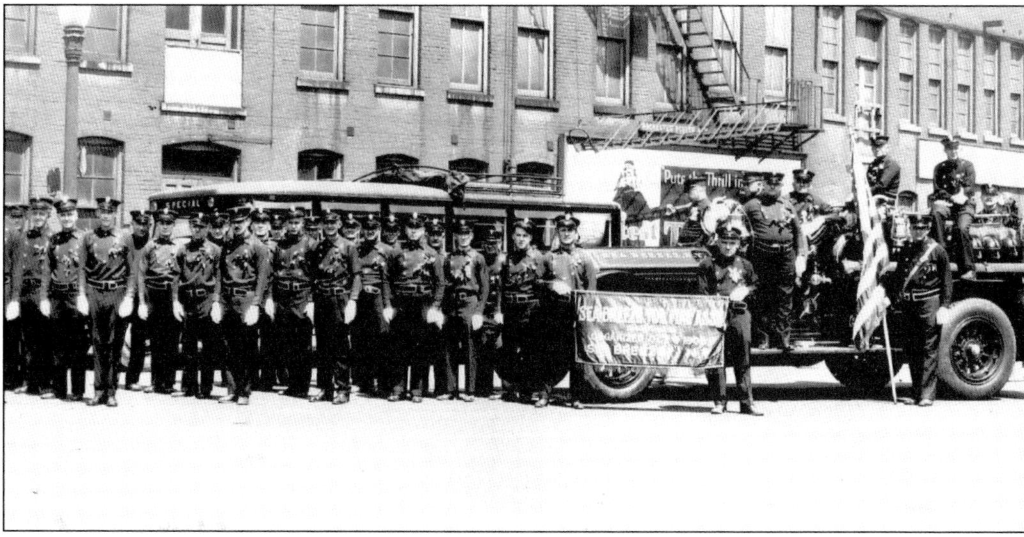

The fire company from Sea Breeze, all dressed up in formal uniform, was about to parade in Rochester. The department was formed in 1908, and early fireman Jeff Champion once said that a boy who has a father in the fire department is destined to become a firefighter. That is true not only at Sea Breeze but in the other volunteer units.

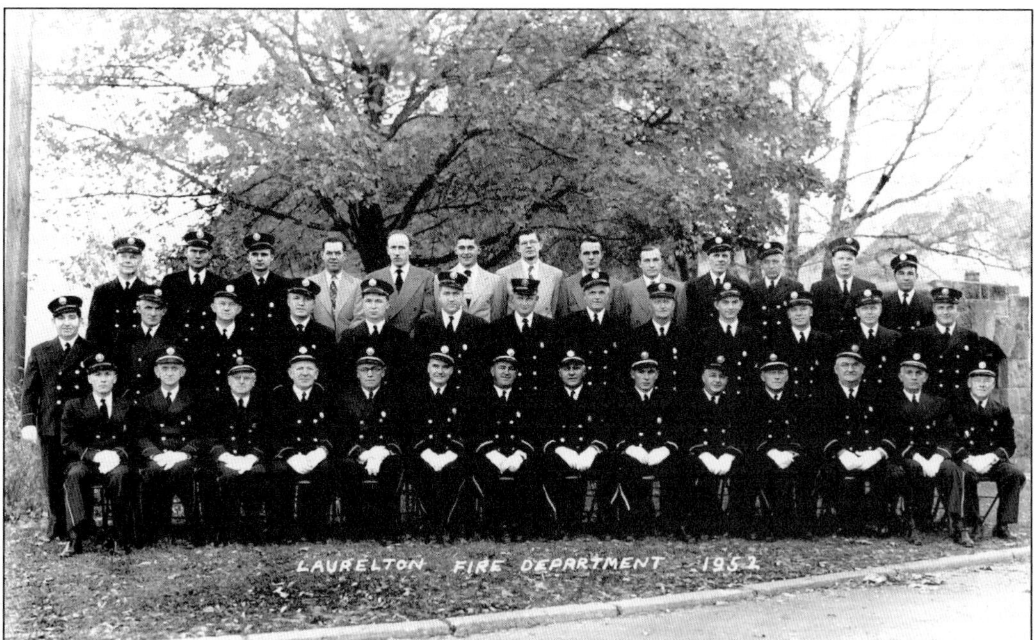

The Laurelton Fire Company was formed in 1927. Even though some fire companies now hire professionals there is still a community spirit and every fire hall is full of fond memories and heroic stories.

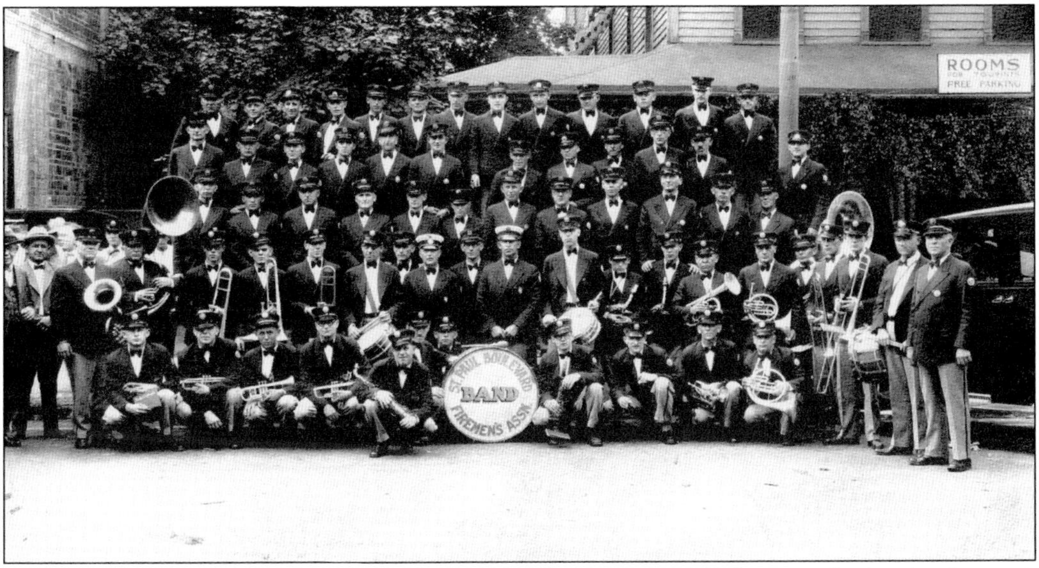

The St. Paul Fire Company was formed in 1924, and in August 1927 they marched at the firemen's convention in Niagara Falls accompanied by their own band.

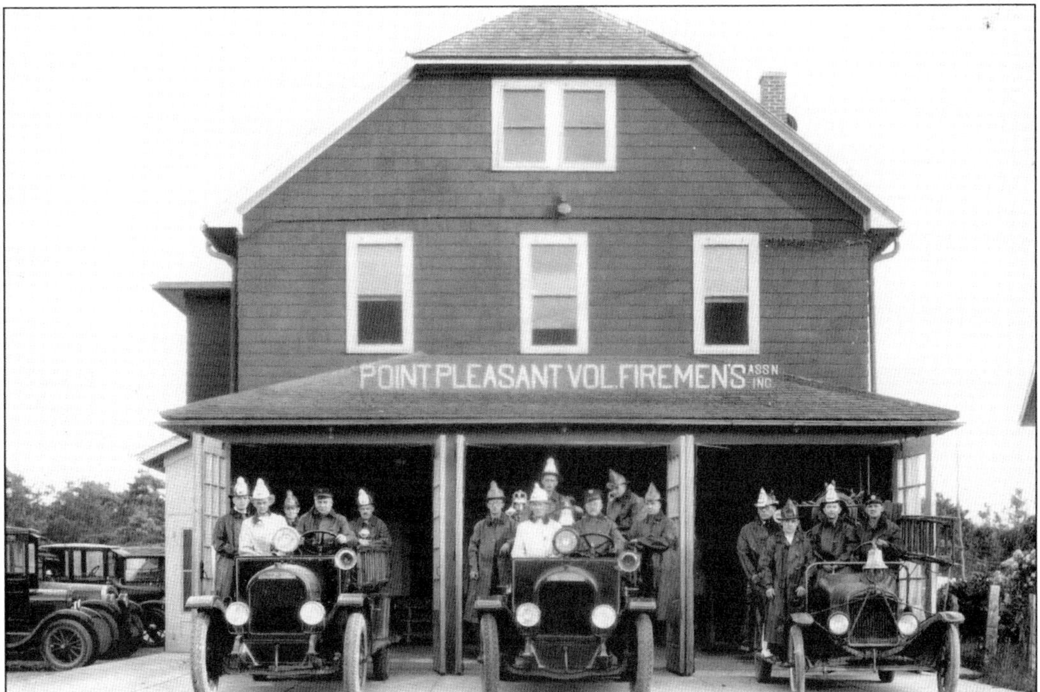

The Point Pleasant Fire Department was formed in 1915 and became known as "the pea pickers." In this 1924 photograph, they showed off their equipment and new firehouse.

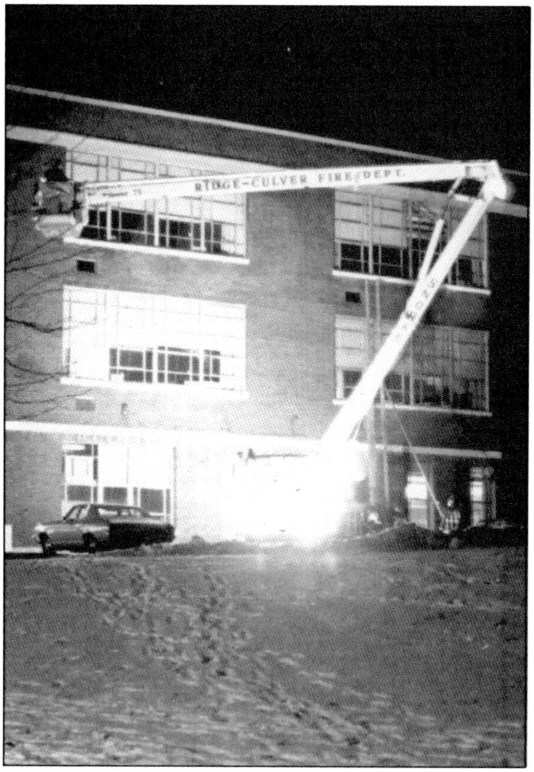

During the ensuing years, fire departments took on other duties such as ambulance and rescue services, plus educational programs. More sophisticated equipment meant more intensive training. The Ridge Culver Fire Company formed in 1924 and is shown here practicing their skills at Ridgewood school.

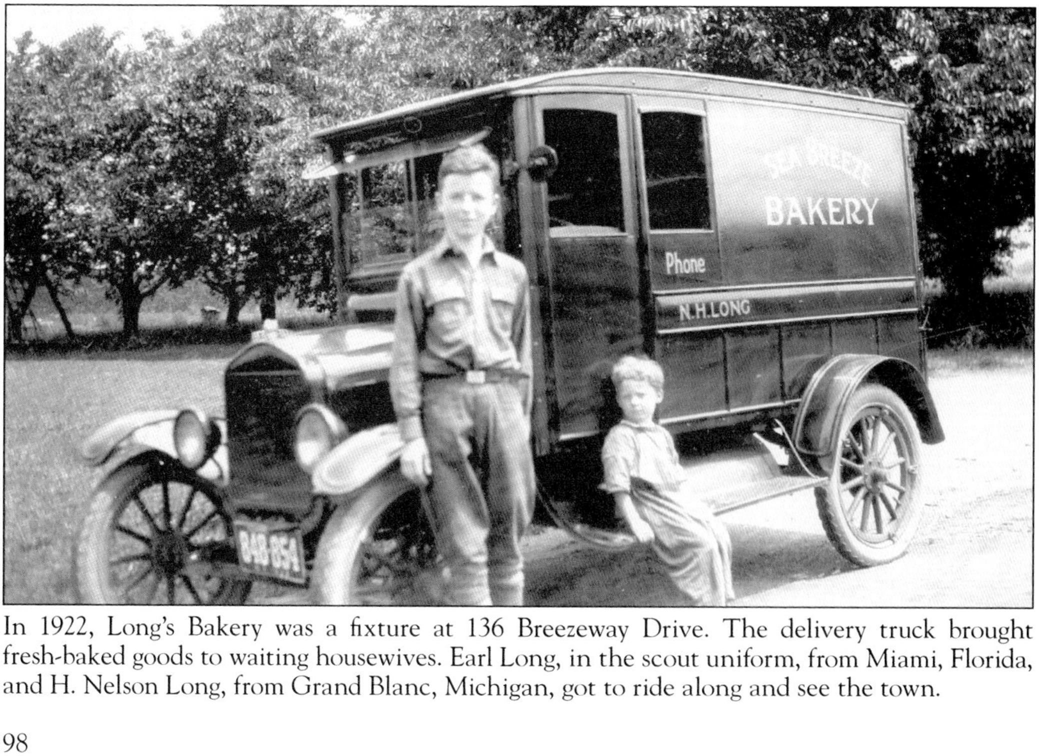

In 1922, Long's Bakery was a fixture at 136 Breezeway Drive. The delivery truck brought fresh-baked goods to waiting housewives. Earl Long, in the scout uniform, from Miami, Florida, and H. Nelson Long, from Grand Blanc, Michigan, got to ride along and see the town.

In 1939, Irondequoit celebrated its 100th birthday. Many residents dressed in costume. Among them were John Everett Bonn and his wife Laura Thompson, cousin of Laura Leake Thompson

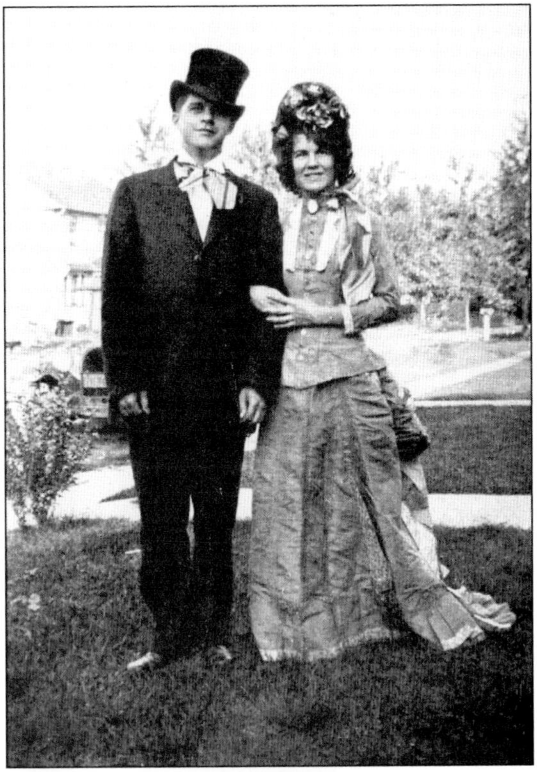

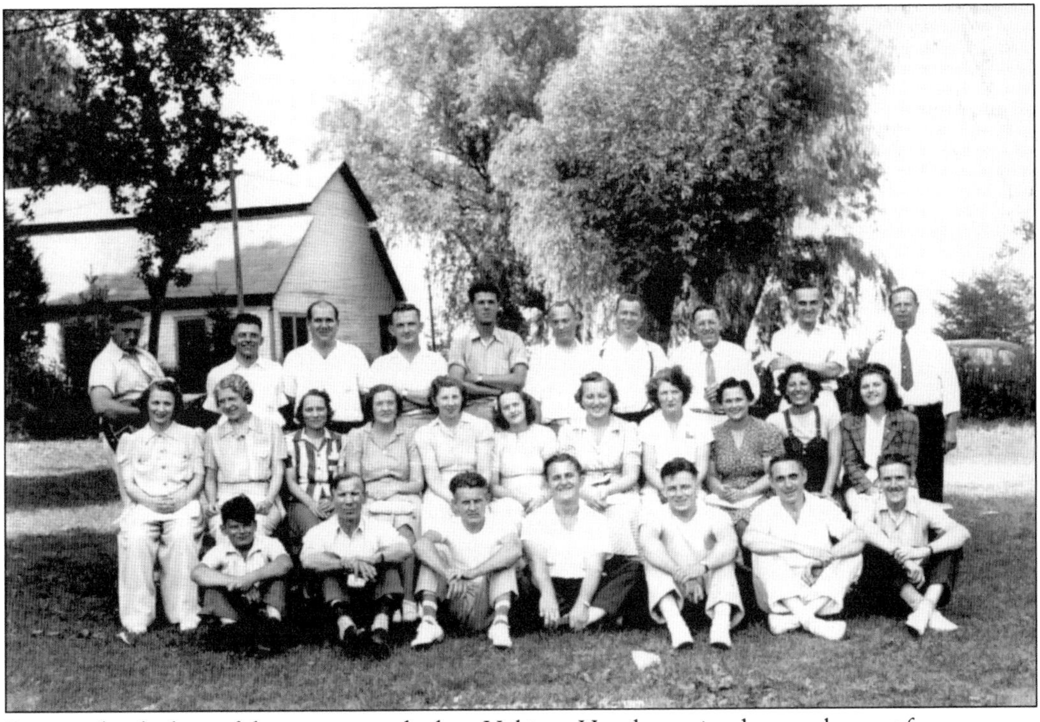

Despite the decline of the resorts on the bay, Hebings Hotel remained a popular spot for company picnics such as this department picnic from Bausch & Lomb in August 1940.

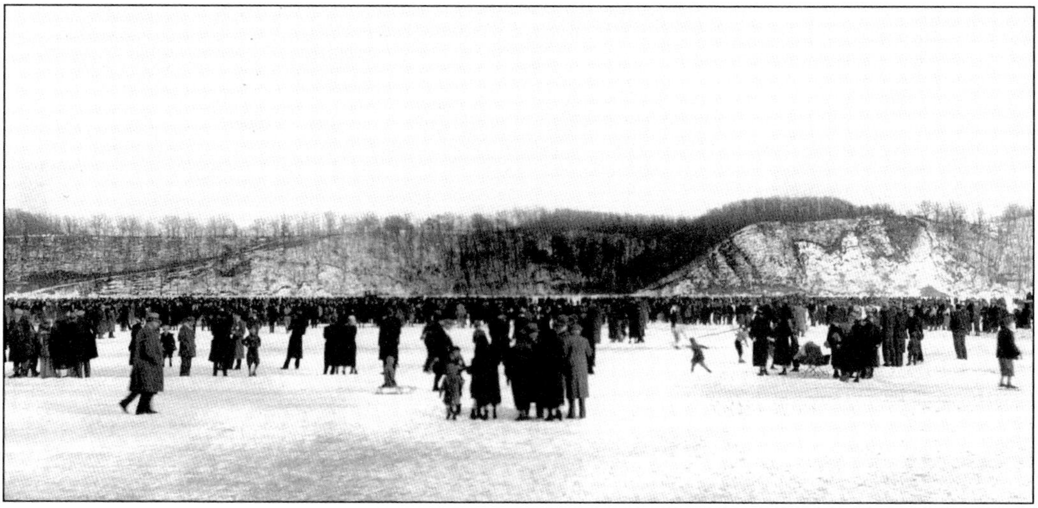

W. Dennington of Keating Drive snapped this photograph of the crowds enjoying a winter carnival on the bay in the early 1930s.

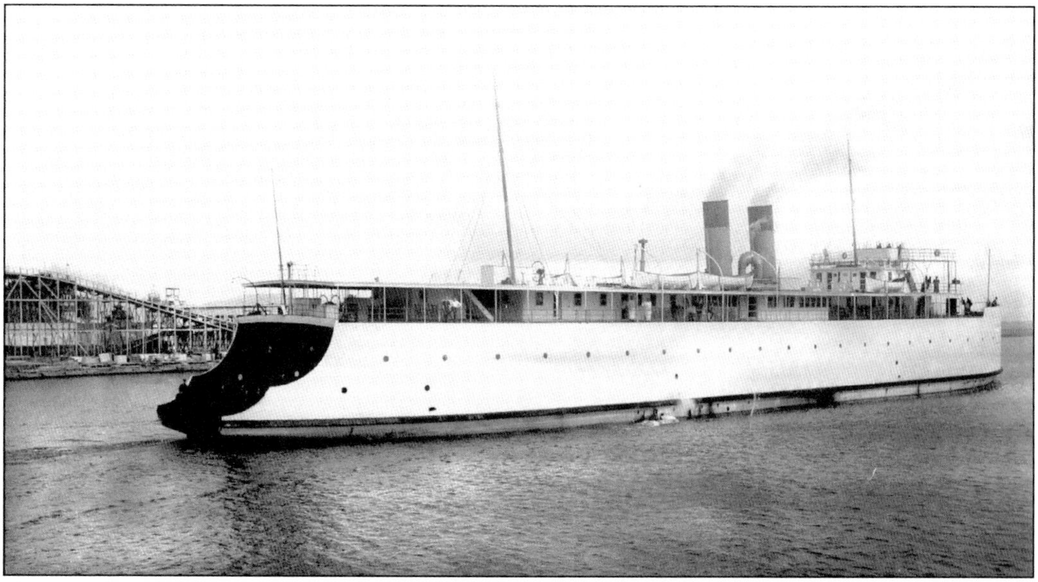

Ontario One and her sister ship *Ontario Two* sailed from the port of Rochester with coal and passengers who made the trip to Coburg. For many Irondequoit families this trip was a summer tradition. Passengers could board the ship at 8:00 a.m. and return at 8:00 p.m.

Ontario One was not primarily a passenger ship. Its first priority was hauling coal to Coburg. This shot shows the business end of the voyage with loading of flat cars at the Boxcar Street wharf.

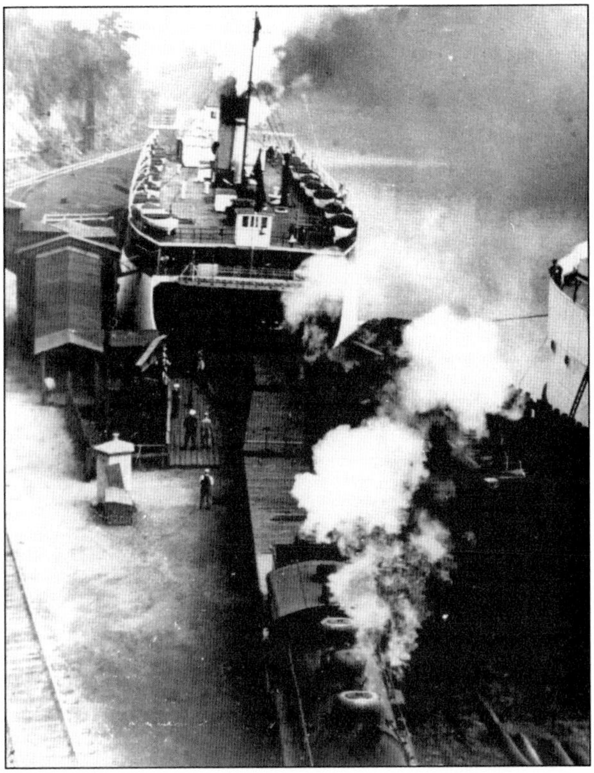

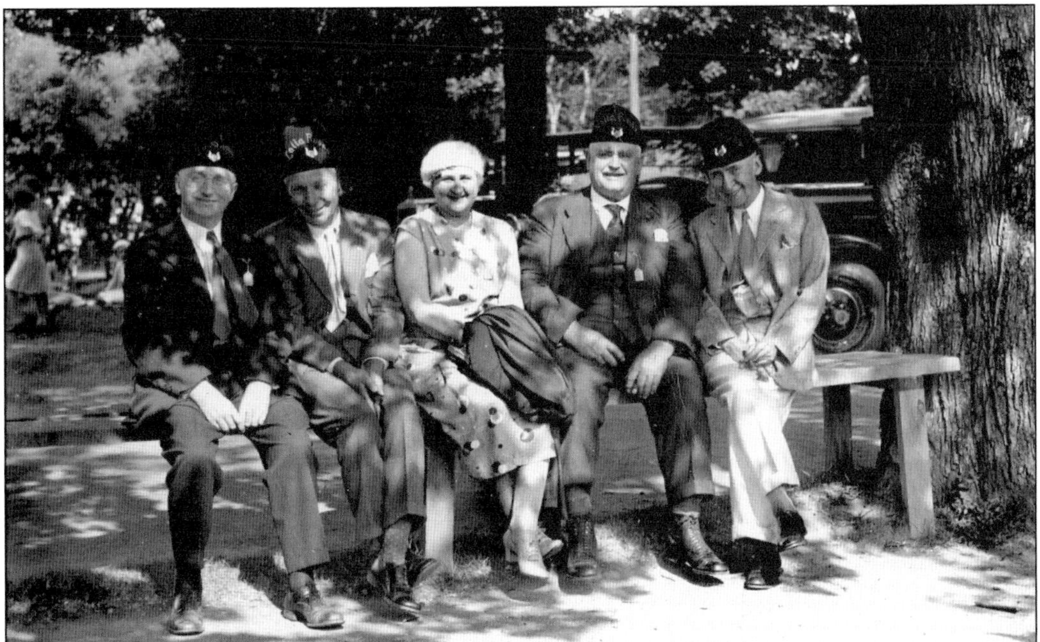

Named after the romantic Thomas Moore poem, the *Lalla Rookh* group was a sub-group of the Freemasons that helped form, strengthen, and sustain social ties. Edward "Ted" Cole is second from left and appears with four unidentified fellow members.

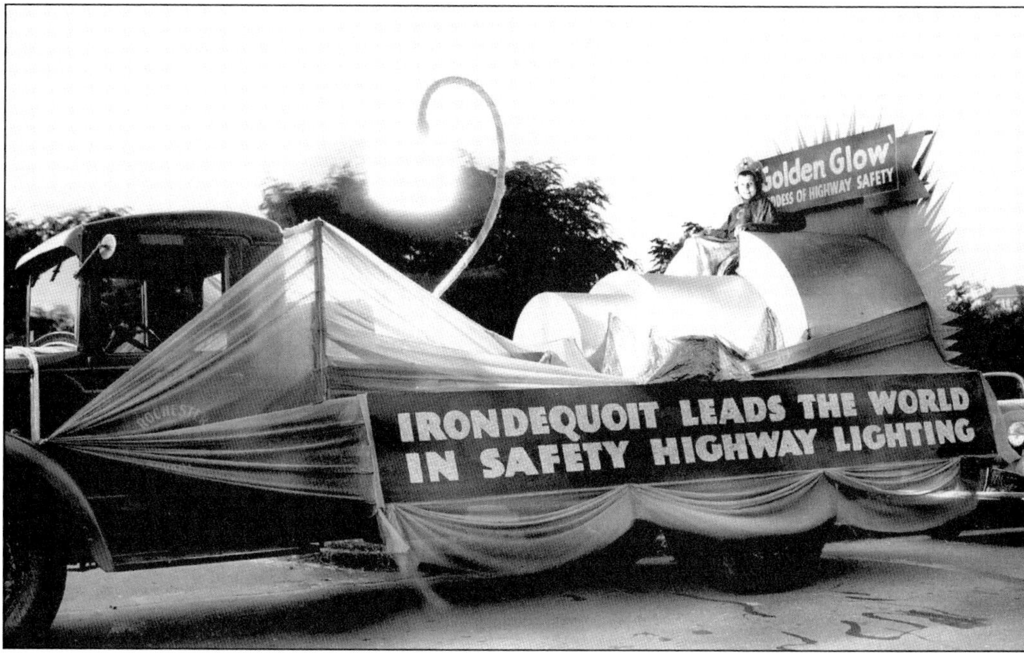

Irondequoit's Myrtle Reisig Bantle was "Golden Glow, the Goddess of Highway Safety," atop a float sponsored by Rochester Gas and Electric in a July 1936 parade celebrating the new sodium lights installed on St. Paul Boulevard. The lamps provided brightness to the pavement and broad, reflected light with an absence of glare and a minimum use of poles.

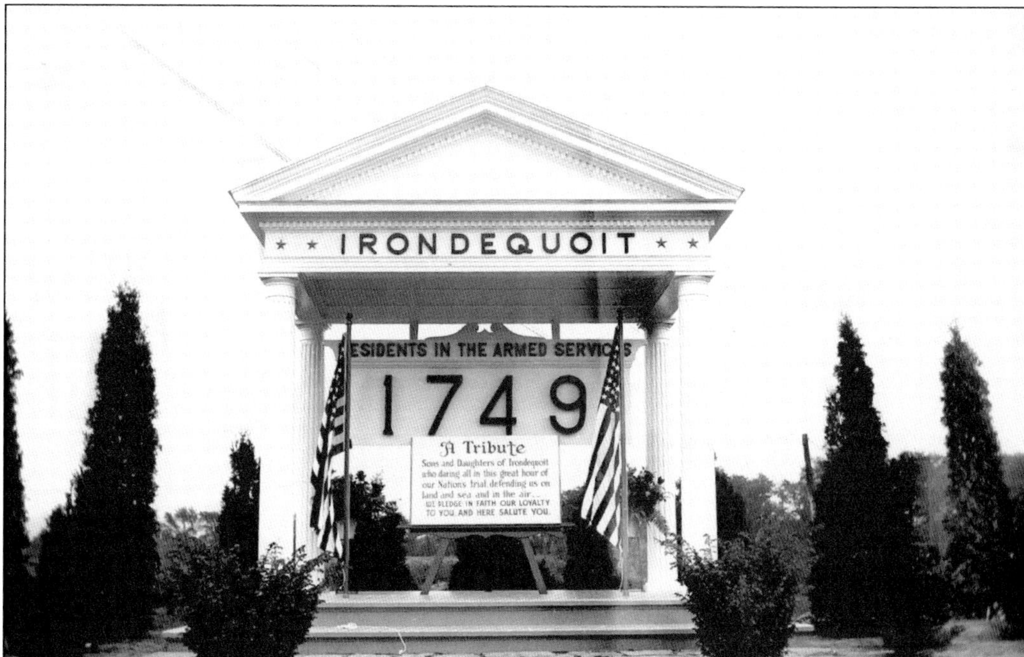

December 7, 1941, the day the Japanese bombed Pearl Harbor, prompted the United States to enter World War II and changed Irondequoit forever. The servicemen's plaque on Ridge Road bears the names of those who served during the war.

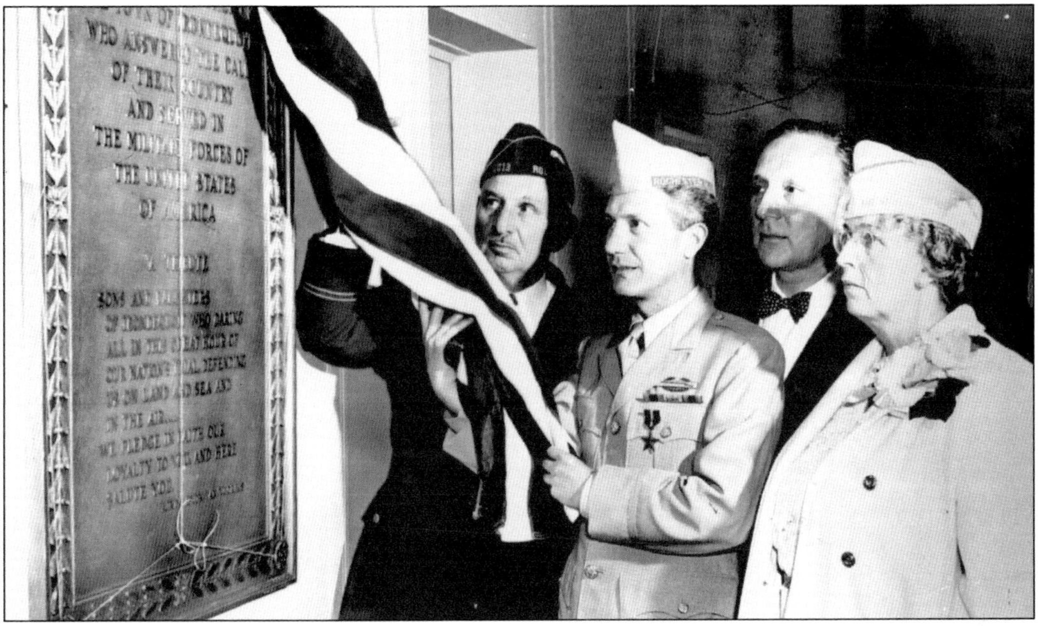

In 1951, the people of Irondequoit remembered their sons and daughters who went off to serve with a memorial tablet in the new town hall. Conducting the service, from left to right, were Franklin Seltman, commander of the Warren Claudius Legion post; Nicholas Pronio of the Culver Veterans of Foreign Wars post; and Jacob Ark, post state commander of the legion. Edythe Reynolds (right), a Gold Star Mother, attends the unveiling on May 30, 1951.

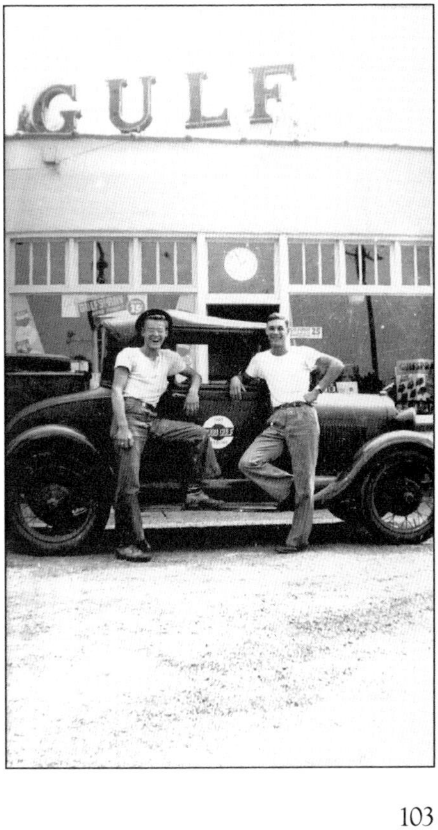

In 1943, young Jim Bircher (left) and Norman Bachman hung out at Wilbur Donovan's Gulf station in Summerville and posed next to their "doodle bug." They were typical of the young men who would leave their teenage years behind and serve their country far away from Irondequoit.

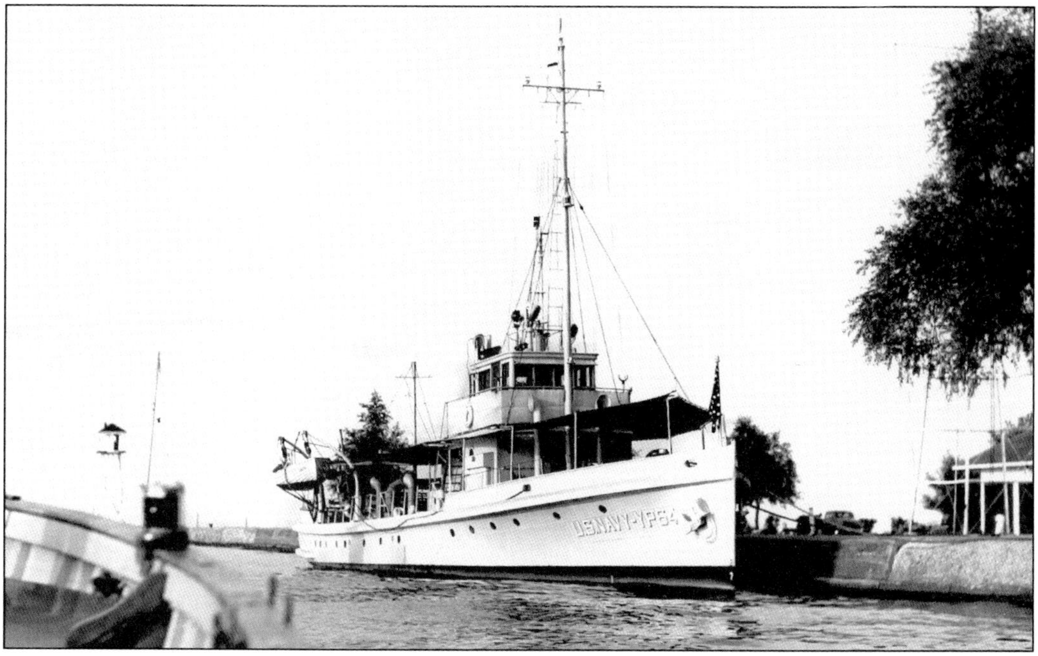

Many naval reserve members would be called up to serve after the United States entered into the war. Some had received training on a U.S. Naval Reserve training ship stationed on the river from 1922 to 1937. In 1937, the sub chaser became the first government ship to be buried in fresh waters. It was sunk about five miles off Durand-Eastman Park in 265 feet of water.

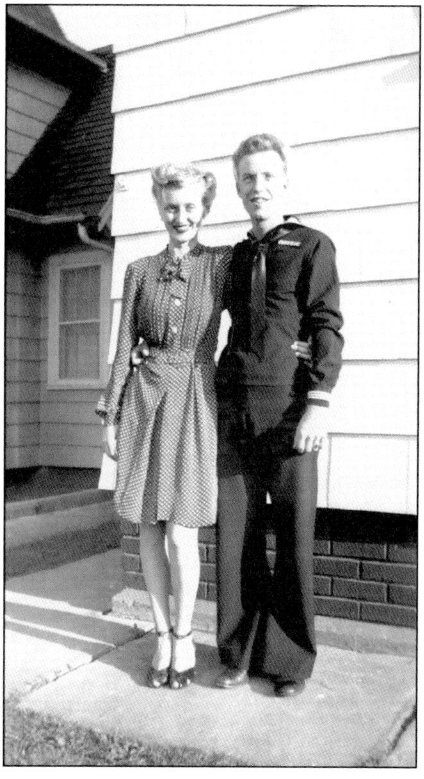

Edward "Bud" Cole, a descendant of the pioneer Cole family, served in World War II and is pictured here with an unidentified woman in 1947.

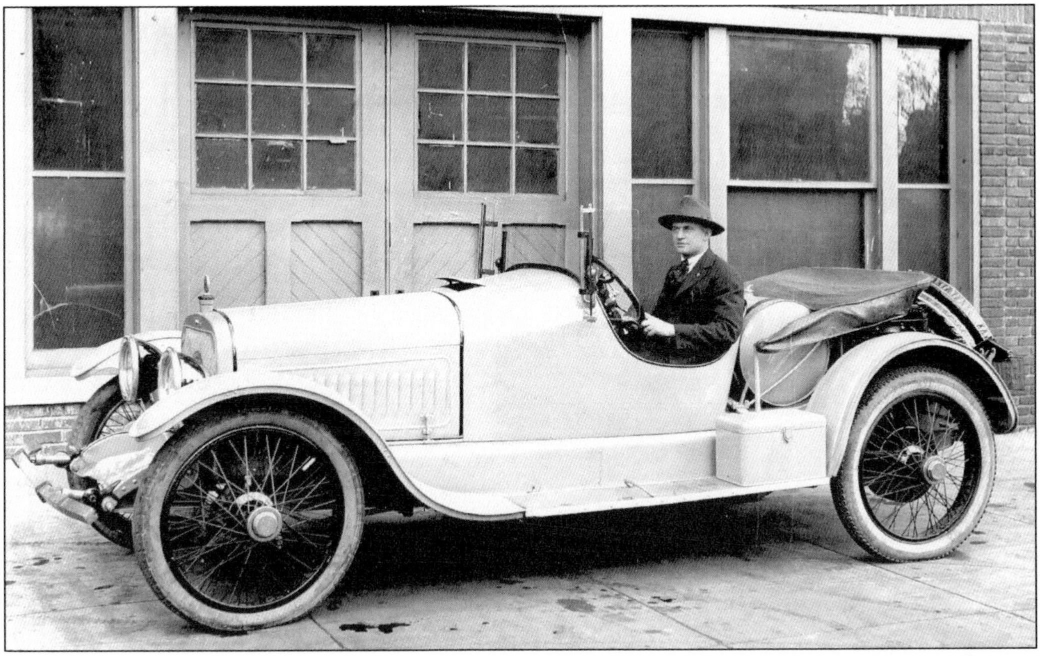

Resorts on the lake disappeared but Raymond "Silky" O'Loughlin's bar and restaurant on the pier at Summerville still remains a landmark for many young people who have left their hometown and those that still remain.

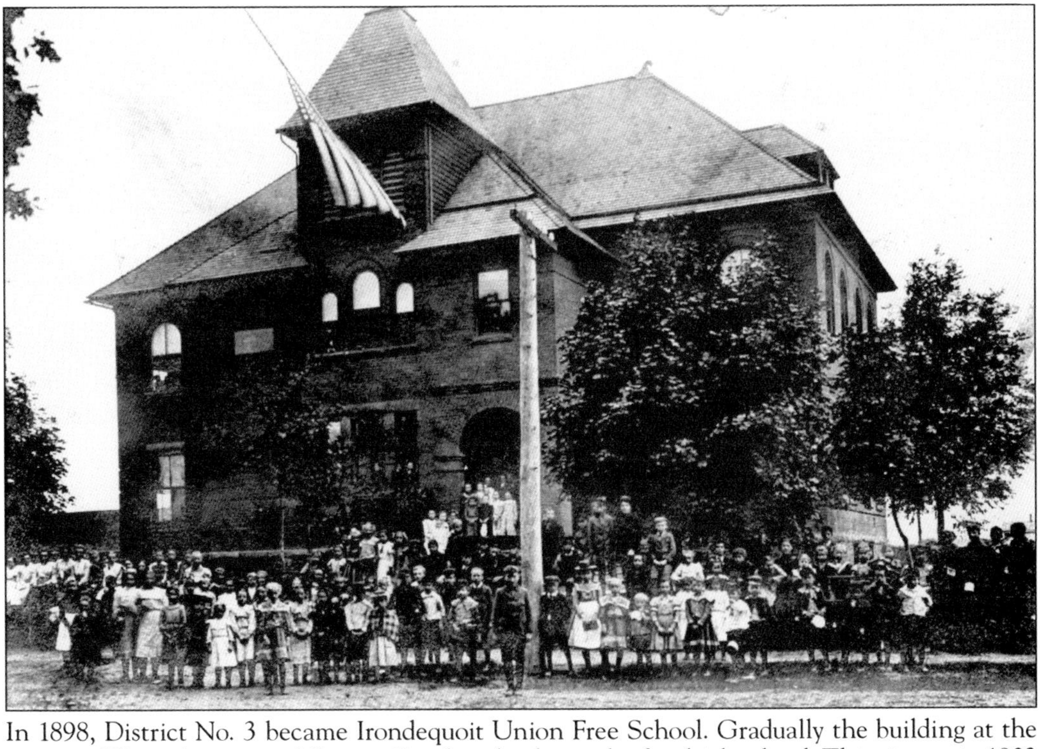

In 1898, District No. 3 became Irondequoit Union Free School. Gradually the building at the corner of Titus Avenue and Cooper Road evolved into the first high school. This picture in 1903 shows all the young students gathered outside.

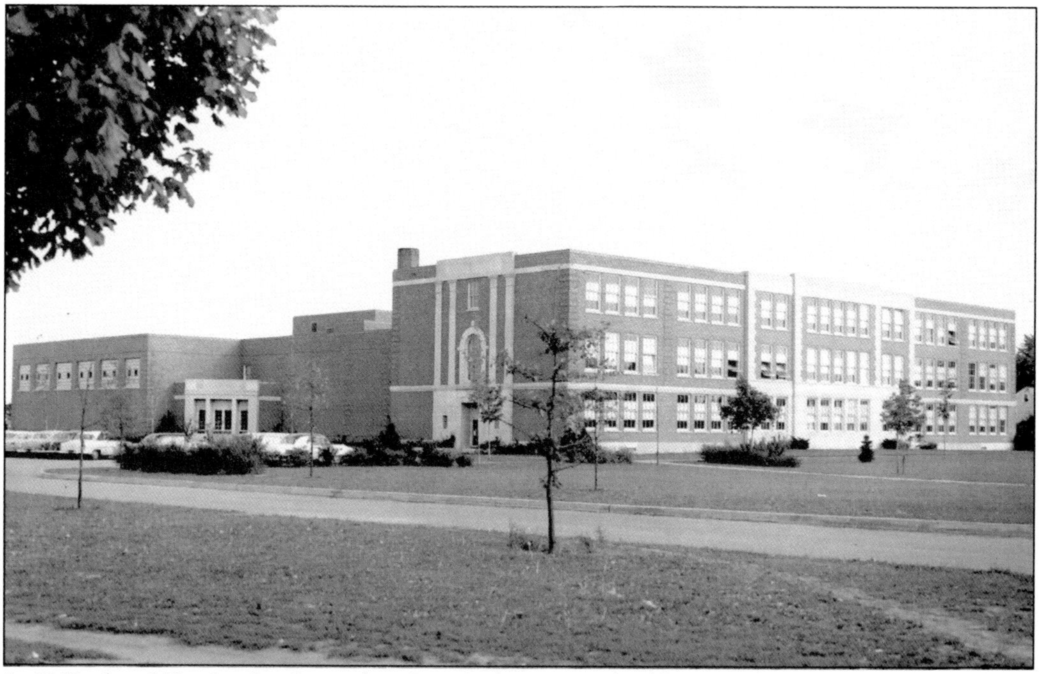

In 1950, the old high school was abandoned when a new building was built on Cooper Road at a cost of $1 million. As the community grew, so did the school, which has seen many renovations in recent years.

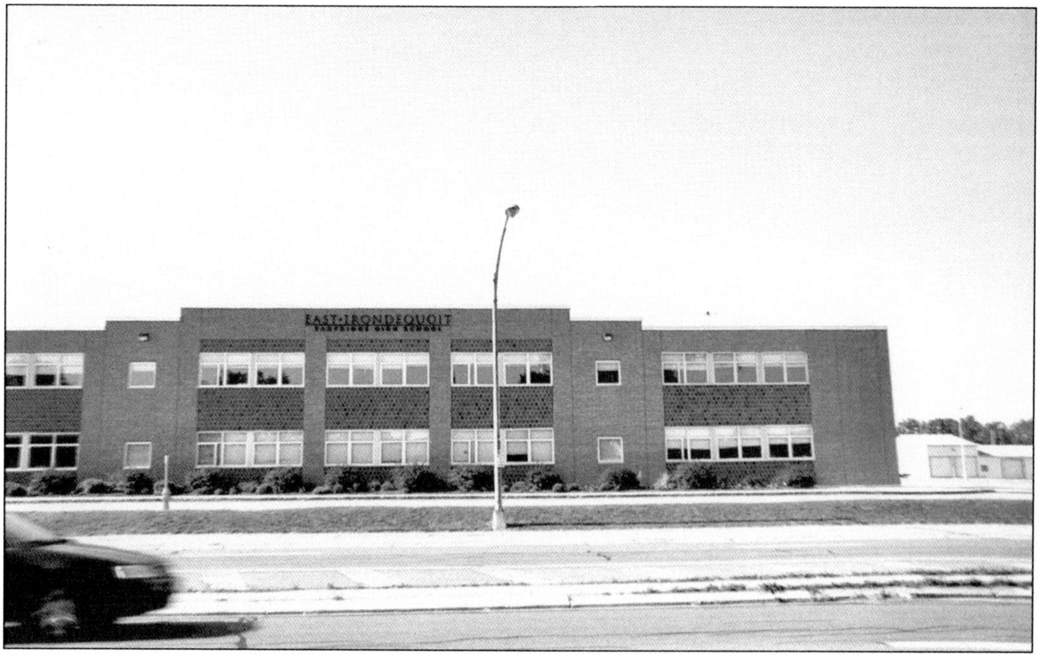

On November 15, 1956, the East Irondequoit school district approved a plan for a new high school on the east side of Irondequoit, and Eastridge High school was built at a cost of $3.58 million.

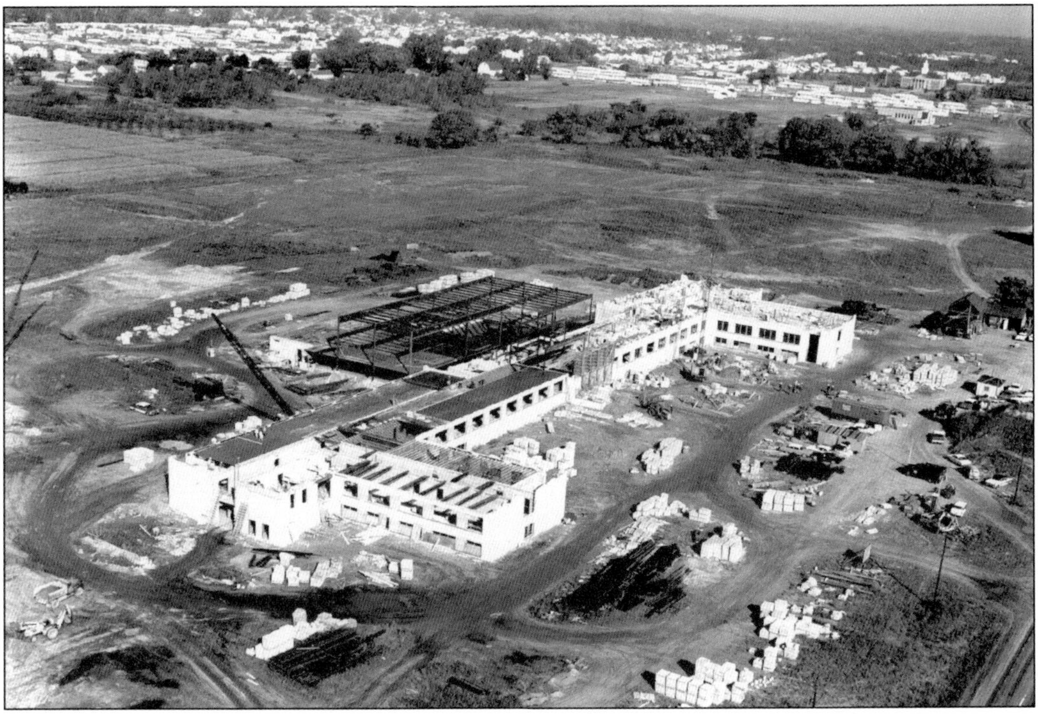

By October 1961, construction on a third high school was well underway. Bishop Kearney is a Catholic high school serving the northern part of Monroe County.

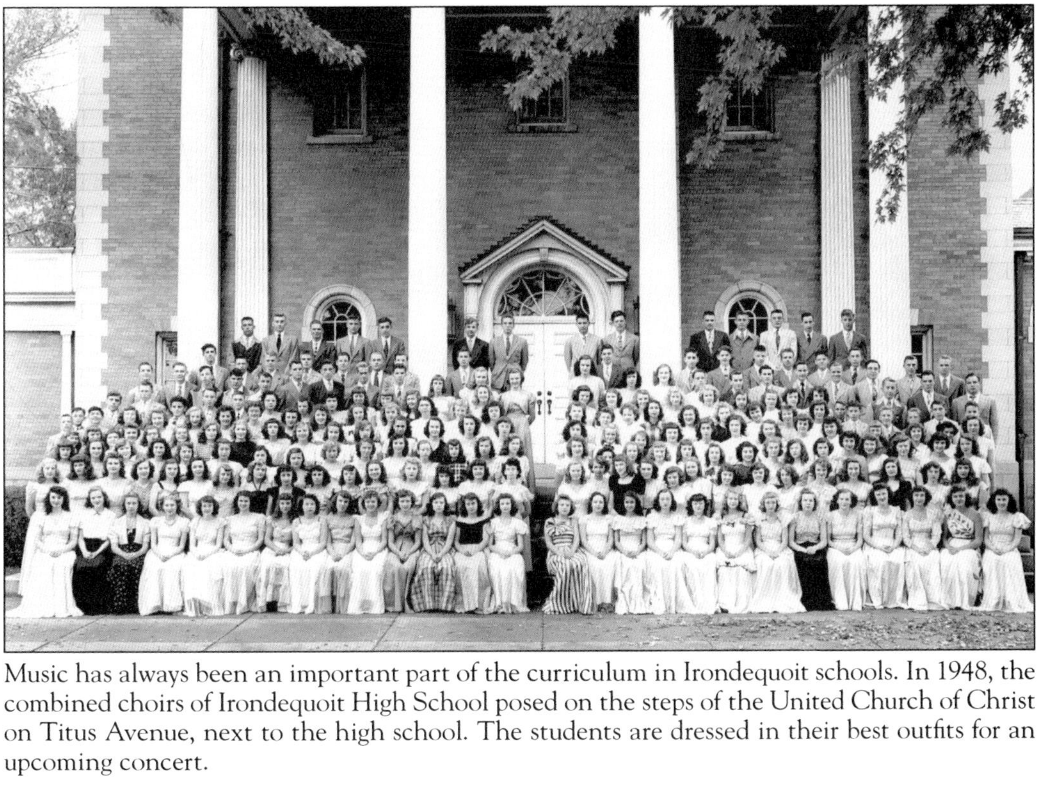

Music has always been an important part of the curriculum in Irondequoit schools. In 1948, the combined choirs of Irondequoit High School posed on the steps of the United Church of Christ on Titus Avenue, next to the high school. The students are dressed in their best outfits for an upcoming concert.

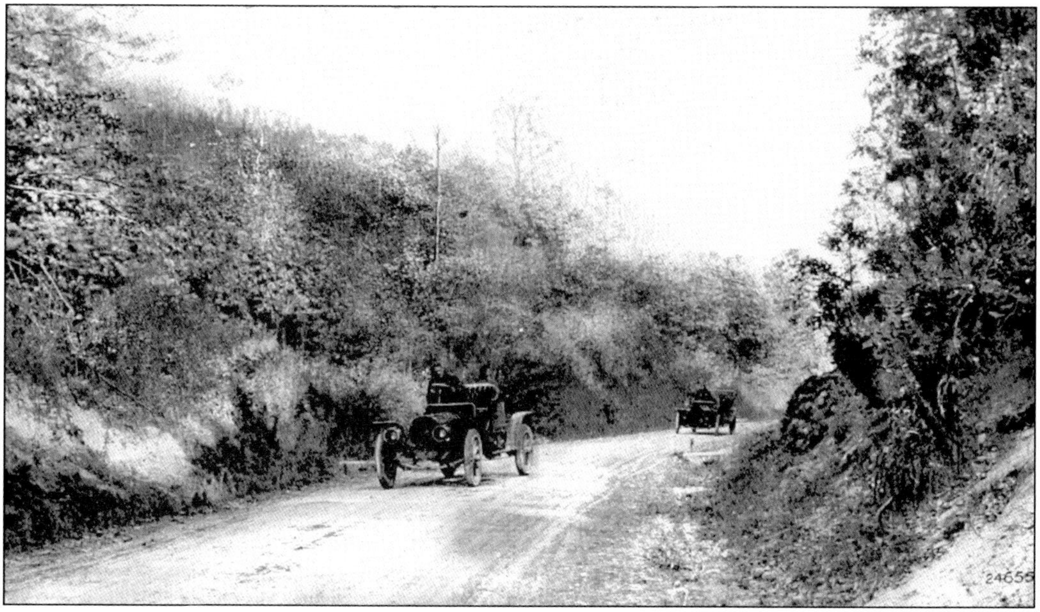

One cannot underestimate the role of the automobile in the changing course of Irondequoit history. This 1915 postcard with a 1¢ stamp shows cars traveling the Dugway at the end of Irondequoit Bay between Irondequoit and Webster.

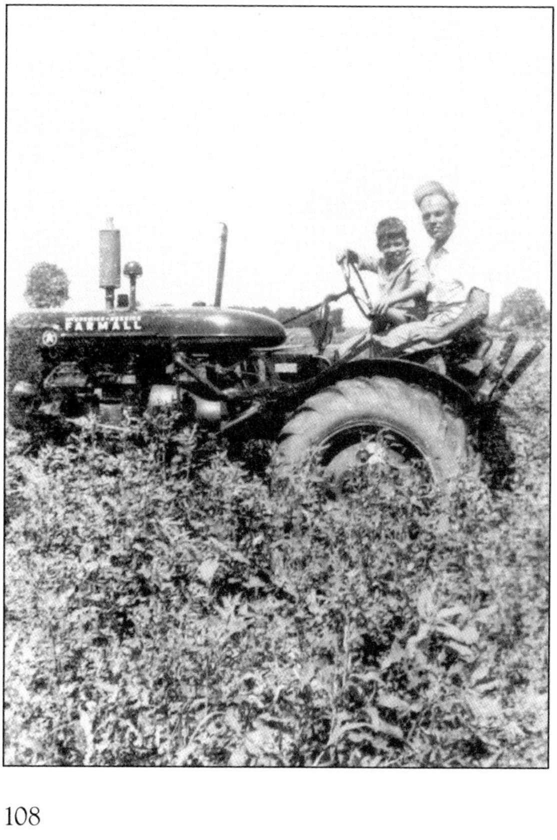

By 1940, even the small market gardening farms in town had started to mechanize. The La Croix family added a small Farmall tractor to their tool shed, and across the town, poor old "Dobbin" went out to pasture.

Ward West represented the fourth generation of a family who emigrated from England in 1842. In 1960, he shifted gears from farming to greenhouse horticulture, eventually owning 13 greenhouses at the corner of Ridge Road and Portland Avenue. African violets became his specialty, and he was also noted for his industrial plantings featuring interior landscapes.

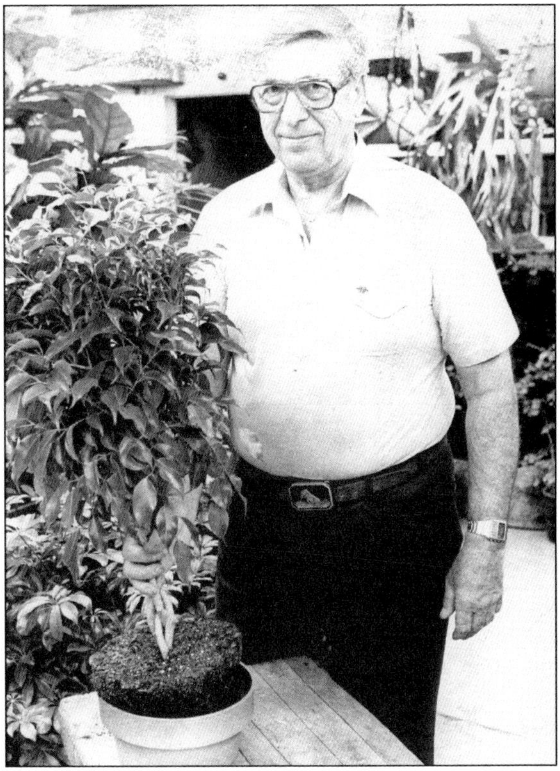

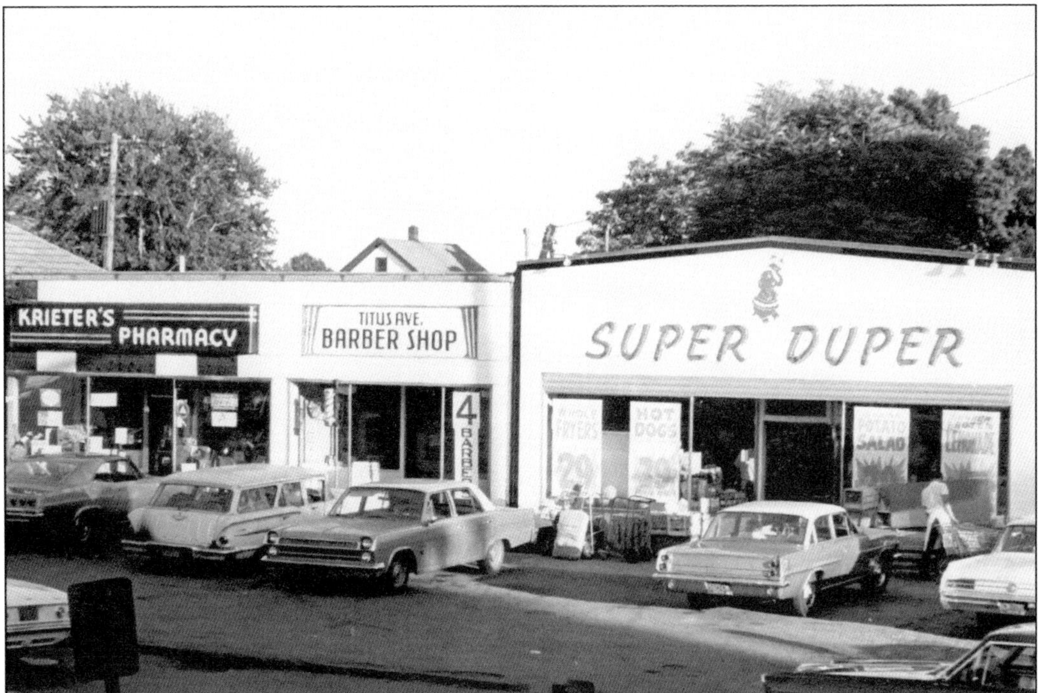

By the 1950s, the landscape of Irondequoit was changing from farms to subdivisions and from farm stands to strip malls, the forerunner of plazas on Titus Avenue.

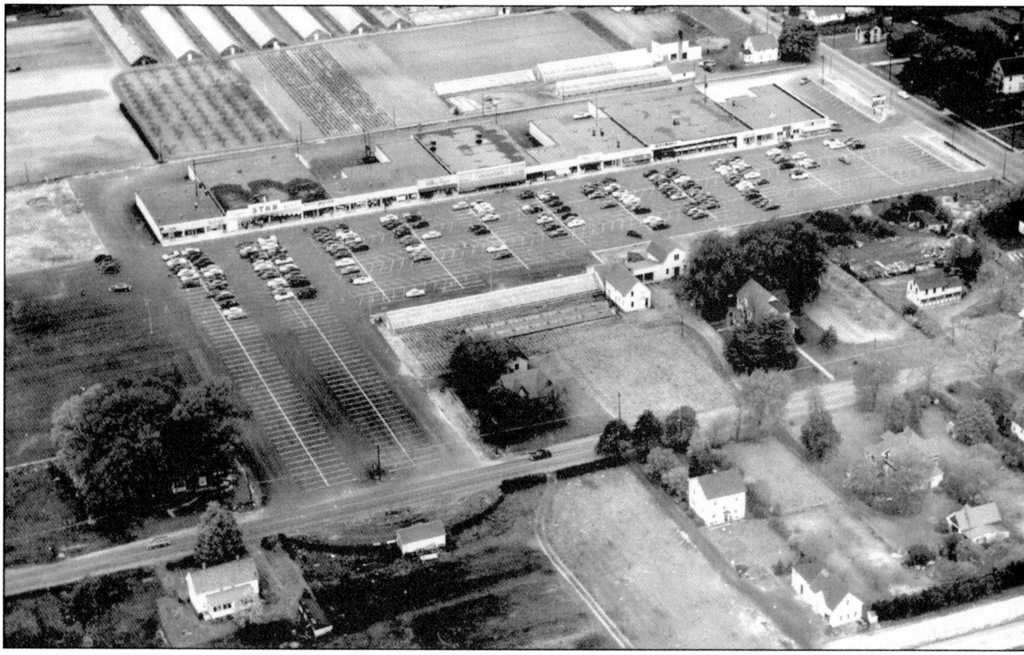

This aerial view of the mid-1950s dramatically illustrates the changes the next few decades would bring. It tells a story of change with the growth of subdivisions shown at the top of the photograph, then the greenhouses, farmhouses, and fields, and in the middle the wave of the future with Irondequoit Plaza.

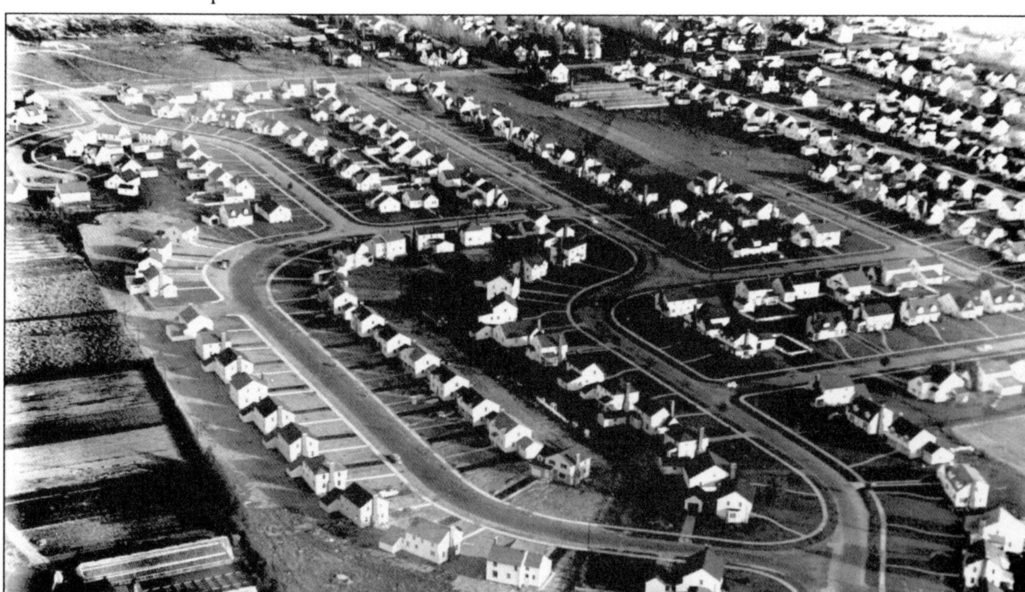

The end of World War II in 1945 brought great pressure to small towns like Irondequoit. There was a demand for housing, and returning GIs were anxious to assume home ownership. Farmers were offered astronomical prices for their land and at the same time were being squeezed by higher taxes needed to provide more services for an expanding population. Farms disappeared and were replaced by subdivisions like the Green Acres tract seen here.

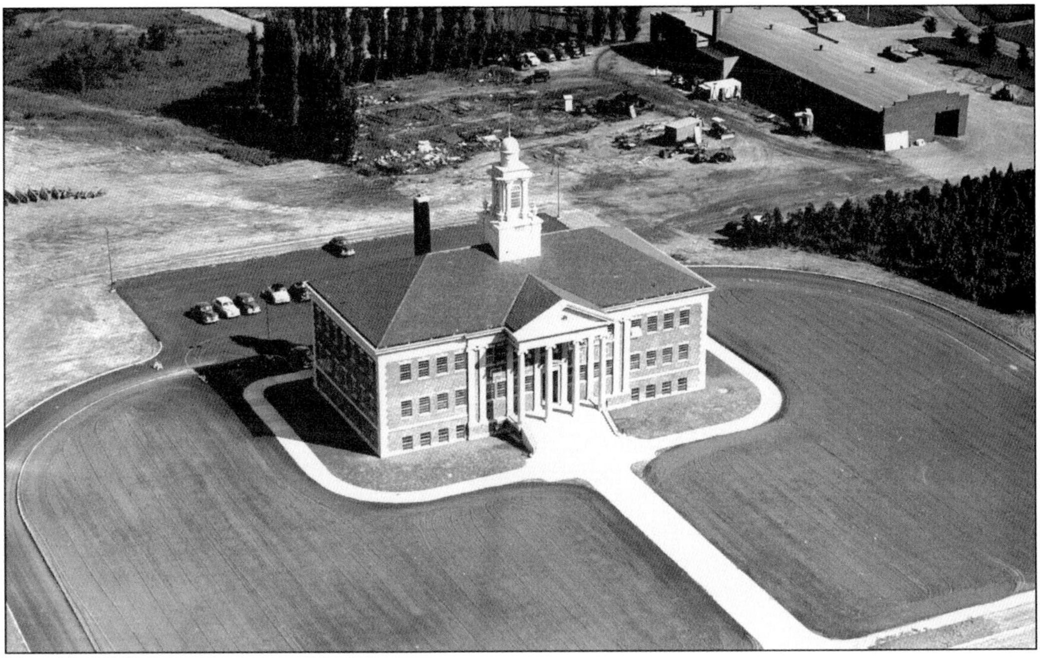

Irondequoit's historic colonial-type town hall was dedicated on May 29 and May 30, 1951. Through the foresight of longtime supervisor Thomas Broderick, it was built at a cost of $500,000 without any increase in taxes. Through the years, Broderick had set aside funds for the new building, but he died in 1949 and did not live to see the dedication.

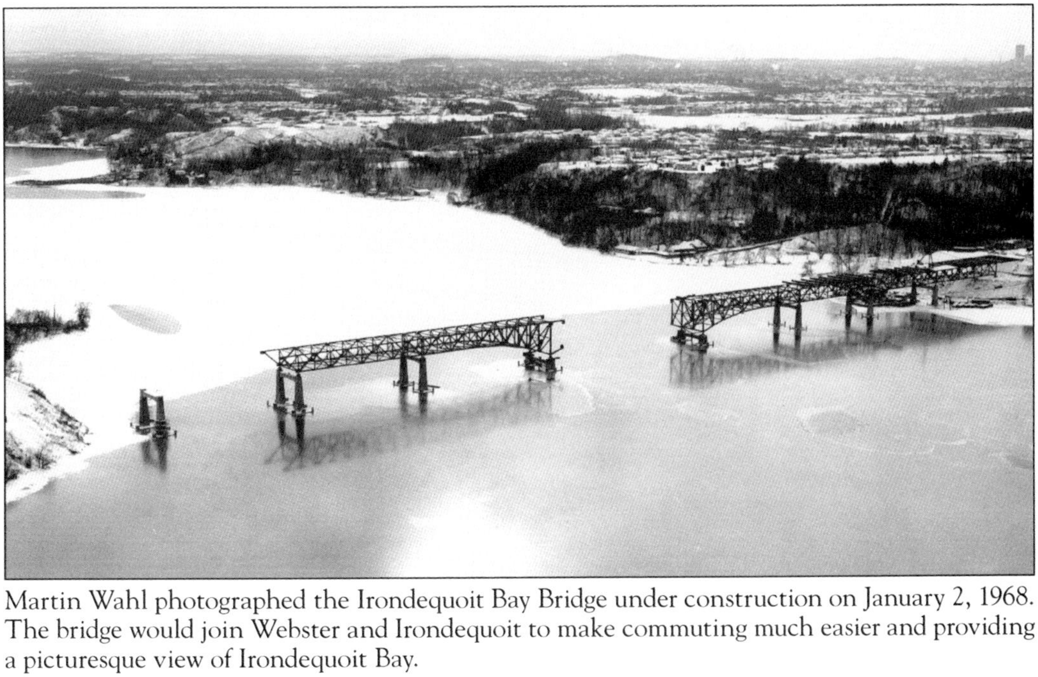

Martin Wahl photographed the Irondequoit Bay Bridge under construction on January 2, 1968. The bridge would join Webster and Irondequoit to make commuting much easier and providing a picturesque view of Irondequoit Bay.

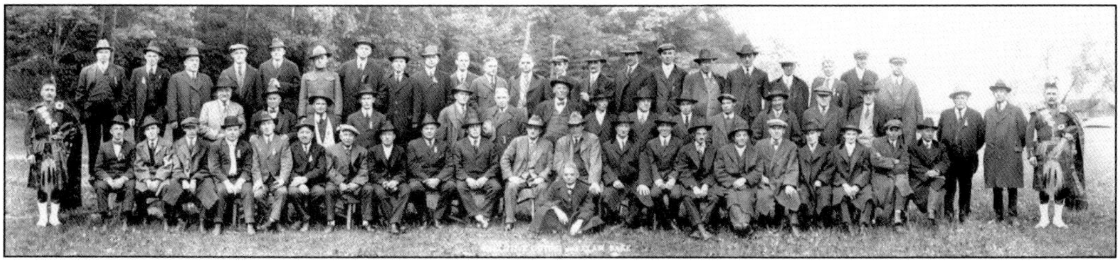

In the early 20th century, a clambake was usually an all-male affair. In this picture taken on September 21, 1918, the guests at a Point Pleasant clambake are dressed for the occasion in topcoats, hats, and business suits. Seated, at the center of the group is Rochester's number-one citizen, George Eastman who, according to the people at the George Eastman House, favored the Point Pleasant location for outdoor events. An intriguing aspect of the picture is the piper. The gentleman in a kilt appears on both sides of the picture. This phenomenon was the product of the circuit camera developed in 1904 by Frederick Brehm, an employee of Mr. Eastman. The camera was mounted on a tripod and rotated. The camera started at the left and, as soon as the piper was photographed, he sprinted to the other end of the group to be photographed again.

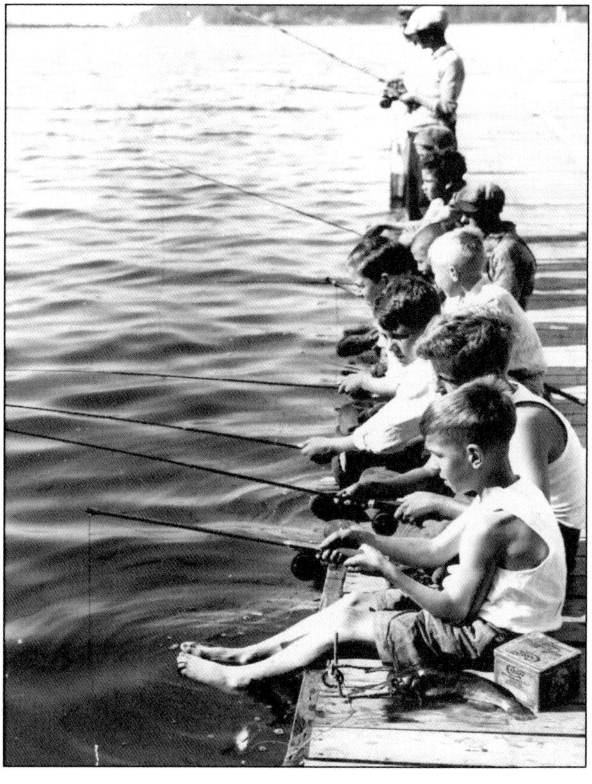

While there were many changes, some things stayed the same. Kids still went fishing on Irondequoit Bay. This group was having Saturday morning fun hanging out on the Hebing Hotel pier hoping to catch sunfish, perch, or bass. The young man in the front of the picture seems to have been successful already and spent time dangling his bare feet in the water.

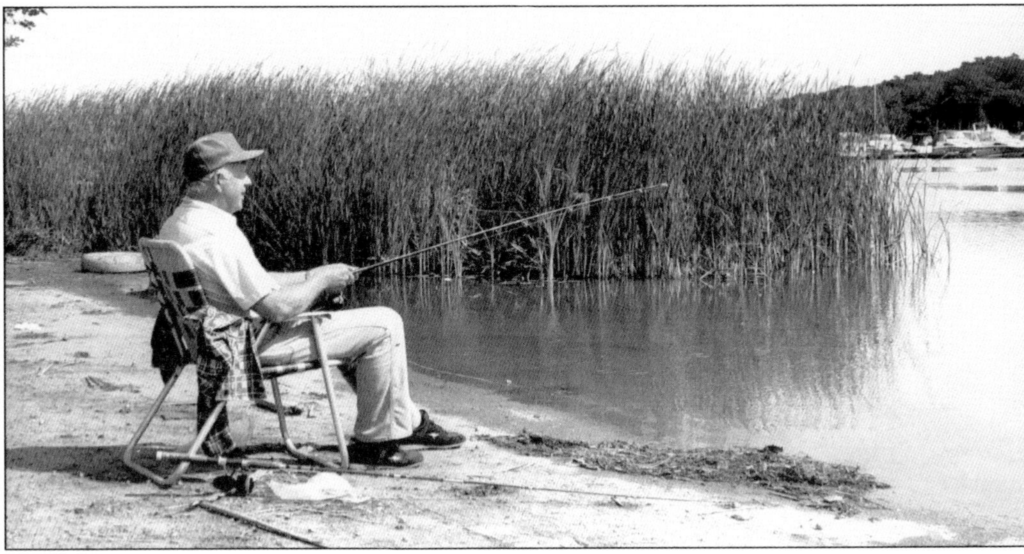

In 1989, Bill Norton found a good spot to relax and fish behind the tall rushes on the bay that had been cleaned of pollutants and had seen the return of game fish.

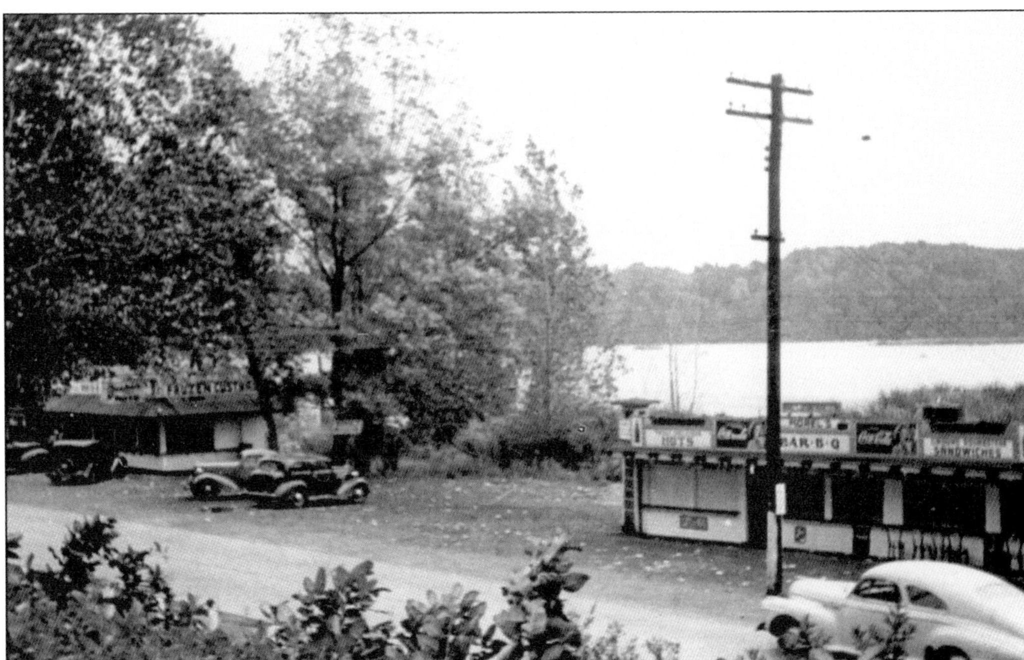

In 1946, the land between Irondequoit and Webster was a prime location for what is now called fast food and is still referred to as Hot Dog Row. Vic and Irv's is still an old standby for a white-hot or a barbecue. Bill Gray's has joined the row with a new facility.

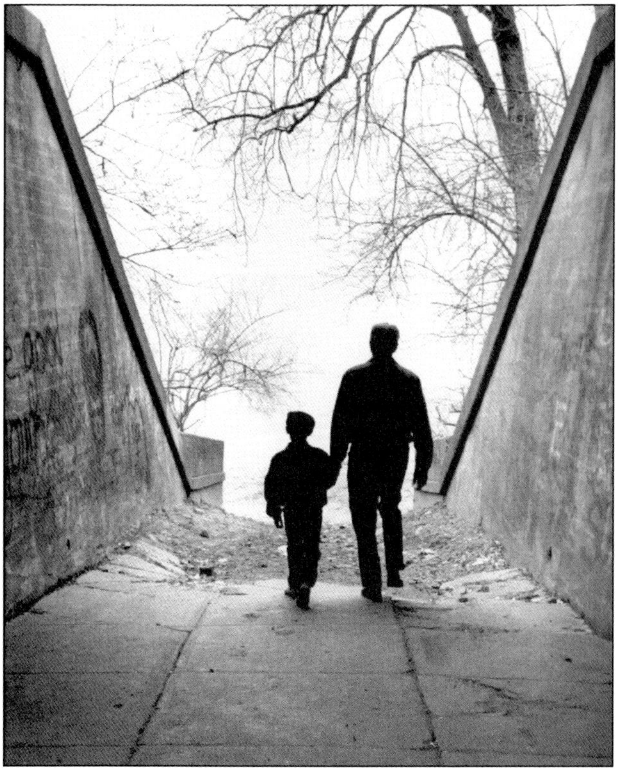

Adam Murphy and his grandpa, Frank Marsden, stroll through the tunnel to Durand-Eastman beach early in the spring. The tunnel has been torn down and an easier access to the beach constructed.

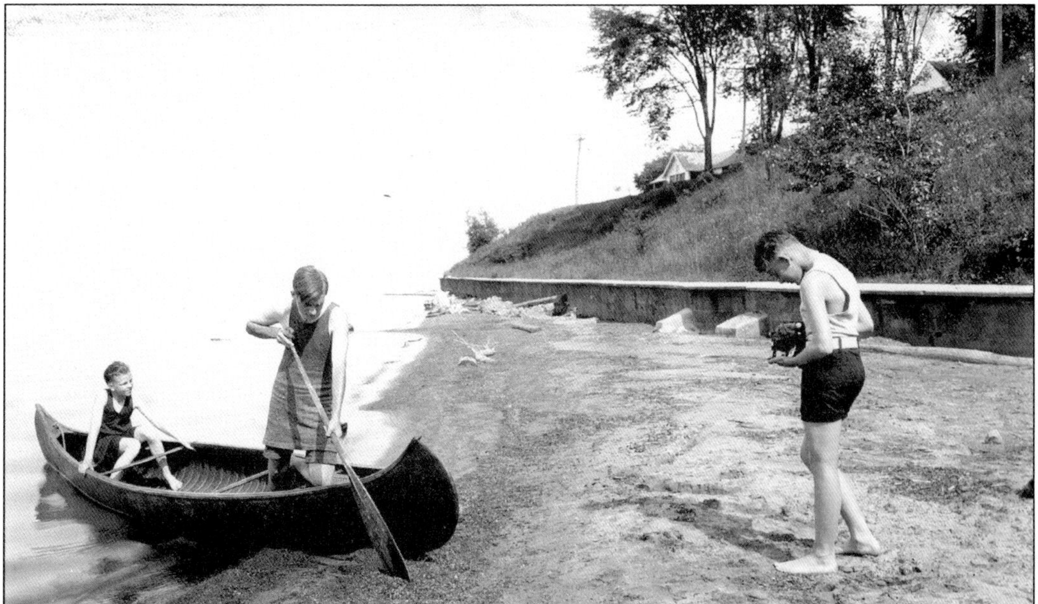

About 1920, Lawrence Morrow (standing in the boat) borrowed a canoe from his neighbor but failed to put it high enough on the beach. A storm washed it east and it broke up on the rocks. Presumably, Lawrence owed his friend the price of a canoe. Lake Ontario can be destructive and unpredictable. The break wall in the background fell apart in 1929.

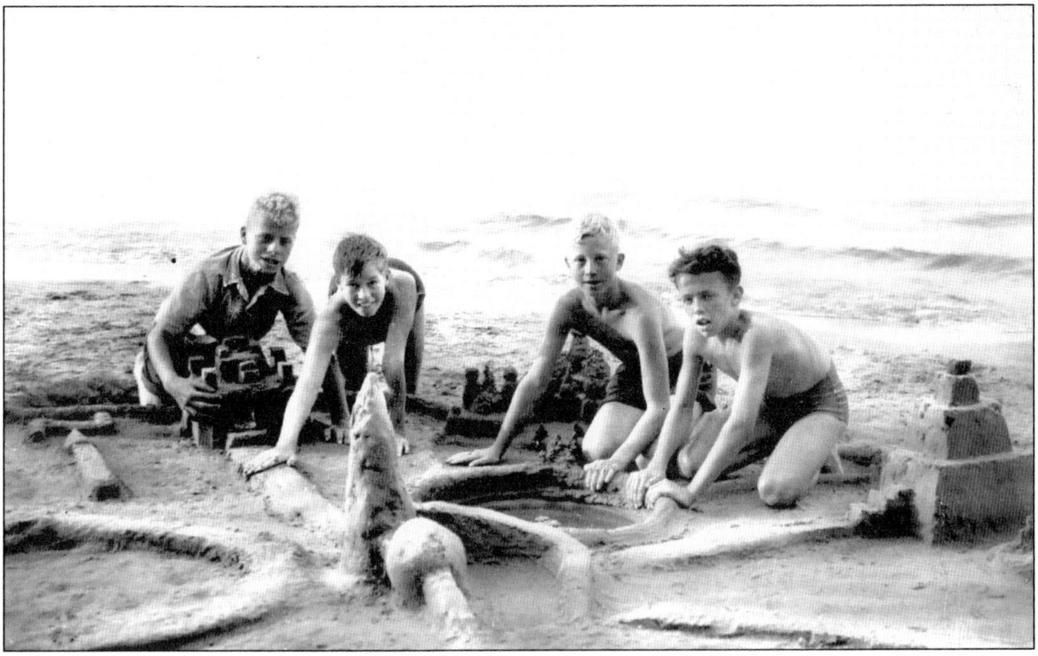

While most of the beach on the lake is made up of small stones, some sand has periodically been brought in to the delight of local kids. Seen here, from left to right, Charley Moscowitz, Jim Spelman, Barry Moscowitz, and Eric Kent built their version of a replica of the New York World's Fair of 1940.

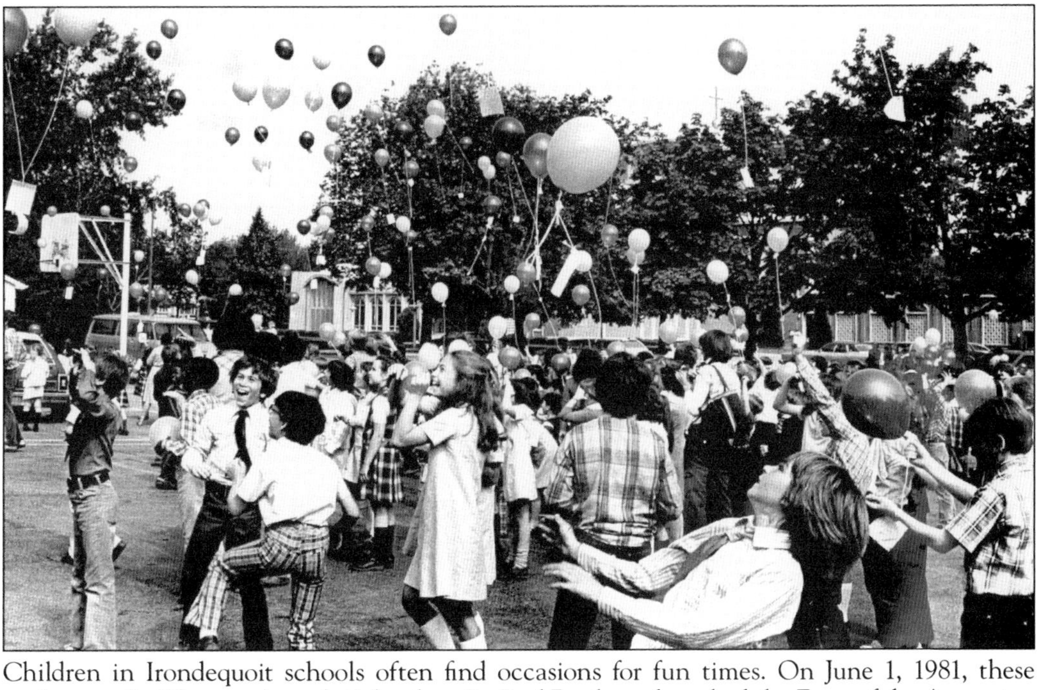

Children in Irondequoit schools often find occasions for fun times. On June 1, 1981, these students at St. Thomas Apostle School on St. Paul Boulevard marked the Feast of the Ascension with this symbolic balloon launch. Notes were attached to the balloons to let the finder know where they were launched from.

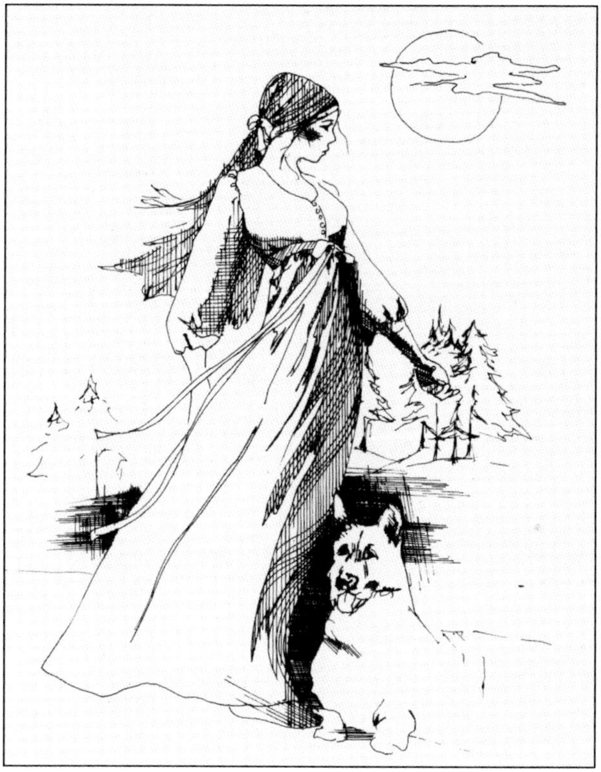

Times have changed, but the white lady of Durand-Eastman Park is still a fascinating legend and a challenge to the local historian. Supposedly, she lost her daughter who walked to the lakeshore in the early 1800s and never returned. According to the legend, the ghost of the distraught mother glides up and down the beach on misty nights with her German shepherds, still looking for her daughter and protecting young girls from over-zealous boyfriends. Despite repeated attempts by the historian to convince people that no disappearance or abduction occurred, the white lady continues to be sighted by visitors at the Durand-Eastman beach area.

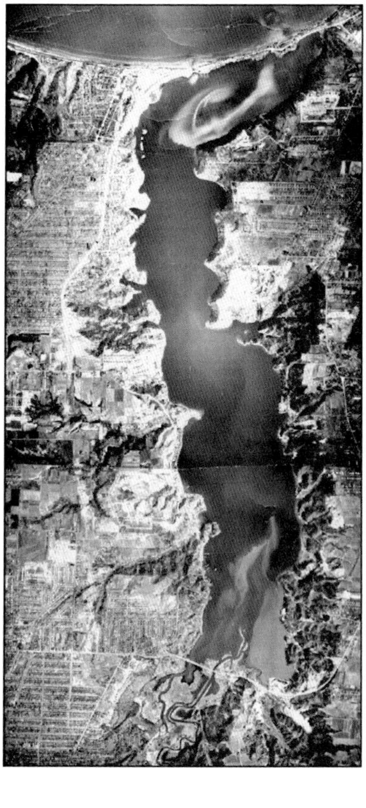

This aerial photograph, taken in 1957, of the Irondequoit Bay area reveals the growth of suburbia and the demise of the agricultural community in Irondequoit.

Six

PRESERVING THE PAST FOR THE FUTURE

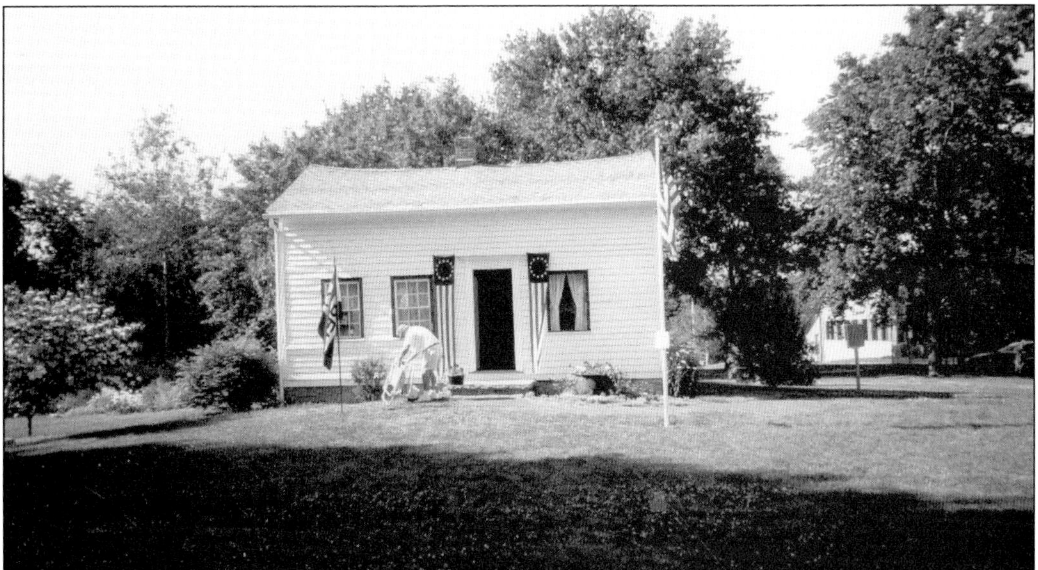

"Recognizing that the Town of Irondequoit's rich and varied history and vibrant present are evident in its commercial and residential buildings and surrounds, it is hereby declared as a matter of public policy that the protection, enhancement and perpetuation of landmarks and historic districts is necessary to promote the economic, cultural, educational and general welfare of the public." This excerpt is from the Historic Preservation Law of the Town of Irondequoit. Above is the Pioneer House which is now located behind the town hall and operates as a pioneer museum.

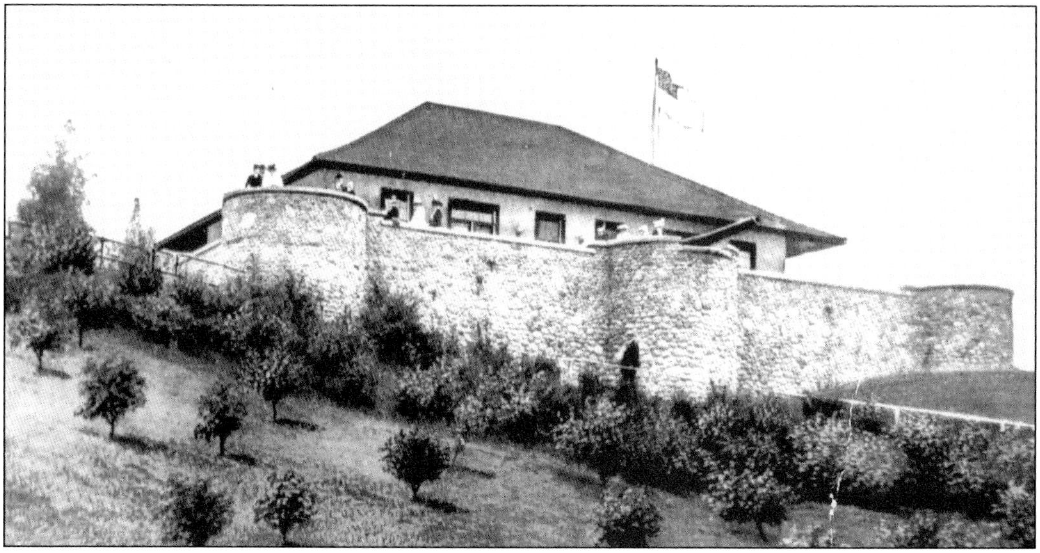

Some historic buildings disappear because of fire, demolition for land usage, or deterioration. Others were remodeled beyond recognition. The refectory or dining hall was built in 1911, and started serving refreshments in 1912 in Durand-Eastman Park. The cannon was moved to Highland Park after many thought it was pointed to our Canadian neighbors. The building was demolished in the early 1930s during the Depression because there were no county funds to maintain it. Many inquiries to the historian's office seek information about what some people believe are the ruins of the white lady's castle.

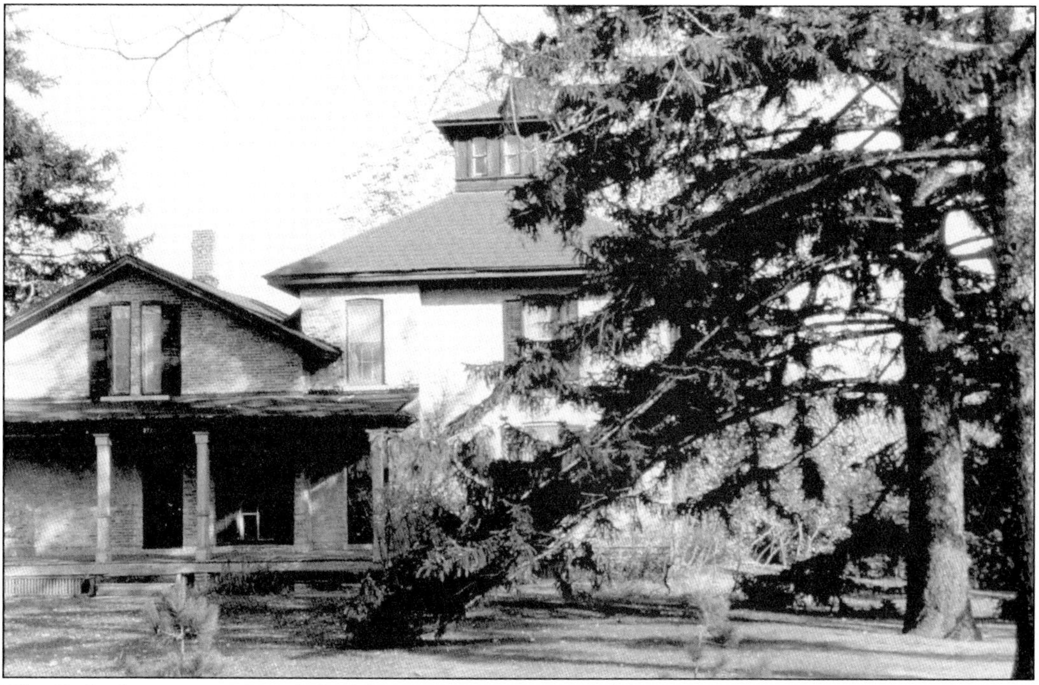

The Dake house was demolished because it was impossible to remodel it for a parsonage since there was no way to access the two wings of the second floor. The home was owned by the pioneer Dake family and was once a trolley stop.

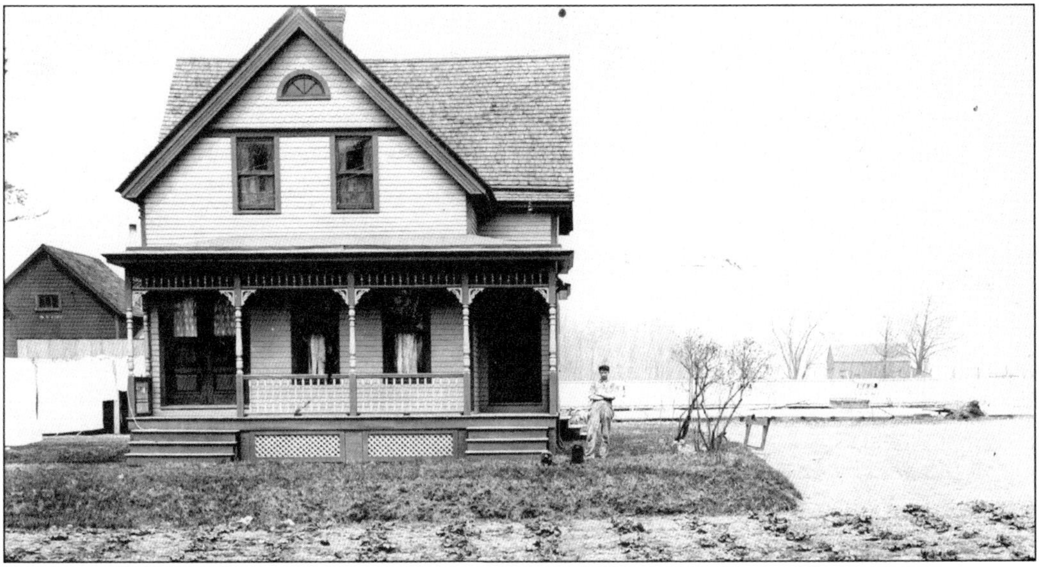

A recent demolition brought down the Josh family home on Ridge Road when the property, with its greenhouses and flower shop, were purchased for a medical center. The house had been remodeled several times and had lost its historic integrity.

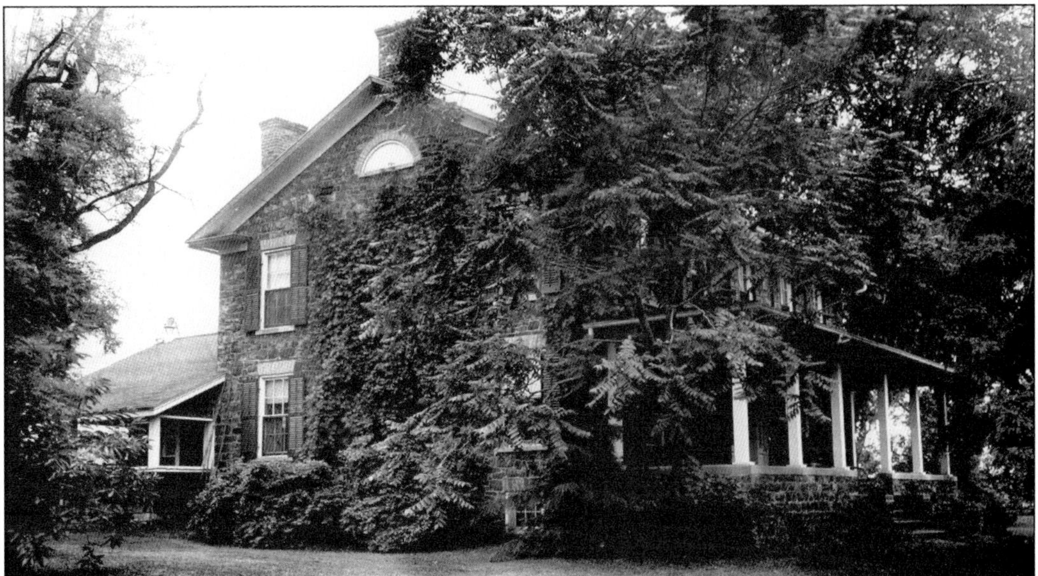

The saddest loss for the community was the destruction of the Hooker mansion in July 1967. The red sandstone house was built by the prominent pioneer and organizer of the town of Irondequoit, Alexander Hooker, in 1828. Despite efforts of the Landmark Society, the New York State Historical Society, and the Irondequoit Historical Society to save the home, St. Ann's home had the building razed because of complaints from the town board that saw the structure as a fire hazard.

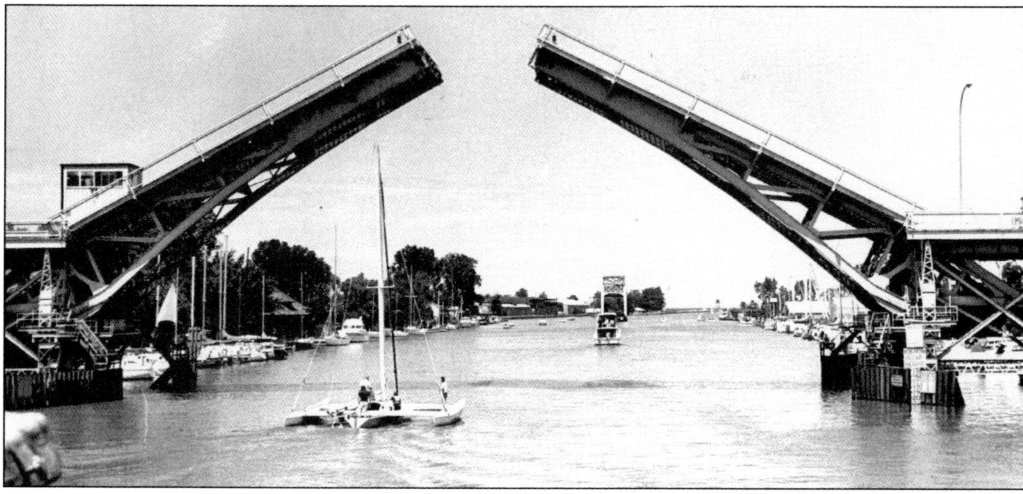

The Stuston Street Bridge was named after two brothers and opened in 1918, but by 2005 had become obsolete. Many times it got stuck in the upright position, backing up traffic, and sometimes it did not go up at all.

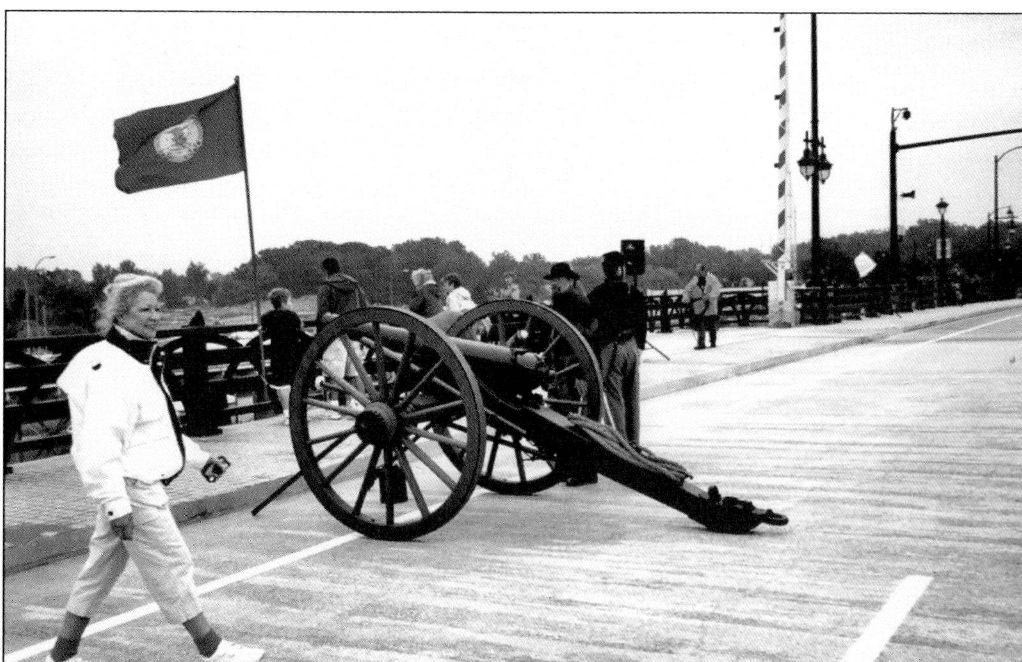

In 2005, a beautiful new bridge was completed and named after the Civil War hero Patrick O'Rorke who died at the battle of Gettysburg. O'Rorke was the first Irish American to graduate from West Point Academy. The new bridge was dedicated in October 2004.

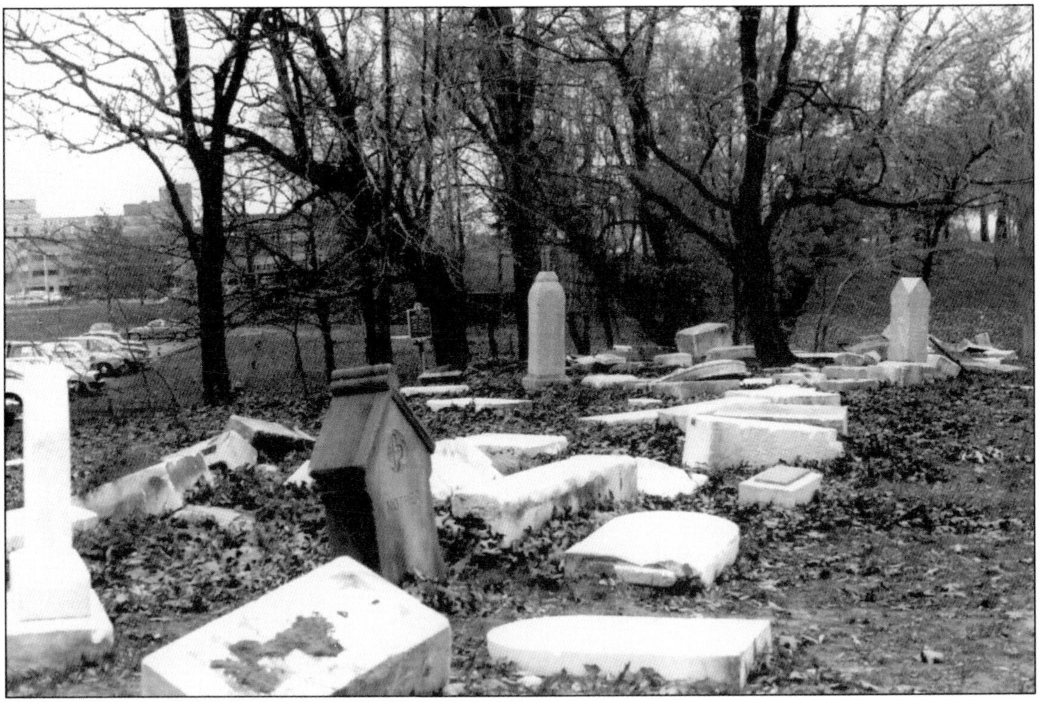

In 1840, Alexander Hooker gave the young town of Irondequoit the land behind his house that had been used as a burial ground. Hooker cemetery functioned as the last resting place of pioneer families until 1895. Through the years the cemetery was neglected and vandalized.

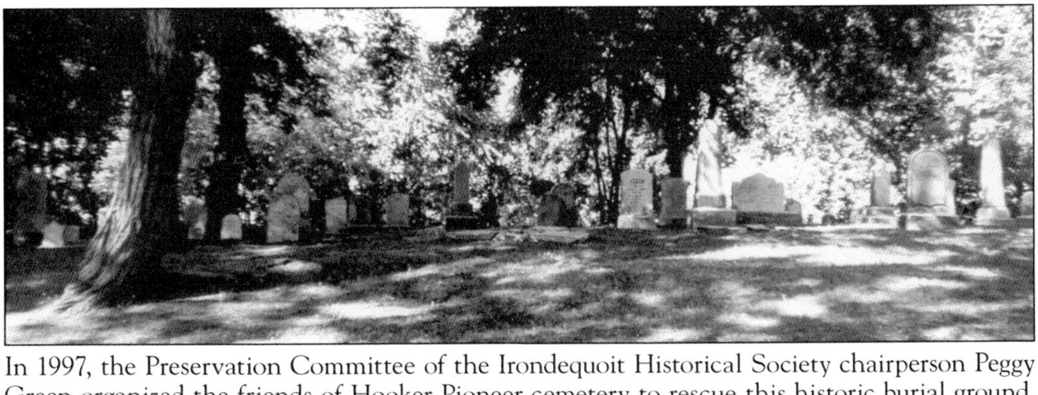

In 1997, the Preservation Committee of the Irondequoit Historical Society chairperson Peggy Green organized the friends of Hooker Pioneer cemetery to rescue this historic burial ground. In September 1999, the cemetery was dedicated as a memorial park and on Memorial Day 2001, local veterans led by George Reitter designed, donated, and installed a marker honoring the 15 veterans buried there.

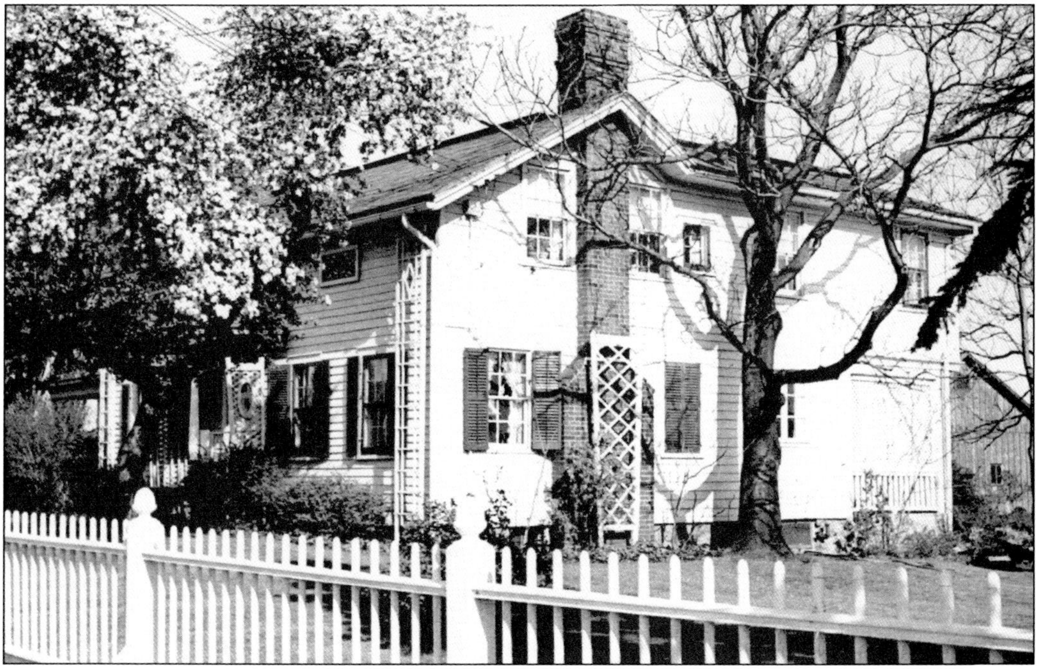

The Isaac Butts farmhouse was saved at the same time as the pioneer house and was moved to a new location on Kindlewood Lane.

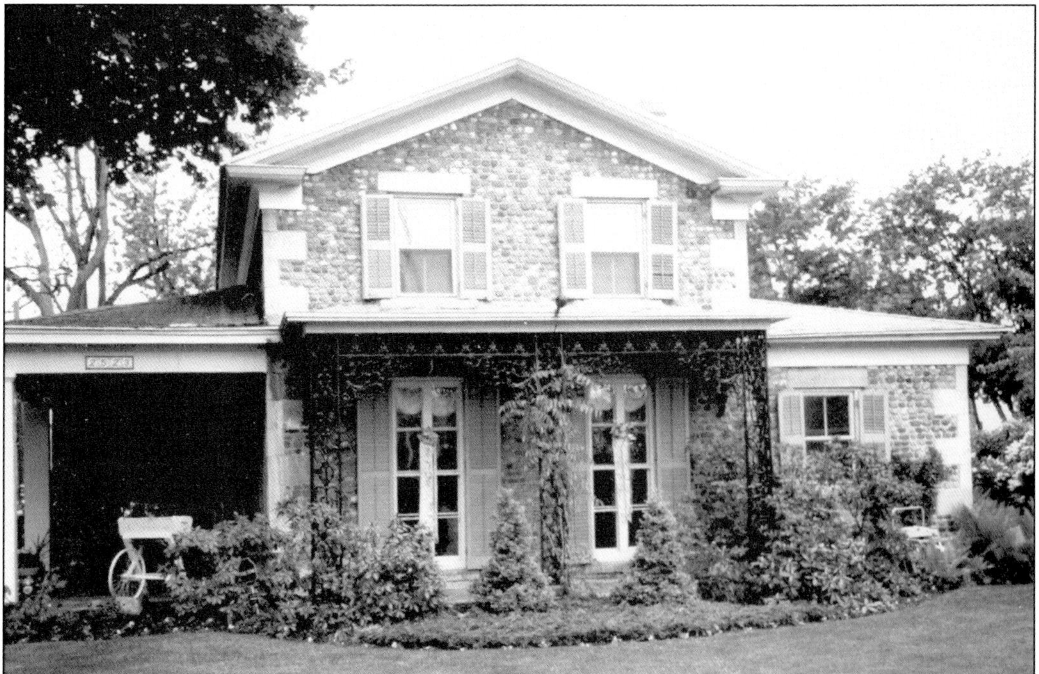

Cobblestone homes are indigenous to western New York, and one of the loveliest examples is the St. Paul Boulevard home of William and Elaine Royer Troutman. The house was built in the 1830s and has been placed on the local historic site list by the present owners.

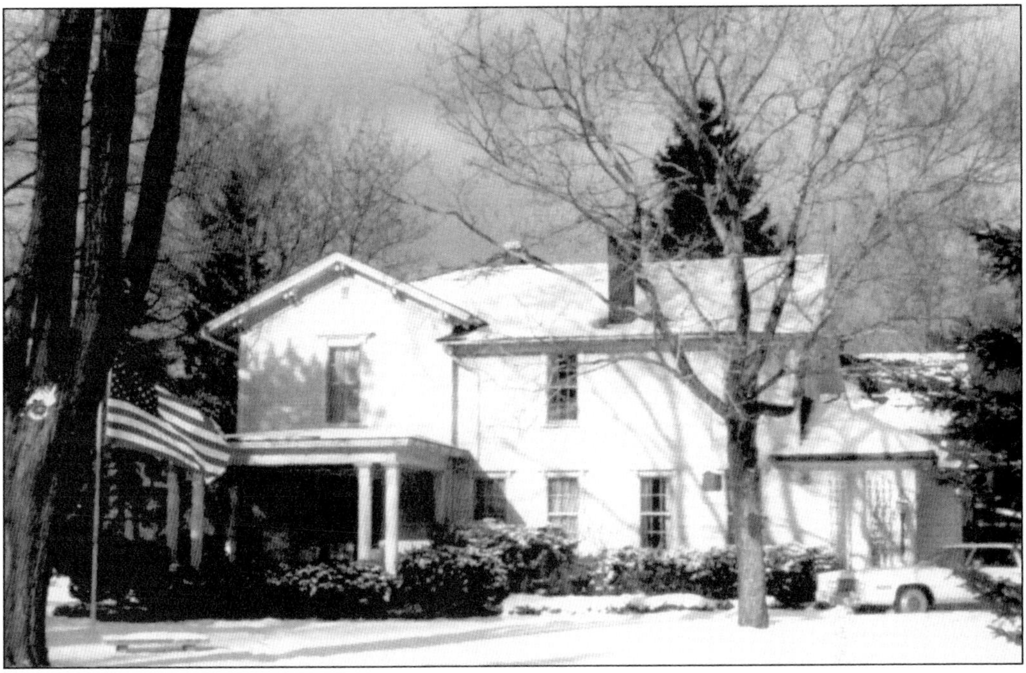

The Walzer family needed a large farmhouse for their 14 children. Their gracious home still remains on Culver Road and was lovingly restored by former owner Frank Kehoe. The house is an excellent example of preservation like the cobblestone houses.

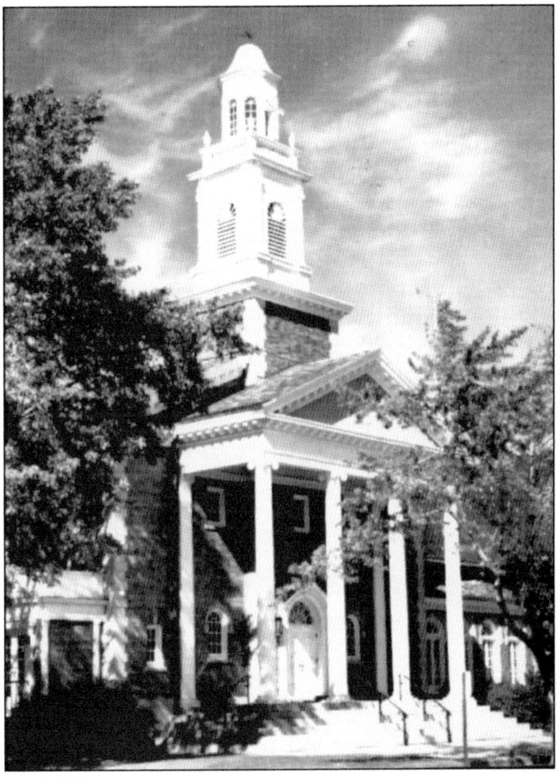

The first church in Irondequoit was the United Church of Christ, built in 1911 on Titus Avenue. It is listed on both the state and National Register of Historic Places.

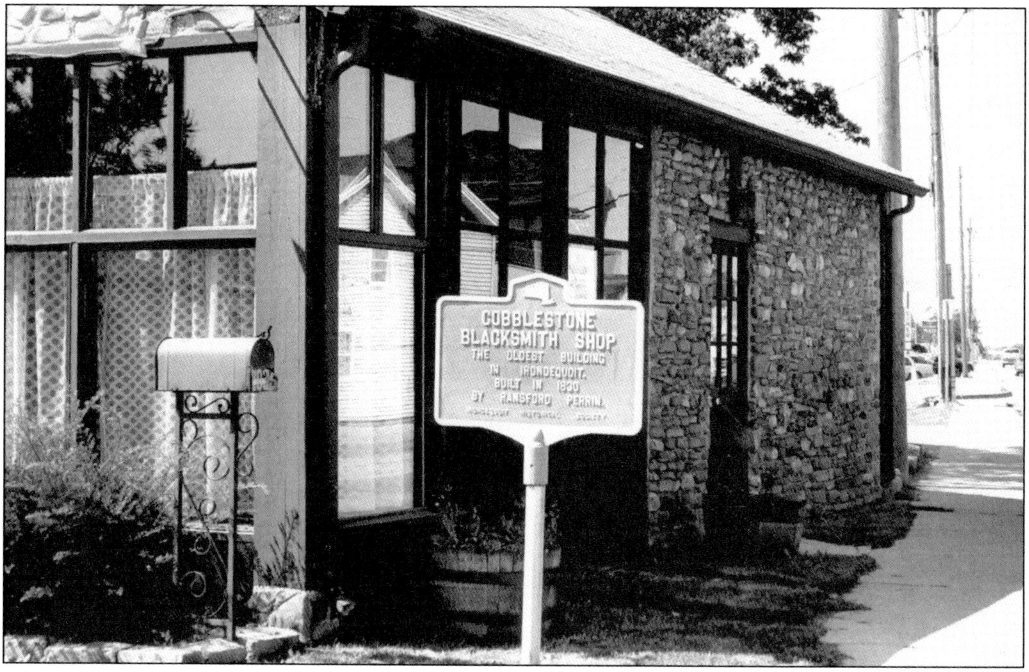

The cobblestone blacksmith shop on Ridge Road East is the oldest building in town. Built by Ransford Perrin in 1820 to fulfill the needs of a small settlement in a wilderness, it is protected as a local historic site but needs to be relocated.

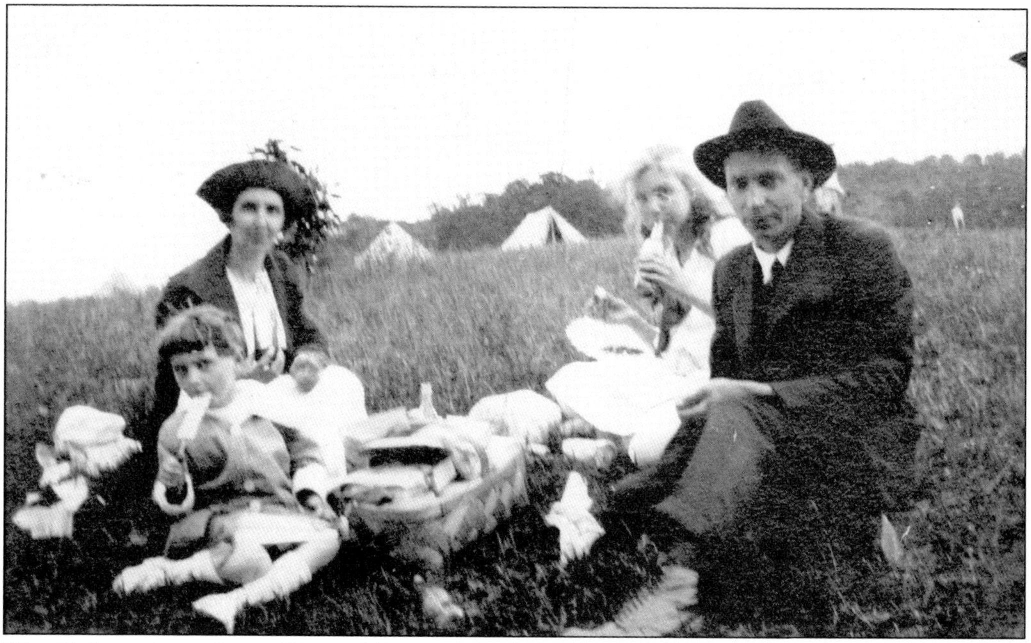

The Coles enjoy a day at Durand-Eastman Park in the early 1900s. The house built by Josiah Cole still stands on Colebrook Road and is being restored by its current owner. The Firemen's Exempt building on Thomas Avenue is the only other building remaining from the Cole's numerous farms in Irondequoit. Pictured here from left to right are Phyllis, Luella, Audrey, and Ted Cole.

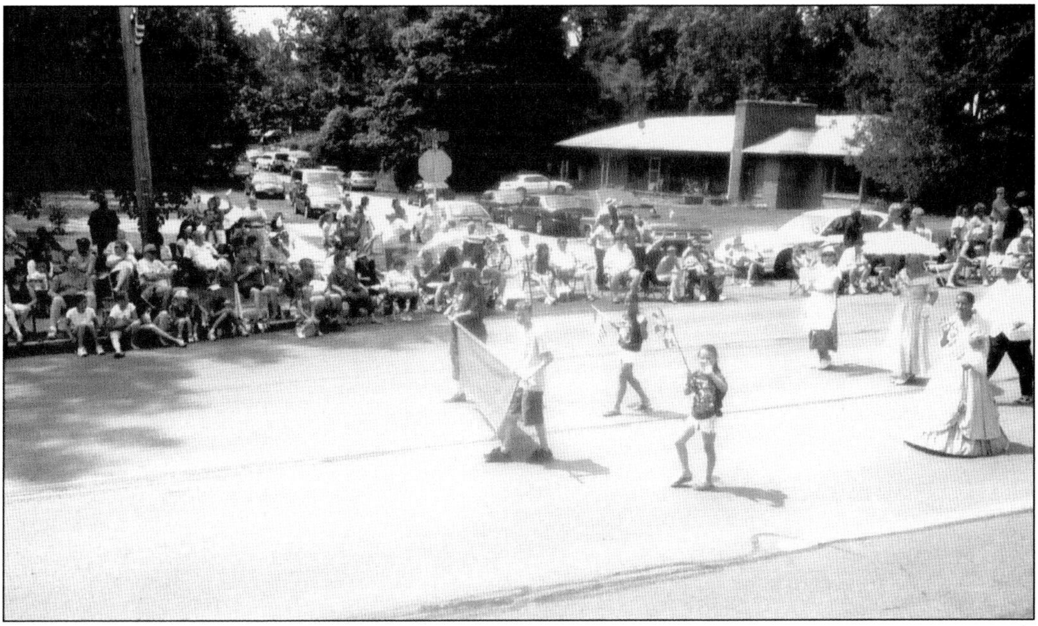

While landmarks may disappear, traditions remain. In 1974, the town began to sponsor a Fourth of July parade and celebration which centers on the campus of the Irondequoit Town Hall. This celebration fosters community spirit and brings in visitors from all over the county. It also gives the Irondequoit Historical Society a chance to raise awareness about local history and remind people of the need to preserve the past.

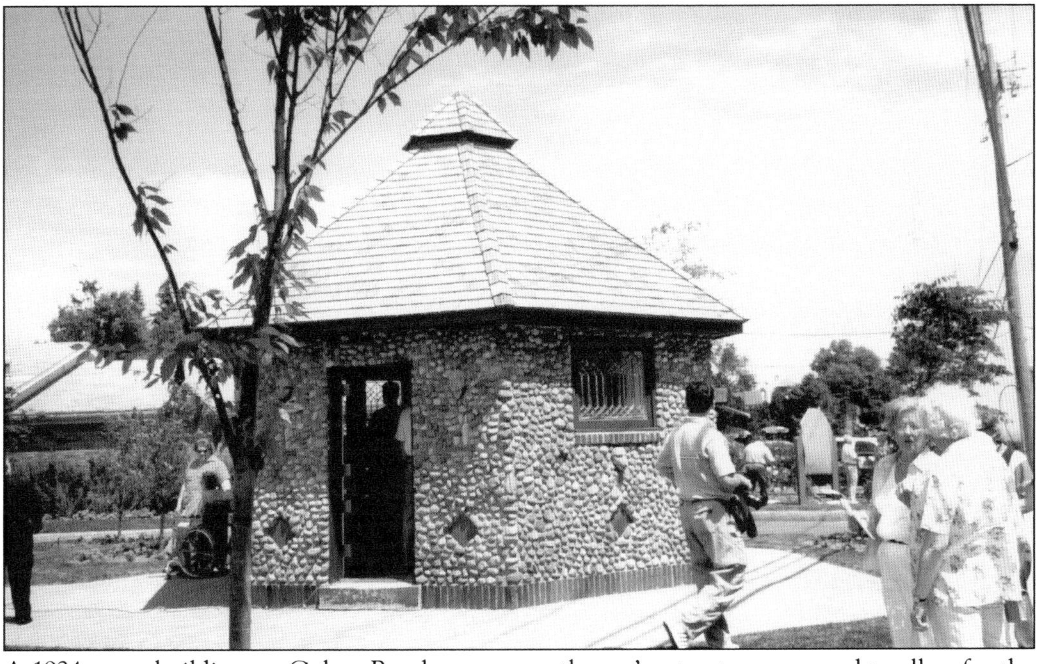

A 1924 stone building on Culver Road, once a gentleman's retreat, was moved to allow for the expansion of the Ridge Culver firehouse. The stone building found a new home at a pocket park in Sea Breeze dedicated to Oscar Roth. The rehabilitated house is very popular with residents and illustrates what preservation can do to add to community spirit.

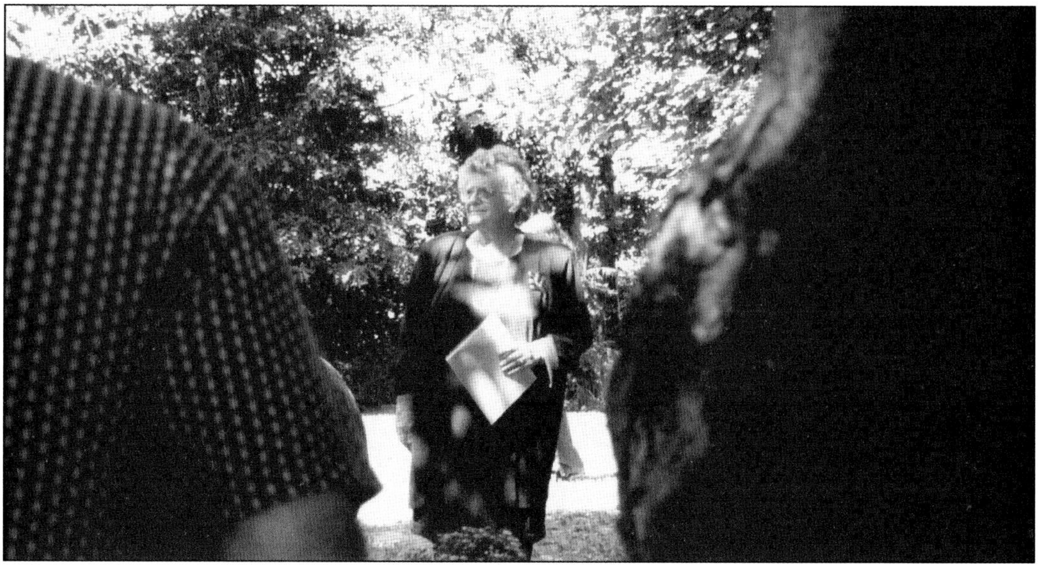

Preserving historical heritage often means patience, persistence, and perseverance. Peggy Green, former chairperson of the Preservation Committee of the Irondequoit Historical Society had these attributes. Soft-spoken and deliberate in her research, she engineered the movement of the small pioneer house, now the Pioneer House Museum, to the grounds of the town hall and supervised its change to a museum, then launched a drive to rehabilitate the Hooker cemetery which was renamed the Pioneer Cemetery. All of these projects heightened resident's interest in the history of Irondequoit and the support of a strong preservation ordinance to protect remaining historical sites.

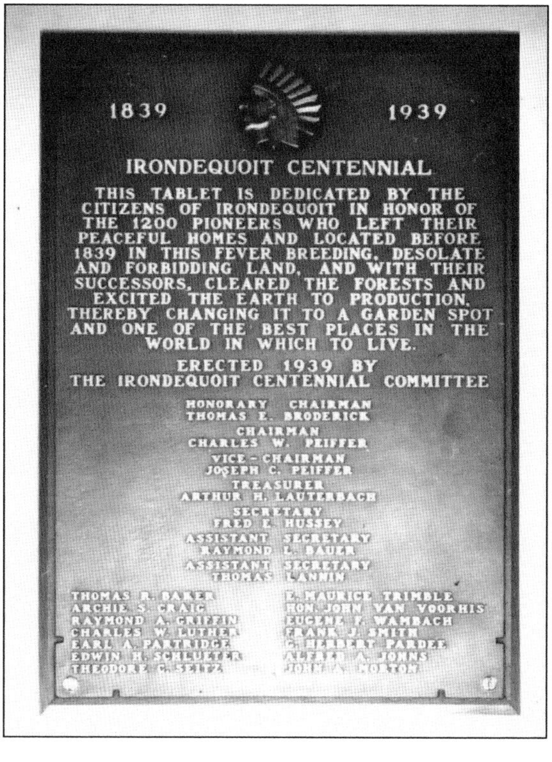

The centennial plaque, part of the 100th birthday celebration in 1939, is now mounted on a large boulder in the Pioneer Cemetery. Its tribute to the pioneers is as meaningful today as it was in 1939, and it is their memory that gives preservationists the drive to keep the town's heritage alive. Despite all the changes Irondequoit has seen, it is still "one of the best places in the world in which to live."

Bibliography

1788 – 1877 History of Monroe County, New York: Everts, Ensign & Everts, 1877.

Carpenter, Edmund S. *Two Essays: Chief & Greed*, North Andover, MA: Persimmon Press, 2005.

Day, David H. *The Life and Death of a Family Farm, Second Edition*, Rochester, NY: Kendall and Hunt, 1993.

Fink, Carol, Joan Frenzel, Anne Rehbach, and Patricia Wayne. *Early Irondequoit Memories*, Irondequoit, NY: Irondequoit Historical Society, 1997.

Fink, Carol, Kathy Taddeo, and Patricia Wayne, *Hooker Pioneer Cemetery*, Irondequoit, NY: Friends of Hooker Pioneer Cemetery, 2001.

Gates Historical Society, *Gates*, Charleston, SC: Arcadia Publishing, 2005.

Judkins, Russell A. Ph.D, *Lewis Henry Morgan's League of the Iroquois; The Ethnographic Core*, North Andover, MA: Persimmon Press, 2004.

Lewis Henry Morgan Chapter of the New York State Archaeological Association. *Genesee Country 1687–1937, Denonville-LaSalle 250th Anniversary Celebration, Official Pictorial Legend*, Rochester, NY: 1937.

Stanton, June L. C., Kathleen Stanton Wedman, *Cole Family History*, Rochester, NY: Cole Family Collection, 1983.

Stanton, June L. C., *Cole Family Memories*, Rochester, NY: Cole Family Collection, 1973.

West, Maude I. *Irondequoit Story; a History of the Town of Irondequoit, 1839 – 1957*, Irondequoit, NY: The Town of Irondequoit, 1957.